Charley Burley

and

The Black Murderers' Row

Charley Burley

and

The Black Murderers' Row

Harry Otty

1st edition 2002
2nd edtion 2006
This edition 2010

Published by Tora Book Publishing
ISBN 0-9543924-2-6

Cover Design by Roger Williams and Harry Otty © 2010

charleyburley.com

Dedication

To my wife Sandra for putting up with my boxing obsession (and the countless hours away) and to my children Hannah, Jake and Lewis.

Contents

Foreword

A number of years ago I spoke to the late Hank Kaplan in order to request his assistance in filling in some gaps for the first edition of this book. As the owner of the largest collection of boxing data in the world I felt Mr. Kaplan would be just the man to assist me - and indeed he was - but, he was also a little puzzled. While Hank was a fan of Charley Burley, he wondered what there would be to write about and why anyone would want to write it. What did Burley ever do? He never saved a baby from a burning building and he most certainly never won a world title. In fact he didn't even contest one.

For me personally, it was not about what Burley did or didn't do, it was how he went about it. I had been a boxing fan for a number of years when I read about his induction into the Ring magazine Hall-of-Fame in 1983. I had never heard of him, but I liked what I read and attempted to find out more. Being from England, this proved a difficult task as not too many people had heard of him here either. His name was curiously missing from every boxing history book I looked at.

About three years later Charley featured in an article by O. F. Snelling in the Boxing News (the British weekly). This piece provided me with a little more information and piqued my interest further. I wrote to Angelo Prospero, the 'Old Timers' columnist for Ring magazine and Angelo was good enough to provide me with more information on our man, including a contact address for him in Pittsburgh. The rest, as they say, is history.

From 1988 I was in touch with Charley on a decidedly irregular basis, birthdays etc, and I was fortunate enough to meet him at his home in September 1992. Speaking to this very soft-spoken gentleman I found it difficult to picture him in the ring with championship calibre fighters from welterweight on up to heavyweight. After all, here was a relatively small guy, admittedly quite ill at the time, who looked like an old, wise uncle yet had traded punches with Fritzie Zivic, Archie Moore and Ezzard Charles. I mention these particular fighters because they are usually the only ones most boxing fans recognise. But, his record didn't lie and, if anything, it totally failed to tell the real story of this remarkable man. As most boxing people in the know appreciate, a fighter's record is only part of the story and the win-lost column means nothing if taken out of context.

I was saddened to hear of Charley's death just a couple of weeks after my visit. I think it was then that I made the decision to cobble together something that would highlight to the rest of the boxing world just how special this man was. It may have been a case of hero worship, but I got a little bit angry every time some so called boxing fan said "Charley who?"

On a return visit to Pittsburgh and the Burley family in 1995 (and many subsequent visits), I started to gather information that would help me with this task. Initial attempts at research lead to an essay on Charley being published by the Cyber Boxing Zone on their web site. I have since written essays on Charley's contemporaries Holman Williams, Eddie Booker, Jack Chase, Lloyd Marshall and other great fighters who, to one extent or another, featured in the life of Charley Burley. Thankfully my research has moved on somewhat from that initial attempt, but it has taken a number of years.

What I didn't want to do was write something that resembled report-age and just reflected Charley Burley's fights, dates, locations and oppo-nents. Charley's own career memorabilia was limited to documenta-tion such as press clippings, letters, telegrams, contracts, certificates of induction and a very non-descript looking championship belt buckle. Julia Burley very kindly gave me access to all of these things. She was as generous with her hospitality and time and is a remarkable woman. Who better then to offer some real life background and help put some flesh on the flat image that stares out at us from so many years in the past?

Maybe the people that knew Charley best could help tell his story. This was a reasonably simple idea and the best way to go about this would be to interview people who actually knew him. Sadly, there are few of them still around from his fighting days and their numbers dimin-ish with time. The stories they shared were not always about boxing or Charley's fights and, with regard to 'painting a picture', I feel this is a good thing.

Julia Burley was the closest to Charley. For over fifty years she was his wife, lover, friend, the mother of his children and his rock. He always referred to her as "My Julie'. It is obvious that they were made for each other. He was a lucky man to have such a woman by his side and he knew it. Bobby Lippi knew Charley Burley from a number of perspectives, mentor, friend, role-model, confident and constant companion. A.J. 'Blackie' Nelson was also a dear friend and was a sparring partner during the West Coast years and beyond. David Jordan worked with Charley on the garbage trucks and was on the Pittsburgh fight scene from the late 1940s onward and knew Charley very well. Irving Jenkins travelled to the Barcelona Olympics with him in 1936 and observed Charley under extreme circumstances. Many others that knew him in one form or another have also made a contribution and each provided a little piece of what is both a complex yet simple jigsaw-puzzle. Their memories, while maybe not 100% accurate with regards to dates and places, help provide a more balanced view of Charley, as a fighter and as a man. The task was a difficult one, for myself and those interviewed, as Charley Burley was essentially a very private person who allowed few people in.

When we look at his record and the history of the fighters he met in the ring, we get a good idea of how good he was at his chosen profession. When we begin to wonder how he failed to achieve the ultimate goal of world champion, we only have to look at who he was, what he stood for and how he conducted himself, both in and out of the ring, in order to find a partial answer.

Introduction

Since the early to mid 1930s, when crime in the United States was very much well organised, certain nefarious figures no longer had a piece of a prize-fighter purely for status and street credibility. The end of prohibition in America meant that other, more traditional, avenues for earning money had to be explored; loansharking and gambling were among the usual favourites. Professional boxing, a sport whose machinations existed out of the public eye, was often viewed as an ideal business enterprise. Fighters, and to an extent their managers and trainers, became commodities that could be bought, sold and traded. Into this arena entered a number of individuals who, using 'legitimate' managers as a front, infiltrated and eventually ran the professional fight game in America for over twenty years.

With vast amounts of money to be made from the betting on medium - to high-profile fights, a certain amount of control was necessary and connected promoters, managers, and sometimes even the fighters themselves, were 'doing business' in almost every gym and arena. At the helm of this operation were underworld figure John Paul 'Frankie' Carbo, aka ' Mr. Grey', his chief lieutenant, Frank 'Blinky' Palermo and several of their cohorts. History tells us that Mr. Carbo in particular was not a guy you would want to cross. Previously a member of the notorious 'Murder Incorporated', Frankie was not too shy about using deadly violence as a means to an end.

Through Mike Jacobs and his 20th Century Sporting Club at Madison Square Garden, Carbo controlled the sport and a farm system of promoters, managers, trainers and fighters was developed. Eventually, practically every manager worth his while and every fighter signed to that manager was connected to Palermo and company in one large, ugly, nation-wide web of corruption.

Throughout the 1930s and 1940s Mike Jacobs became one of the most influential men in professional boxing. Born in 1880, Jacobs was a hustler from the outset. Unafraid to tackle anyone that threatened his patch as a newsboy in the tough Hell's Kitchen area of New York, he quickly moved on to ticket touting, selling refreshments on the Hudson River excursion boats and even sold tickets for the Metropolitan Opera. The Opera set

I

him on the road to his first fortune as he signed up, and promoted tours for, Enrico Caruso, Lionel Barrymore and a host of other celebrities of the day.

In his mid-thirties Jacobs moved into professional boxing and never looked back. He loaned trail-blazing promoter Tex Rickard the money needed to set up a world heavyweight title defence for Jess Willard, a favour that earned him tickets for some of the better seats; all of which he sold for a profit. The Jack Dempsey versus George Carpentier million dollar gate at Boyle's Thirty Acres in Jersey City in 1921 was made possible due to a collaborative effort between Rickard, Jacobs and a syndicate of ticket brokers. This ensured that he again had access to the choice tickets and put his foot firmly in the door of Madison Square Garden on Eighth Avenue and 48th Street, where Rickard was the promoter.

Mike Jacobs had started his fast-growing empire from a little ticket office situated in the Normandie hotel in New York. As he became richer he moved to a small office on West 49th Street in New York, but in reality was already conducting business from inside the Garden. When Tex Rickard died in 1929, Mike Jacobs was already in a sufficient position of power to be a natural choice to fill his shoes. In a surprise move, depending on who you were and who you knew, the garden executives decided instead to give the job to ex-fight manager Jimmy Johnston.

As the 1930s progressed Jacobs plugged away at the fight game and began to buy up promotional rights on some of the country's top fighters. Before long, Jacobs could boast such popular pugilists as Barney Ross, Billy Petrolle and Jimmy McLarnin as a part of his roster

In 1933, Jacobs capitalised on what was essentially a huge mistake by new Garden boss Jimmy Johnston, when the manager at the Garden cancelled the venue's participation in charity events and fund-raisers. The Garden would no longer donate a percentage of the arena's revenues to the several worthy causes it had previously supported. One of the affected charities was the Milk Fund for Babies of which Mrs. William Randolph Hearst, wife of the newspaper tycoon, was a patron. As Johnston's biggest opposition, Mike Jacobs was approached by a number of the Hearst group's reporters, Edward J. Frayne, Bill Farnsworth and Damon Runyon, who proposed the formation of a promotional company that would operate in direct opposition to Johnston at the out-of-favour Madison Square Garden. To this end, they rented the New York Hippodrome on 44th Street and Ninth Avenue and the 20th Century Sporting Club came into existence. The three reporters would now write up glowing pieces on the promotions of the newly-formed club, which would pay a percentage of their profits from boxing promotions to the Milk Fund and Mike Jacobs would be the public face of the Club. The three scribes remained at their usual jobs and, as silent partners, received an income from their fledgling club's promotions. To raise the profile and develop the long-term prospects of the club, Jacobs added the fast-rising heavyweight star Joe Louis to the ever-expanding roster and the new enterprise continued to go from strength to strength.

In 1937 Jacobs promoted the Carnival of Champions at Yankee Stadium, a bill that featured reigning world champions Marcel Thil, Lou Ambers, Barney Ross and Sixto Escobar defending their titles against Fred Apostoli, Pedro Montanez, Ceferino Garcia, and Harry Jaffra respectively. The presentation of four world title fights on one bill demonstrated Jacobs' influence over main event boxing. By October of the same year, Jacobs had negotiated a leasing agreement with Madison Square Garden giving him total control of the major fight arenas in the New York area. Jacobs could now boast sole promotional rights to the Garden, Yankee Stadium, The Polo Grounds and Long Island Bowl.

With colourful, and highly popular, world champions Joe Louis and Henry Armstrong as part of his promotion package, it seemed that everyone wanted to fight for Mike Jacobs. He branched out to develop boxing as a weekly attraction on the radio, and if Madison Square Garden was booked for a Circus or a Rodeo on a Friday night, he transferred the boxing activity to the St. Nicholas Arena. Here Sam Taub and Bill Stern described the action for the radio listeners and later, when Gillette were the weekly event's main sponsors, Don Dunphy and Bill Corum took over the microphones. By 1938 Jacobs had an even better deal with the Garden signed, as he took the corporation in as a partner. He now paid fifty percent of the profits from his promotions, whenever he held them, instead of rent. The monopoly that Madison Square Garden once had on boxing now belonged to Jacobs and the 20th Century Sporting Club.

"Jacobs was the boss of boxing, not only in New York, but throughout the United States. Promoters in other states had to go through him for talent."

Nat Fleischer (founder of Ring Magazine)

With Jacobs' control over the heavyweight champion of the world, Joe Louis, he maintained a very tight grip on the professional fight game. During the 1940s, if you weren't connected in some way or didn't fight for Jacobs, you didn't have a great chance of reaching the top. This is not to say that all of the top fighters were crooked, though several were, or that they were personally involved in fixed fights. The better fighters would usually have to 'play the game' in order to progress and while there is practically no evidence of Joe Louis, the jewel in Jacobs' crown, ever taking part in a fixed fight throughout his championship years, it has to be said that other champions were not so lucky as to practice their trade without some kind of outside influence. That there is little doubt cast over the integrity of the Brown Bomber and his championship reign is probably due to the fact that Jacobs, in order to maintain Louis' clean, respectable image, would not have tolerated interference in heavyweight title fights. Such a scandal involving the widely respected and well-liked heavyweight king would have spelled disaster for boxing in general and Jacobs in particular.

If a top-flight fighter was connected to Czar Jacobs and his boxing empire then, more often than not, large chunks of his winnings were divided up amongst people that he had never met or even heard of. World champions and contenders took all of the risks, but received little of the spoils.

One well-documented tales of woe concerns Ike Williams, a Hall of Fame fighter and one of the greatest lightweights who ever lived. In his interview with boxing historian Norm Meekison for his International Boxing Hall-of-Fame interviews in 1991, Ike explained his own experiences.

"Seventy-five percent of it was controlled by crime. They were pretty fair to the fighters, they just stole their money.

Ike Williams, 1991

Williams became connected to Palermo, who had a manager's licence, because he had been black-balled for sacking his manager Con McCarthy. The irate manager, through his own connections in the sport, had Williams ostracised. There was then the unusual situation of a fighter, a reigning world champion, who couldn't even go into a gym and get a sparring partner, let alone a fight and a payday. After McCarthy reported him to the Managers' Guild, the lightweight champion became persona-non-grata in boxing circles.

Philadelphia-based Palermo offered to help Williams get fights if he would let him take care of his affairs. Williams did so and soon found himself virtually penniless, eventually working in a warehouse for less than $50 a week, the $77,000 that he earned from three fights under Palermo's guidance nowhere to be seen and not one cent of it in the fighter's own pocket.

"He said he would straighten it out with the guild, I couldn't get any fights, I signed a contract with him and he gave me some money, but it was the worst money I ever made."

Ike Williams, 1991

With close to one 150 boxing venues across America and with many of the major cities having two or three arenas with at least one fight card each week, a decent preliminary fighter could earn a reasonable living. In New York City alone, one could go and see boxing maybe six nights out of seven and even some small towns managed one fight card per week. Professional boxing was as popular in the United States then, as the National Football League, National Basketball Association and National Hockey League are today.

Television, at the time, had still not developed sufficiently enough to beam boxing events into the living rooms of America and the crowds at fights were still large. Because live gates were still substantial, the sport was big enough to accommodate and support close to 60,000 registered fighters, although it is nigh on impossible to pinpoint the actual numbers with any degree of accuracy.

With such a high level of participation, the potential for generating vast amounts of money through gambling and skimming off fighters' purses was phenomenal. Usually, the men in the know had the inside track on who was going to win and bets would be laid all over the country on bouts of sufficient interest. Within this environment many managers and their fighters prospered, while many more suffered. While palookas and journeymen plied their trade against each other with little interference from outside influences, the fighters with talent and desire eventually had to pay the band.

Good preliminary fighters might find themselves eventually opposing a genuine up-and-comer and while talent would usually win through, in some cases it had to be assured. Promises of decent future pay days and regular competition, in return for little or no real effort against a built up fighter, usually won the day. Of course anyone not willing to take the money, sign with the manager or otherwise comply with instructions would be ostracised and very little opportunity would come knocking for them.

Because of the way in which the sport was being run many talented fighters were left out in the cold and although some of them eventually had to 'do business' in one form or another, merely to get some work, they were never afforded the opportunities that their skills deserved. Holman Williams of Detroit, Jack Chase, Lloyd Marshall, Aaron Wade, Bert Lytell, Billy Smith and Eddie Booker of California and the determined Archie Moore were some of the more talented fighters around during the 1940s. Sadly, some of them became involved in business fights in order to further their careers and at one time or another they had to 'play ball' in order to get ahead. Unfortunately for a great number of these and other unheralded great fighters of the time, talent and a certain amount of integrity played a part in them being denied a chance at making history. In addition, it has to be said the colour of their skin was also a factor.

In order to make a living, black fighters like Holman Williams, Chase, Lytell, Wade and Smith had to battle amongst themselves, and very seldom did they get to fight any of the big name white fighters or receive anything like a good pay day. Most of these men, and many more like them, mostly long since forgotten, were fighters in possession of real talent. In terms of ability some of these men were simply too good for their own good. And when their sense of what was right and what was wrong would not allow them to become involved in games that destroyed the careers and lives of honest men, they were ignored and avoided. One such man was Charley Burley of Pittsburgh.

Many who observed Burley in action marvelled at his skill, his grace, his body control and his sheer athleticism. Charley Burley appeared to have it all, and while some fighters were great defensively, but could not punch, and others were explosive or concussive punchers, but didn't have the defence, Burley was capable of both. A boxer-puncher whose style, though unorthodox, was extremely effective, if at times rather dull. Called the greatest fighter of all time by such authorities as eventual world light-heavyweight champion Archie Moore and legendary trainer Eddie Futch, Charley Burley was a man admired by his peers for his prodigious talent in the ring and for his gentle and honest demeanour out of it.

"You know, people ask me who was the best fighter I ever met and I tell them Rocky Marciano, because that's what they want to hear.

Hell, Marciano beat me when I was 42 and I gave him a great battle. Eddie Booker and Charley Burley were the best. They beat me in my prime. Booker broke my ribs and Burley gave me a boxing lesson."

Archie Moore

"He was something to see. He was a master at slipping punches, counter-punching. He walked to you with a good jab, feinted and made you miss. He didn't move his legs too much, he'd just slide over, make you miss and he was right there on top of you with either hand punching."

Eddie Futch

"He was a good old guy, a good husband and a good father to his children. He used to say 'I don't bother no one and no one bothers me.'"

Julia Burley

Charley Burley developed his skills in the gloomy gymnasiums and smoke-filled fight halls of his adopted home of Pittsburgh, Pennsylvania during some of the toughest and most competitive years of boxing the famous 'Smoky City' had seen. Harry Greb, Patsy Brannigan, Frank Klaus, Johnny Ray and the Zivic brothers were some of the more famous fighting names to come out of the city during the first few decades of the 1900s, but the 1930s and 40s could also boast some of the toughest names in the history of the game. Teddy and Tommy Yarosz, Fritzie Zivic, Ralph Chong, Billy Conn, Jackie Wilson and Harry Bobo, were just a few of Charley Burley's contemporaries, amongst many others, and during the years that they were all vying for recognition, Pittsburgh had a reputation as being one very rough fight town indeed

Pittsburgh scene by Sean Odega from a photograph by Peter Krumel.

Charley Burley

Scourge of the welterweight and middleweight
divisions between 1936 - 1950

Chapter One

Bessemer, the 'Burgh and Barcelona

Hell with the lid off. A description that writer James Parton saw fit to tag onto industrial Pittsburgh in the early part of the 20th Century. During that time the steel city was a place so dark and broody that 'lighting up time' came several hours before neighbouring towns and cities. The steel mills that lined the Monongahela River constantly spewed forth noxious by-product that trapped man and beast under a semi-permanent frown, with thousands of feet of smoke and soot seemingly woven into an impenetrable blanket, protecting its shadowy occupants from the outside world. If you were born there, you learned to survive. If you deliberately moved there and settled down you also learned to survive, but to do so you had to be desperate to the extreme, or a few bricks short of a load.

Near the outset of the 1930s The Hill District became home to the Burley family as they re-located from Van Meter, Pennsylvania, a small mining town in Westmoreland County, some thirty miles or so southeast of Pittsburgh. The mining industry, operated by various companies such as the Bessemer Coke Company, the Pittsburgh Coal Company and the H.C. Frick Coke Company (amongst many dozens of smaller operations), was the primary source of work for most itinerant workers. There is little to indicate that Westmoreland County or its industry held anything in the way of future promise for its inhabitants and just as numerous other black families from many rural outposts travelled the United States searching for work and a better way of life, so too did the Burleys contemplate pastures new. With nothing more than the clothes on their backs they travelled from one mining community to another, ever hopeful of finding a place to settle.

The seemingly endless journey took in several long-term stopovers, with the ongoing migration held in check by the necessity of working for food and shelter. The dusty streets of coal mining 'patch' towns, that were built up around the mining industry, practically blurred into one rickety, beat-up and run-down hovel after another. Locations such as Van Meter (where the Pittsburgh Coal Company operated Banning No. 3 Mine),

1

Unity Township or the slightly more developed mining community of Latrobe, at one time or another saw all or some of the Burley convoy.

Van Meter, like many mining towns, was not the most salubrious of places. Men and supplies had to be hauled across the river from the village of Jacobs Creek, where most of them lived, to work at the Darr Mine. If getting to their place of employment was considered a dangerous proposition, the labour itself, especially at the Van Meter mine, was deadly. The mine inspector's report for 1906 concluded that ventilation at the Darr mine was insufficient and that gas and dust were a major concern. The report proved prophetic, as the mine at Van Meter was the site of one of the worst mining disasters in the nation, as on December 19th, 1907 an explosion killed 239 miners.

By 1910 the Pittsburgh Coal Company had resumed operations, though the company dropped the Darr name and simply operated the mine as an entry of the adjacent Banning No. 3 Mine. By 1913 Banning No. 3 Mine employed 350 people. That year its miners produced about 155,000 tons of coal and it was here that the head of the Burley family found yet another job. Charles Burley Senior had worked the mines in his birthplace of Virginia - where he had met Angeline O'Brien - and the backbreaking excavations of rural Pennsylvania were nothing new to him. The physical work itself was deadly enough and a miner usually paid with his health for the long days, months and years of breathing in coal dust. After many years as a coke drawer and tippler, Charles Burley was one who paid the price. Born the son of a former slave in Albemarle County, Virginia in September 1875, the head of the Burley clan was considered to be in good enough health when the final civilian draft for WWI was conducted in September 1918 and his army records indicate that there was nothing exceptional or different about the then 43 year-old. He was of medium build, medium height, black hair and brown eyes, married with dependants and no physical disabilities.

With the conflict, by that time, in its fourth year Mr. Burley may have wondered if he would be required to experience the horrors of war and must also have wondered if the trenches of the Western Front were any less hellish than working for H. C. Frick and his coal mining behemoth. A monster as relentless as the war in Europe; seemingly intent on sucking the life out of the green fields of Pennsylvania and the souls that toiled there.

Despite the fact that his health was deteriorating, he struggled on in an attempt to provide for the ever-growing family he and his equally hard-working partner, Angeline O'Brien, had produced. Their only son,

2

Charles, had been born in nearby Bessemer on 6th September 1917 and by the time of his second birthday excavations at Banning No. 3 were slowing as the mine produced less than 30,000 tons of coal. Soon after, Pittsburgh Coal Company closed Banning No. 3 Mine and the old Darr Mine entry. Workers were offered the opportunity to transfer to Banning No. 1, mined by the same company in nearby Fayette County and it would appear that there was little choice.

At that point in his 'career' Charles Burley had progressed sufficiently to be afforded the enviable position of 'tippler' at the mine. Based above ground, his job was to tip the coal into small lorries for the short journey from the tipple to the coke ovens. Although Charles Burley Senior's health was beginning to fail, he decided to make the move and continue in his chosen area. It seems that as the Burleys moved around the mining fields and operations of Westmoreland County, constantly looking for work, their patriarch's health began to give way completely. While the miners strike for better conditions in 1922 may have been successful for some, for Charles Burley it was too late and in 1925 he finally succumbed at the relatively young age of 50.

For a while, Angeline (who, by 1930, was 55 years old), Charley and his younger sister, Zella, lived with Leona Burley (the eldest of the Burley children), her husband Harry Moore (also a miner) and their own two children in the Darr Village at Van Meter. Located on the west bank of the Youghiogheny River in Rostraver Township the village was comprised of about thirty miners houses, a managers' row and a company store. The wood-framed accommodation was cold, cramped and cost $9.50 per month to rent and while there may have been little else of real value there it appears that Van Meter contained the most important element of all - a railroad passenger depot. As the surviving family members looked towards a location that would offer more in the way of opportunity for a widow and her young children, life in the mines went on. The Pittsburgh Coal Company continued to operate Banning No. 1 & No. 2 Mines in Fayette County through the 1940s.

The nearest city was Pittsburgh and while it could never be called large, in comparison to New York or Detroit for example, it held something in the way of opportunity for those desperate enough and the Burleys, like thousands of other families, had little else but hope. As with many other northern cities in America, such as Chicago and Detroit, Pittsburgh received a huge influx of African-Americans during the early 1900s. These sons and daughters of former southern slaves began migrating north in a futile attempt to flee the poverty and degradation of their home cities and towns in the south.

Those that arrived in Pittsburgh discovered a city that was, in economic terms, well past its prime. The boon for industry that was the First World War was long gone and despite the resulting economic decline, many still flocked to the city. The black population of Pittsburgh more than doubled from 20,000 in the first few years following 1900 to 55,000 by the 1930s, (and 100,000 by 1960). Many of the blacks that flooded into the city settled in an area known as 'The Hill District'.

The Hill District first began to develop as a community in 1818 when a group of runaway slaves first settled there. Around twenty years later the district developed further still, as local entrepreneur Thomas Mellon bought the land and sold it off in plots at a good profit. Many of Pittsburgh's well-to-do found The Upper Hill to be an ideal move away from the grimy smoke and soot that emanated from the steel factories along the river fronts.

Soon, The Hill became the first stop-off point for many European immigrants and African-Americans newly arrived in the city. As time passed the Hill District grew to include Armenians, Germans, Jews, Greeks, Italians, Russians, Irish, Syrians, and many other nationalities, mostly living in and around the Bedford Flats. A real 'bed-bug' place, as lice and other parasites were the norm. An environment where grubby hands and shoeless feet were commonplace and shaven heads were popular amongst the young male population in a seemingly constant battle against infestation.

With so many races represented in the area, the intermingling of cultures gave The Hill District a unique character and identity of its own. In its day the area was as glamorous as New York's Harlem. Part of the Lower Hill at one time was known as 'Little Haiti' with Centre Avenue and 10th Street being known as the 'crossroads of the world'.

Coming from the relatively quiet backwoods of rural Pennsylvania it must have overawed the Burleys to be amongst the frenetic activity that existed in and around The Hill District. To survive they quickly had to adapt to their new environment and this they achieved with great difficulty. It took a while before they managed to find a place to call home, at times hopping from one rented squalor to another, and it was a number of years before they were able to find something remotely stable. Eventually Angeline Burley and her children settled on Roberts Street on the lower Hill. Charley's older sisters, Olga, Millie and Viola also lived on the Hill and were relatively established when the rest of the clan caught up with them. Charley was a quiet child and was slow to make friends whilst his younger sister, Zella, had little trouble in that department and was soon in the regular company of local girl Julia Taylor. Julia was Pittsburgh born and bred and she and her family were living on Arthur Street, which formed an intersection with the busy Wylie Avenue and was a stone's-throw from Bedford Avenue and Crawford Street, two of the better known and more densely populated streets on The Hill. She remembers the Burleys from almost the instant they settled on the Hill.

> "Charley come from the country. So, when his family moved to the city his sister came first, she lived down there near 'Jew Town'. You know where 'Jew Town' was – Logan Street, Franklin School. She lived down there. So, she married this guy from the city. Then they sent for them one-by-one, for the sisters and their mother. Their mother came, then all of the Burleys were here in Pittsburgh. They all lived together down there in Elm Street and they moved up to Roberts Street and I lived off Arthur Street."

> **Julia (Taylor) Burley**

Charley's mother, who, according to surviving family members, had emigrated from County Cork in Ireland as a young woman, had a reputation in the neighbourhood as being a 'tough old bird'. Standing barely over five-foot tall, with long, coarse, dark brown hair, a strong jaw and piercing blue eyes she was famous around the neighbourhood for the amount of swearing and cussing that she could fit into an everyday conversation. As an aside, it is worth noting that census returns for 1930 show that Angeline O'Brien claims that she was born in Ohio and her parents in Pennsylvania. Such returns are, of course, 'self-reported'. There may have been a valid reason for Angeline to claim American ancestry, but still, her Irish roots are evident in her own surname and the fact she gave young Charley the middle name of Duane - Gaelic for Black.

Although the area had a rich blend of cultures and races, mostly poor, it must have taken a special character to survive up there on The Hill, a single white woman with five black children, regardless of what part of the world she originated from.

If she were Irish Angeline Burley had the necessary prerequisites, as being Irish and being tough went hand in hand; because if you were Irish you had to have character to last. The lowest of the low as far as the 'Old Pittsburghers' were concerned, those of Irish descent apparently had no place in a city that used to pride itself on its wealthy European heritage.

5

No matter that a large portion of the city's industry was built upon the strong backs of sinewy, Celtic labour. It was somehow a lower class and, like the rest of the so-called lower classes that flooded into Pittsburgh during the early part of the Twentieth Century, The Hill District, and in particular the lower Hill, was the allocated place.

The area appeared to mirror its inhabitants, with thousands of dwellings like odd, misshapen little boxes sitting close enough to each other, upon uneven cobbled streets, to have washing lines strung between them. Families practically lived in each other's pockets with space an ever-dwindling commodity, as the densely packed dwellings were filled to overflowing by the constant flood of migrating hopefuls.

Without a man in the home to be the breadwinner, Angeline Burley and her children, eked out a meagre existence for themselves in the same manner as many of the other poorer families on the Hill, doing whatever it took to get by. Some took in washing, cleaned at some of the more well-to-do homes or worked at the Heinz Food or Clark Candy Bar factories.

A skill that many of the black population of the Hill brought with them from the country was that of chicken plucking and whilst barely his teens this was young Charley's speciality. Plucking the carcasses of dead poultry was laborious, tedious and extremely hard on the hands, but it was also an honest day's work, an ethic that Charley's mother preached often to her children. Living within deprived times - and an equally poor location - meant that stealing and cheating, and just about every other activity thrust upon the have-nots, was rife.

The Hill district in particular was populated with individuals from all walks of life, including; prostitutes, gamblers, thieves, confidence tricksters, drug-dealers and just about every other questionable occupation that enabled these people to survive. Falling into that lifestyle was easy for many, but while the Burley family may not have had much, what they did have was earned by their own honest toil.

"Charley was a chicken-plucker, proud of it too. It was his first job when he came from the country; he plucked a lot of chickens. Years ago children worked, everybody worked, all the immigrants all worked down in 'Jew Town' they called it, the Jews owned almost all of the stores."

Julia Burley

The area around Wylie Avenue, Bedford Avenue and Logan Street was lined with such stores. Kalson's Delicatessen, Gropper's Grocery, Benkovitz Fish Market and the Live Chicken Store. There were also Italian ice cream parlours and coffee shops to add to the mixture of aromas in the air. With most of the poorer families on the Hill the exchanging of food was common practice, as families traded amongst themselves. Jewish dishes for Greek dishes, Greek for African-American, for Italian and so on. The food may not have been plentiful, but the populace of the Hill certainly had a varied diet. This might go some way to explaining Charley's love of pasta and of spaghetti in particular. Charley loved to eat, but the amount of food he put away appeared to have little effect upon his long, lean frame and while he might have been growing up, he certainly didn't grow out too much.

Young Charley attended 5th Avenue High School and his younger sister Zella went to Letsche school, which was on Bedford Avenue opposite the top end of the steep Northward slope that was Crawford Street. Charley lived within a few blocks of Letsche, as did Julia Taylor who also attended the local school. The two were already seeing quite a bit of each other socially due to school and Julia's friendship with Charley's sister. Being the quiet and somewhat reserved kind, Charley usually kept himself to himself and while he was fond of Julia he had yet to let her know.

The winters on the Hill were as bleak and miserable as just about anywhere else you could name. The seemingly ever-present smog only deepened the oppressive atmosphere. "So dreadfully hideous, so intolerably bleak and forlorn, that it reduced the whole aspirations of men to a macabre and depressing joke.", was how writer H.L. Mencken remembered it. As dark as the winters may have been, it seems that the summers were blessed with the constant warm and bright glow of childhood memories. Occasionally, fire hydrants would be opened up for the children to enjoy the cool, refreshing water and Julia Burley remembers many such times with affection. She also recalls that when they were younger they rarely strayed from the immediate neighbourhood. She thinks it funny that back then, for them at least, nothing appeared to exist past Kirkpatrick Street - less than a mile away from their corner.

It appeared that there was always something to do and they entertained themselves as only younger minds seem able. With the water and washing facilities at the local Washington Park openly reserved for whites only and the community pump constantly occupied during the slightest heat-wave, the open hydrants were a blessing relished by adults and children alike. Out of school (and when not earning money dressing chickens), Charley usually busied himself playing baseball down at Washington Park. The sport of baseball in Pittsburgh, especially among black players, has a tremendous history. The Homestead Greys, who won a record number of 'Negro League' titles, and the Pittsburgh Crawfords, owned by local entrepreneur William A. 'Gus' Greenlee (who also owned and operated the famous Crawford Bar and Grill), were two of the most dominant teams in black sports during any era. Julia Burley recalls that Charley was a good all-round athlete and swimmer and that he received an offer to play for the Greys while he was in his teens. This would have been a great honour as the Greys at the time boasted the legendary Josh Gibson (for one) on their roster. Legend has it that Gibson hit the longest drive ever witnessed at Forbes Field when he sent the ball out of sight over the centrefield wall. As far as baseball went, Charley was interested, but he had already found himself another distraction from the daily grind of living to work and this activity was taking up practically all of his spare time.

> "We were movers, we moved around a lot, no special place to go I headed for the gym."

Charley Burley

The gym he found was the Kay Boys' Club, which opened its doors for the first time in the early part of 1931. Situated at 2038 Bedford Avenue in an old, disused three-storey factory, the club was named after the president of the Pittsburgh Newsboys' Home, James Kay. A prominent attorney in the city, James Kay devoted much of his time and money to under-privileged boys. The club that bore his name offered local boys a programme of general recreation, including physical activities and vocational training. This is where Charley Burley began his boxing career and he took to the sport like the proverbial duck to water, dedicating more and more of his spare time to the gym.

The presence of black male figureheads at the club in the form of his coaches, especially one Leonard Payne, cannot be underestimated. From the age of eight, young Charley had no male influences in his life apart from the occasional visit by his two stepbrothers and the time he lived with his brother-in-law Harry Moore. Leonard Payne had a great influence on a young and impressionable Charley Burley and the first photograph on the first page of Charley's dusty, green leather-bound scrapbook shows boxer and coach posed together in mock practice.

The adults and older boys at the boys' club undoubtedly gave Charley the necessary balance in his teenage years providing a counter to the six females in his life. Being the only boy from six surviving children, Charley must have felt the male-dominated sport of boxing was a most welcome change. That is not to say that he did not benefit from being the only boy. According to Julia Burley, Charley was quite spoiled as a child and his mother or one of his sisters always made sure his boxing attire was clean and pressed each time he fought.

Amongst the almost hypnotic, rhythmic noise of bag punching and rope-skipping that resounds around every boxing gym; Charley learned how to box. Skipping and bag-work helped to develop his fitness while the coaching and sparring sessions resulted in the development of a boxing style that may be described by some as relaxed. At the age of 13 and after only a few months of training, he was put into his first contest against an opponent whose name and physical features have been obscured by the passage of time. Wearing swimming trunks and sneakers Charley jabbed and moved his way through several minutes of frantic activity to the end of three rounds of boxing and his first ever win. He was a scrawny 112-pounder at the time, but enjoyed the competition and continued to box successfully as an amateur for the remainder of his teens.

"I found something I was good at, so I stuck at it."

Charley Burley

By the time Charley was 16 years old he had developed his style and skills sufficiently enough under the tutelage of coaches Leonard Payne and Howard Turner, to win a Junior Golden Gloves Championship at lightweight. Even at this relatively young age his ability to defend from a punch while remaining in range to counter was baffling many of his opponents, and even the older, more physically mature and experienced boxers at the boys' club were beginning to struggle with him in the ring. Charley was blessed with the appropriate physical tools for his chosen sport in the form of long, slim legs and extremely long arms for his height and weight.

The variety of amateur clubs that were dotted around the city meant that there was always competition available. The Kay Boys' Club, the

Pittsburgh Boys' Club, the Superior Athletic Club and the Irene Kaufman Settlement, (also known as the 'Ike's'), fought often in an attempt to gain superiority in local boxing circles. The Settlement, while offering as wide a range of sporting activities as possible, was not ideally suited to the sport of boxing. The ring was hemmed-in by three walls, all padded as a safety precaution due to their close proximity to the ring ropes. There was also a speed bag, a heavy bag and a double-end bag. Five guys training and the place would be full. However, boxing was not the Settlement's main priority, as it also catered for vocational skills in addition to the arts and other sports.

A young Charley Burley with his amateur coach from Pittsburgh, Leonard Payne.

Boxing in Pittsburgh, as in many other large cities during the time, was not only a form of exercise and self-defence - it was a way of earning extra money and therefore a living. The numerous young fighters that had aspirations to be as good as the men in the photographs that adorned the walls of gyms and bars throughout the town knew that they had to work hard at their sport. Harry Greb was probably the most famous fighter to come out of the city, becoming world middleweight champion in 1923. Legends of 'The Pittsburgh Windmill' were recounted endless times around the amateur and professional gyms, as were stories of the fighting Zivics from Lawrenceville, one of whom had gone on to win an Olympic games boxing medal.

During the early years of the 20th century Pittsburgh had quite a reputation for producing tough, hard-fighting stock. Frank Klaus and George Chip were the forerunners before World War I broke out and, at that time, the Steel City was a tough place to get a win. In those early days Pittsburgh was a 'newspaper decision' haven, which meant that each writer picked his winner and reported accordingly. There were seven newspapers back around the time of World War I, these were : The Dispatch, Post and Gazette Times in the morning and Press, Sun, Leader and Chronicle-Telegraph in the evenings. The Dispatch and Leader disappeared in 1923 - the same year that the McBride act came into force and boxing moved under state control - and the Post-Gazette and Sun-Telegraph were formed after mergers around four years later. So, if four of the seven reporters went for the local - or their own favourite - fighter then bets would be paid out according to the 'newspaper decision'. It is not difficult to see how coercion and corruption could creep in. When the aforementioned Mr. Greb came to prominence there was some semblance of control within the fight game with regard to the decisions rendered, but it was still not perfect and it would take until 1955 (when the State Athletic Commission made a concerted effort to make the sport 'honest'), before any real effort was made to see-off the more corrupt element.

By the time Charley Burley may have been formulating his own ideas about a career in boxing Pittsburgh was a pantheon of pugilistic activity. There were fights at Motor Square Garden in East Liberty, Duquesne Garden in Oakland, South Side Market House, the old Exposition Hall, the North Side Arena and Hickey Park in Millvale. With so many venues holding fights on a regular basis activity amongst promoters was almost as frenetic as anything that went on in the various boxing rings.

As Charley Burley matured into a welterweight the victories kept coming. However, it appears that hand problems stalled his blossoming career for several months as, in late February - early March 1935, he was forced to undergo an operation on an injured hand. It was reported that by the end of March he was back in training three days a week for a May 10th bout with local rival Leo Sweeney of nearby Lawrenceville and was "socking as hard as ever". Overall the year appears to have been something of a disaster. At the end of October Charley managed to get a bout at the South Side Market House where he defeated Young Brown of the Willow AC.

1936 started on a more positive note, as far as boxing went, as Charley set his sights on the national Amateur Athletic Union championships and a possible Olympic berth. Despite the Saint Patrick's Day floods that devastated the area in March of that year, the worst in the city's history, normality was resumed as soon as possible and the people of Pittsburgh continued with their daily lives. A tournament was organised for April as a 'Flood Relief Fund-raiser' and Charley, as one of the city's top amateurs, was invited to appear. Prior to that, an intercity match was held in Cleveland. The Pittsburgh team came away with a narrow victory and Charley played his part by defeating Jimmie Smith by KO.

For the fund-raiser at the Syria Mosque tickets were available at $1, $2, $3, $4 and $5. With the promise of 14 inter-city fights that would feature top, local talent displaying their skills some 4,500 fans packed the venue. The appearance of guest referees Jack Dempsey and Joe Louis undoubtedly helped swell the takings to an impressive $10,000 for the flood relief fund and the Manassa Mauler made himself very popular with the people of Pittsburgh by covering his own expenses; he also bought 20 tickets and paid for 10 of the watches that were given out a prizes to the amateur boxers. Jack may not have been so popular with local favourite Leo Sweeney who dropped a close bout to Howell King of Detroit in which the former heavyweight champion was the third man.

Other notable bouts on the card included the tall, muscular Elbert Rooison of Detroit who gave the fans something to remember by braking Tony Galento's Pittsburgh KO record by stopping Tony Olercheck in 13 seconds flat; Galento had once won in 14 seconds at the Motor Square Garden against George Panka. Another of the Detroit fighters on show was the murderous-punching Milton Shivers. The hard-hitting Detroiter forced referee Al Greyber to intervene in his bout with Bob Crosby of Superior AC. Charley Burley Apparently did nothing special in a three round decision over Stanley Murszyk of Chicago.

Charley and the rest of the rising amateur stars had done their bit for charity, but there were more pressing matters at hand to attend to as in excess of 250 pugilists descended upon Cleveland to dispute the 1936 national AAU titles. All of the semi-finalists in each of the weight divisions were promised a position in the box-offs for the United States Olympic boxing team, so the competition was intense. With such a massive field to whittle down to 16 eventual finalists it was decided to forego the usual rules pertaining to the national championships and the initial rounds were staged over three two minute rounds instead of the usual three minutes per round. At the end of three days of furious competition (fought in two rings) Charley made the welterweight semi-final along with fellow Pittsburgher, Leo Sweeney. The Lawrenceville boxer had quite a reputation in local amateur circles and had previously been Pennsylvania state champion at featherweight, lightweight and welterweight. In his series, Sweeney defeated James Pattisall of Danville, Virginia and Sweeney Byers of Chilocco, Oklahoma (both on points), whilst Charley defeated Mario Duchini of Sacramento, California and George J. Morrow of Philadelphia (also on points). KO artist Vincent Solders of Baltimore was looking to be the favourite for the competition as it approached the semi-final stage as he had disposed of both his early round opponents via the short route. Howell King of Detroit was also in contention for the title. In his semi-final, Leo Sweeney was drawn against King, whilst Charley appeared to draw the short straw as he was matched with the dangerous Solders. Leo Sweeney beat King on points to reach the final and Charley stopped the hard-punching Solders in the third round. Thus the final pairing was not just about a national championship, it was also about local pride as the Pittsburgh Boys Club (Sweeney), fought it out with the Superior Athletic Club (Charley Burley). Regardless of the result, the city of Pittsburgh was guaranteed its first national champion in ten years. With advantages in both age and experience Leo Sweeney was a little too good for his young rival and he gave Charley an effective demonstration of jabbing on the move. The Associated press said of the evening's proceedings:

"In the 147-pound division, two Pittsburgh boys fought it out and the victory went to Leo Sweeney. He decisioned his team-mate, Charley Burley, in a cautious bout that showed each fighter knew what the other had."

After the loss to Sweeney in the AAU finals in April Charley, along with Sweeney and 108 other hopefuls, entered the Allegheny Mountain Association Golden Gloves in May. The event drew amateur boxers from Morgan Town and Wheeling West Virginia to Oil City, Monaca, Erie, Kittaning, Butler and East Liverpool. Over three nights of boxing at Duquesne Garden Charley defeated Al Anderson of the Curry Rox Club on points and Lou Gendle of Miami AC on a first round stoppage before he was eliminated in the regional finals by the boxer who definitely had the hex sign over him - Leo Sweeney. Charley's nemesis then lost to Johnny Barbera, who then lost in the national semi-final to team-mate Howell King. Chester Ruteki defeated Vincent Solders in the other semi-final before winning the national Golden Gloves crown by out-pointing King in the final.

After a very brief professional career Sweeney became a well-respected and much-liked police officer in Pittsburgh. Most cops in those days had to be big, because once they were out on the street they were essentially alone and respect was usually gained by virtue of sheer physical presence. The force that patrolled the Hill District in particular, were famous for their size, as they all measured over six feet. There were no radios to call in for back-up if they ran into trouble, so respect on the street was a necessity when trying to get the job done. At five-feet ten-inches and less than 160 pounds, what made 'Irish' Leo Sweeney a successful cop was his fearsome fighting reputation. It was reported (around the time of the 1936 national championships) that Charley Burley had failed to beat Leo Sweeney in seven attempts (if this is true, the Lawrenceville stylist appears to have been the only fighter to have beaten Charley Burley as an amateur). The meetings with Sweeney and his honesty about the manner of his defeats was one of the reasons why Charley was very popular with the Pittsburgh police force in later years.

"I said to Charley, 'How did Leo beat you?' And he told me, 'The best damned left hand you'd ever wanna' see.' And when Charley told you it was the best, we're talking about a left hand that was educated and that's what beat him. Charley couldn't handle that left, he had no bones about telling the truth."

Bobby Lippi, friend and protégé

Immediately after losing to Sweeney in the local Golden Gloves Charley took up an invitation to box against the national AAU middleweight Champion Jimmie Clark in Titusville. The bout was to be top of the bill on the local club fund-raiser, but things didn't work out a planned as the American Olympic Committee pulled the plug on Clark who was a favourite for an Olympic berth and the upcoming Olympic box-offs (as a national AAU finalist Charley was also entitled to compete in the box-offs to be held in Chicago that June). The fact that the Olympic Committee insisted Clark not box, but didn't place the same demands on Charley Burley may be some indication as to how early in the game Charley had decided not to try out for a place in the U.S. team.

It has been suggested that Charley decided not to compete in the box-off because of his own moral opposition to the racial and religious discrimination being promoted in Nazi Germany. If so, this can only be considered a rare sense of morals and political awareness in one so young. Part of the answer may lie in the build-up to the games themselves.

The eleventh Olympiad was awarded to Germany by the International Olympic Committee in May, 1931. The award was viewed as part of Germany's continuing re-integration into European and world affairs in the aftermath of WWI. However, within two years of the gesture Germany came under the control of the National Socialists. Adolf Hitler's appointment to the chancellorship saw the instigation of nationwide campaigns boycotting Jewish businesses. An escalation of these racial policies saw discrimination against Jewish students in schools and universities along with the intimidation and exclusion of Jews in the professions of medicine, education, and law. Sadly, the German sporting community would not be immune to these trends as the two men largely instrumental in bringing the Games to Germany, Theodor Lewald and Carl Diem, were removed from the German Olympic Committee presidency because of the own or their wife's 'partial Jewish heritage'.

By April 1933, Hans von Tschammer (Hitler's appointed replacement for Lewald and Diem) had ordered an "Aryan only" policy in all German athletic organizations and Jewish and Gypsy athletes were excluded from sports clubs, public pools, gyms, and other sports facilities. Between 1933 and 1936 debates raged across America questioning the wisdom of sending U.S. athletes to a sporting event hosted by a country whose political regime was sworn to racist ideology. The controversy encompassed not only athletes and leaders of amateur sports groups but also labour and religious organizations. Rallies and public meetings in several U.S. cities called for the re-instatement of German Jewish athletes or for a complete boycott.

Charley's coach and mentor Phil Goldstein undoubtedly had his charge's ear when the subject of Nazis and their racial and religious persecution of Jews came up. Conversely, Pittsburgh's African American newspaper, the Courier, believed that the U.S. should send a team as not to do so would deny many black athletes the opportunity of a lifetime. Whatever his reasoning, the final decision was that Charley Burley did not attend the competition in Chicago or subsequently make the team that travelled to Berlin that summer. The disappointment of practically de-selecting himself from the national team for a once-in-a-lifetime event must have been bitter, but it was also short-lived. Judge Jeremiah Mahoney was a longtime member of the AAU, a former Olympian and former New York supreme court justice. Mahoney was opposed to the U.S. sending a team to Berlin as he believed that participation in the Games would damage the Olympic movement in the long term and would also violate the American Olympic Committee's own national rules against discrimination on account of race or creed. Mahoney had resigned from the AOC in a dispute with Committee head Avery Brundage and went on to form the Committee for Fair Play in Sports.

In May of 1936 invitations to an alternative event to be held in direct opposition to the Berlin games had been sent out by the Spanish Government to the United States and every other country that was considering sending a team to Berlin. Barcelona had been selected as the venue to host these games as the city had been the main contender to host the Olympiad scheduled to begin in Hitler's Germany that August and the infrastructure for a large-scale athletics event was already in place. In June, 1936 Charley was the recipient of a surprise telegram from a Mr. Chamberlain on behalf of the 'Committee for Fair Play in Sports' - would he be interested in representing his country at an alternative event to the Berlin Olympics?

Charley's invitation may have been the result of a recommendation by Phil Goldstein or the labour movement of which Charley appears to have been a supporter. The official position, in the pen picture of Charley that was part of the team sheet for the Barcelona Games, helps further illuminates the situation:

CHARLES BURLEY - 57 Fullerton Street, Pittsburgh, Pa. - BOXING. 147-pound class; Golden Gloves Championship 1936; Golden Gloves Junior Championship 1934; National Runner-up, Cleveland, 1936; AAU tournaments. Was asked to try-outs for Olympic team, 1936, refused to compete on grounds of racial and religious discrimination in Nazi Germany.

Committee for Fair Play in Sports

An additional note at the bottom of the team sheet indicates the team selection process:

Above-mentioned athletes, save two, have been elected by their

organizations - all of them trade unions or labour - in elimination contests here in New York City. Irving Jenkins and Charles Burley selected
by organizing committee for the Barcelona Olympiada because of their
outstanding records and because of their sympathy to the labour sports
movement.

Charley decided to accept the offer and to travel to Spain to compete for
his country in what was generally felt to be a fairer and less oppressive
environment. There had been rumblings throughout athletics as to the
corruption that had infested the prestigious Olympic tournament and it
was believed that bribery, favouritism and commercialisation were ruin-
ing what was essentially an event for amateur sports persons.

The alternative 'Workers Games', which were being promoted by the
Spanish government, had originated in 1925 as direct opposition to the
restrictive and corrupt practices of the modern Olympics. Successful
meets had taken place in Frankfurt and Vienna with upwards of 100,000
in attendance and it was anticipated that the meeting at Barcelona would
be equally well attended.

Charley requested that his coach be allowed to travel with him to the
games, but the committee could not allow him to take his mentor for fear
of setting a precedent they could not uphold for the rest of the team. With
travel funds wired to him at the end of June, Charley left Pittsburgh and
the comfort and familiarity of his family and surroundings and headed
for New York. Upon his arrival in the city, he reported to the offices of the
Fair Play Committee in Vesey Street, just across from City Hall, where he
met Mr. Chamberlain and the team coach Alfred Chakin. The committee
had put together a team of nine athletes, all of whom, apart from Charley,
were from the city or its immediate environs. The only other boxer on the
team was a heavyweight from Cornell University by the name of Irving
Jenkins. The six-foot plus, fair-haired collegian also played football for
Cornell.

After a couple of days of getting to know each other and to witness
the constant blur of movement that is New York City, a party of twelve
– nine athletes, their coach and two committee members – boarded the
SS Transylvania at the dock on West 57th street. Shortly after noon on
July 3rd, 1936, their ship slipped out of the Hudson River and into the
Atlantic Ocean, headed for Europe. None of the party could have known
that as they watched the New York skyline disappear behind them, the
adventure that lay in store for them would dramatically alter their lives
and many of them would never be the same upon their return.

During the trip across the Atlantic, Charley became acquainted with his team mates, although it was probably a lengthy process due to his essentially shy and reticent nature. Snapshots taken during the trip show a rather stern-looking Charley Burley and Julia Burley believes the reluctance to smile for the camera was just plain shyness. When the athletes had settled on board and had found their sea legs, team coach Alfred Chakin began to put them through their paces. Charley and the heavyweight boxer, Irving Jenkins (a student at Cornell), managed to get in some training and sparring with each other and Charley more than held his own despite the disadvantage of four years in age, 45 pounds in weight and five inches in height

> "He had a terrific punch that Charley Burley, I tell you. We used to box on the upper deck of the ship going over."

> **Irving Jenkins**

To his sparring partner, it appeared that Charley genuinely had no fear of bigger fighters, something that would hold him in good stead later in his boxing career, when he would be forced to fight out of his natural weight category. On board ship he set about the heavyweight as if Jenkins were no more than a welterweight. Jenkins remembers that the coach, Alfred Chakin, was not happy about the hell-for-leather sessions.

> "The coach said, 'Hey, you guys will kill each other, don't you dare."

> **Irving Jenkins**

The remainder of the American contingent consisted of working-class amateur athletes from various disciplines. For the track events were Harry Engel (a dress cutter), Myron Dickes (teacher), Eddie Krauss (labourer), Frank Payton (teacher) and Dorothy Tucker (the only member of the team to list her occupation as an athlete). Cyclist Julian Raoul (waiter) and gymnast Bernie Danchik (a clerk). Charley Burley's occupation was listed as 'labourer'.

William Chamberlain assisted coach Alfred Chakin in the care of the youngsters along with Francis Adam Henson, a delegate for the

Committee for Fair Play. Charley Burley, Dorothy Tucker and Frank Peyton were the only black members of the team.

After ten days at sea their vessel docked at the Irish port of Dublin before moving on to Glasgow in Scotland the following day. It was here that the cyclist Julian Raoul left the party to travel independently to Spain. The team's journey was scheduled to take them through France and Raoul had personal concerns in regard to visa restrictions.

The trip from France through to Spain appears to have been an enjoyable one for the party. In Paris Charley recalled seeing the glamorous American star Josephine Baker and was surprised at the amount of spending money that they had each been allocated for the trip. To someone from a deprived background such as he, Charley must have felt that five dollars per day was a small fortune. It was certainly a good sum for the time, as five dollars would have enabled a young boxer to purchase a skipping rope, a pair of bag gloves and a set of hand wraps.

On July 16th they arrived in Barcelona. Charley and the rest of the team set about enjoying themselves as only teenagers know how, utilising the two days prior to the commencement of the games as each of them saw fit. Some of the athletes must have thought that they were in heaven. A beautiful country, sunshine, the relative splendour of the Europa hotel on the Plaza de Catalunya, curious and inquisitive locals, plenty of pocket money and the prospect of representing their country in a sporting event must have left the team feeling like gods. Recalling some of his better memories of Spain, and Barcelona in particular, Charley said that the most beautiful women in the world were the olive-skinned, dark-haired Catalonians.

However, Spain was not to be totally idyllic for the visiting team. In addition to the worries of the upcoming competition they soon learned that tension was extremely high throughout this wonderful-looking country. It appeared that Barcelona and its beautiful inhabitants were expecting trouble and during their time in the city the team members had become increasingly aware that something was not quite right. They knew that General Franco's army was looking to continue its uprising against President Manuel Azana, they had heard as much on the voyage across the Atlantic, and the rumours persisted as they travelled though France on Bastille Day. They could not have thought for one moment, however, that any kind of political and social unrest would interfere with their reasons for being there.

The day before the games were due to begin, Saturday 17th July, Charley and the rest of the competitors were at the purpose-built

Montjuiic Stadium. The athletes had a light work out at the oval arena and looked around the facilities in preparation for the formal speeches and introductions that would form part of the opening ceremony the next day. The stadium, where most of the events were to be held, was originally constructed for the exhibition of 1929 and a revamped stadium would later be used for the 1992 Olympic games.

After a busy and rather full day the athletes returned to their hotel seeking the comfort of a good meal and a decent night's sleep. Unfortunately, jangling nerves of anticipation ensured that sleep was not forthcoming for most. Those that did manage to drift off found their slumber rudely awakened by a very uncommon sound. Charley recounted the incident to reporter Wendell Smith of the Pittsburgh Courier.

> "I was awakened at 5 o'clock in the morning by the sound of a lot of shooting and yelling. I thought they were celebrating the games by shooting off firecrackers. I got up and looked out of my hotel window, and I had no sooner done that than a bullet came crashing by my head, just missing me by inches. I dropped to the floor, then rushed out to where the rest of the fellows on our team were staying, and found out what it was all about."

Charley Burley

The Spanish Civil War had started and the 'Workers Games' were over before they had begun. The American team had seen all that it was going to see of Barcelona and what had promised to be a very exciting and rewarding time for a small group of talented athletes had turned in to a nightmare. They watched out of the windows, dumbstruck with horror as men, women, and children were fired upon. They watched as the Spaniards took pot shots at each other and they could do very little as a once beautiful Barcelona was turned into a bloody battlefield, its churches burned and age-old buildings left in ruins.

Members of the Hungarian and Swiss teams that were travelling to participate in the games were already stranded just outside of the city as the train carrying them and tourists for the games was unable to continue with the journey past the outskirts of Barcelona. They remained stranded for a day and a night on the crowded train before eventually being allowed to continue on.

When lulls in the fighting permitted, several members of the American team ventured outside under the necessity of looting for food. Wearing their blue team jackets for identification, members of the squad helped build barricades along the cobbled streets and became appointed food collectors for some of the women and children trapped in the hotel. During subsequent military mitigations the team, who were the first Americans to become directly involved in the conflict, were able to take part in a colourful flag-waving demonstration at the stadium with some of the other international teams.

Brief forays and flag-waving aside, Charley and the rest of the team were prisoners, trapped in the hotel and unable to escape. Despite the pleas of many of the teams, the games were cancelled. The athletes staged a final parade in honour of the fighting dead, an event for which they all dressed in black. The situation was worsening by the hour and the athletes had every reason to be in fear of their lives. A member of the French team ventured outside the safety of the hotel and was killed by a sniper's bullet, prompting the rest of the team to take their chances by attempting to return home immediately.

Finally, on the night of July 24th, a group of Spanish soldiers came to the hotel and escorted the American team for the twenty-minute walk down La Rambler to the docks and to the relative safety of a ship. They then sailed, with the Hungarian and Belgian teams for company, under cover of night to Seté, the first major port in France, and from there they travelled to Paris. Once in the French capital, William Chamberlain was able to contact Harry Leiper, chairman of the Committee that had sent the athletes on the doomed trip. Leiper then alerted the media as to the plight of the American team and frantic arrangements were then made for the athletes to return home. On July 27th Charley and the remainder of the American team sailed on board the luxurious passenger liner S.S. Normandie to New York. Upon their arrival, relieved family and friends welcomed the athletes home. Also at quayside were members of the press and what boxer Irving Jenkins believes was a Pathé News crew.

"The newsreels, they interviewed us when we got back. We tried to tell them what was going on, to tell them the truth, but you know that film was never released."

Irving Jenkins

Dorothy Tucker and Harry Krause travelled to an alternative meet in Prague, returning safely to the US on board the Champlain in August. Julian Raoul was still missing and he had not been seen by any of his team since he had left them in Glasgow. The propaganda exercise had not worked out as expected for the organising committee or the reigning Spanish government and it had cost them dearly. Not least in terms of the money that was spent covering all of the expenses for each visiting team. With this disaster, the 'worker' or 'popular' games were finished as a serious rival to Pierre de Coubertin's modern Olympics.

Back on home soil, safe and sound, though disappointed that they had not been able to compete, the athletes returned to their homes and their families. Charley had the furthest to travel before he was back in familiar surroundings and he made the return trip to Pittsburgh alone with his memories and thoughts; free to contemplate what had and what was still occurring in Spain. Charley's mother must have been most relieved to see her only son safe and sound as She had already endured the heartbreak of losing a teenage child - Angeline - during their time in the mining towns of Westmoreland County

It is very difficult to determine what effects those scenes of horror must have had upon the psyche of this young group. Irving Jenkins seriously considered returning as a volunteer to help fight the fascist regime, fortunately for him he was talked out of such a move by his father. Team coach, Alfred Chakin, could not be dissuaded from returning to the war-torn country and he returned to Spain to fight with the Abraham Lincoln Brigade. Sadly he was killed in action along with many other American volunteers.

Upon his arrival back home, Charley found that he was even more of a celebrity than he had been previously. Newspapers were looking to interview him so as to report his war stories to the people of Pittsburgh. The whole Spanish episode had been a great adventure for Charley, but he was relieved to be back in the relative safety of Pittsburgh, the Hill and his mother's house at 57 Fullerton Street. After his recent disappointments, Charley must have felt that the timing was right to turn professional. His only steady form of employment, chicken-plucking not withstanding, had been of the mop and bucket variety at a downtown department store. The prospect of remaining in menial employment at that stage of his life somehow held less appeal.

Charley had been able to contribute towards the upkeep of the family by boxing on inter-club tournaments and in local and national championships for merchandise cheques, which could be exchanged at stores for goods. The occasional 'watch fight', where the contestants received a wrist or pocket-watch as a prize and then sold it back to the promoter of the show for cash, had also enabled him to earn tangible rewards from his hobby. That kind of money however was scant recompense for the long and punishing hours spent in training and Charley yearned for the big money that fellow African-American fighters Joe Louis and Henry Armstrong were earning. He knew he had a talent for the fight game, what he needed now was a manager.

18 year-old Charley Burley around the time of his adventures in Barcelona, Spain (1936) when he was part of the USA 'Friendly' Olypmics team.

Chapter Two

The Hill District Holocaust

Phil Goldstein, known to most on the Hill as "Chappy", was born on the East Side of New York in December of 1909. His parents moved the family to Pittsburgh not too long afterwards and settled into premises on Colwell Street in the Hill District. As a youngster Chappy was a newsboy with a pitch on the corner of 5th and Wood Street and such work was a constant battle as the most lucrative patches were also the most sought-after. Young Goldstein's idea of physicallity was the relatively safe environment of the Ketchel basketball team on the Hill and the rough-and-tumble world of the newsboy was something of a shock to him. He soon learned that if he wanted to sell papers and keep his money, then he would have to fight back. Despite his frail and sickly appearance Chappy was scrappy and soon the bigger and older boys gave him the respect he demanded. So much so in fact, that one day when they were at the newspaper's offices cashing up, one of his buddies requested an entry form for the local boxing tournament for him. With no instruction and no experience of a boxing ring, save for the times he used to sneak into the Academy Theatre to watch Al Greyber contest four-rounders for pay and practice, young Goldstein thought twice, but ultimately didn't want to lose face. He was even more concerned when he received an instruction to appear for his first bout at the Westinghouse Club in nearby Wilkensburgh on December 16th, 1922. Upon his arrival at the club with his only supporter - and corner man for the night - Bobby Platt, Chappy was somewhat deflated to discover that the very boys that cajoled him into entering the tournament were nowhere to be seen. Young Goldstein recalled the evening's events a few years later:

"I looked across the ring as we were getting ready and was startled by my first glimpse of my opponent. If anything he was taller and thinner than I and he seemed to have three days growth of beard and, if I remember rightly, plenty of hair on his chest. And I would not be 16 until two days later. I think I should have collapsed if a man sitting right down alongside the ring had not asked in a kindly sort of voice: 'What's the matter kid, are you scared?'

I pulled myself together realising I must have shown my fear in my trembling limbs and the bell rang and we went at it. I didn't know anything about the science of boxing, but I managed to keep my arms and fists moving and carried off the decision at the end of three rounds. I was so happy I didn't notice how tired I must have been after setting such a hot pace."

Phil Goldstein

That first opponent in the 100-pound class was William Seihl of Johnstown, who had been champion of Western Pennsylvania in the same class two years before Chappy's debut. The elation of that first win was only to last until the following day when Pittsburgh's newest boxing star was defeated by Marty McHale of McKeesport, who in turn lost out in the final at Charleroi to future state flyweight champion, and fight judge, Willie Davies.

"That was my start in the boxing game. I stuck as an amateur for three years and engaged in 89 bouts, of which I won 79. I lost nine decisions and suffered one technical knockout when Jackie Williams of New York floored me twice in the second round and the referee stopped the bout. That was in the Olympic games trials in New York in the spring of 1924."

Phil Goldstein

The highlight of Goldstein's amateur career was probably the five bout series he had with Tony Canzoneri. The Pittsburgh fighter won three of those meetings in inter-city tournaments. Canzoneri of course would go on to have the more successful professional career winning world titles at featherweight, lightweight (twice) and junior welterweight, whilst Goldstein lost almost as many as he won over a four-year, and some 70 fight, career.

As a manager Goldstein was a little more successful and he had been doing a fair job with local middleweight Al Quail. The fact that the ex-professional had also had involvement with a young Charley Burley at the tail-end of his amateur career also made the choice of manager a foregone conclusion. The initial contract that was drawn up between Goldstein and Charley definitely favoured the manager over the fighter. So much so in fact, that a local reporter made a point of highlighting the conditions of the contract in a city paper. The report was written by way of a warning to any of the city's amateur stars considering a professional career, and therefore requiring the services of a manager, to be aware of just how little money there might be in such a move.

The contract called for enough fights to provide a minimum income of 1,000 dollars a year gross, this would give Charley slightly more than 80 dollars a month or 20 dollars a week. With the deductions for training expenses and equipment as well as the needs of the family this would not leave very much for Charley himself. The average weekly wage at this time was around 15 dollars per week and sometimes some heavy or demeaning forms of employment were endured by many thousands of workers for what was a pittance. Fighting for a living was no less demanding or demeaning and 20 dollars a week was also meagre reward for risking life, limb and potentially serious injury in the toughest of all sports.

If expectations for a fighter are high, then the initial contract would usually favour the fighter during the early stages, with the manager and the rest of the retinue, should there be one, earning a greater amount as the fighter became more established. A fighter of true world class and standing could earn himself a good living in the ring, especially with title fights and subsequent defences. As Charley had been a star amateur, with a reported (according to the official paperwork of the Fair Play Committee), 43 wins from 49 contests and several amateur titles, it could be argued that expectations of even a moderately successful professional career should have been high. Of course, the manager would not make money if the fighter did not fight and if that were to happen, the manager would end up carrying the fighter. So, it was in the best interests of all to keep Charley busy. With the usual split of two thirds for the fighter and one third for the manager, if the terms and conditions of the contract were adhered to and reached the guaranteed minimum of $1,000, the manager would stand to gain around $300 to $400 per year. Obviously, it would be in Goldstein's best interests to make matches and develop his fighter as quickly as possible. What should be taken into consideration is that while a fighter usually has only one manager, the manager has no limit on the amount of fighters that he guides. The potential for a substantial income on the manager's side is apparent.

Initially making matches would not be a problem. The problem would come when the career of Charley Burley developed to the stage when matchmaking at a higher level would prove to be a near impossibility. Chappy approached several managers and promoters immediately upon signing Charley and attempted to set him up for his professional debut. Eventually Goldstein arranged for Charley to meet a welterweight by the name of George Leggins on a September fight card at Hickey Park, on the north-side of the city. There was little time to prepare for his opponent and getting in shape meant working out every day throughout the month. Charley had not trained seriously since the ill-fated Barcelona trip and the few weeks he had to prepare for his professional debut was scarcely enough time. It may be that the regime was a little too much as Charley injured his shoulder and the debut had to be put back to 28th September.

When the day of the fight arrived both fighters weighed in for the evening show, which was to feature future world lightweight champion, Sammy Angott, against Lee Sheppard. Charley came in at slightly over 150 pounds while opponent George Leggins scaled 145. Charley was undoubtedly nervous about his first professional outing but, as usual, he had total confidence in his own abilities. However, any increasing anxiety was swept away by the howling weather conditions as Mother Nature intervened and a heavy shower of rain resulted in the fights being postponed. The card was rescheduled for the following night, indoors at the Moose Temple on Penn Avenue.

The bout itself proved to be something of a breeze for Charley as he had little trouble in landing his shots from the outset. His economical, gliding footwork enabled him to slide into range where he feinted for openings with shoulders, head, eyes and feet. Charley's most devastating punch, a left hook to the body, was employed frequently as he scored a clean knockout in the fourth and final round of his bout with Leggins. The referee, Ernie Sesto, tolled the ten-count at one minute and 27 seconds of the round with the pole-axed fighter out for considerably longer from the right-hand punch that finished him. The previous year Leggins had gone four rounds with another local fighter considered one of the city's great boxing prospects, handsome young Irish middleweight Billy Conn. It looked as though the latest addition to Pittsburgh's impressive array of fighting talent may live up to the "local 'colored' amateur sensation" tag that had been bestowed upon him by the Pittsburgh Post Gazette.

With his paid debut completed, Charley Burley had taken his first tentative steps in the world of professional boxing, a world that in September 1936 boasted only one Black champion, the likeable light-heavyweight champion, John Henry Lewis, who was under the management and promotion of local 'entrepreneur' Gus Greenlee.

Charley had earned his first pay day from his new profession and he made sure that the people who counted in his life were treated in some manner, no matter how small. Charley's younger sister, Zella, had increased her circle of friends and in addition to Julia Taylor, whom Charley saw whenever possible, she was now spending time in the company of another neighbourhood girl, Daisy Wilson. Daisy had a string of admirers, as she was a very attractive girl, with long curly black hair and beautiful brown eyes. Julia looked just like her, although she was smaller, petite one might say, at around one hundred and twenty pounds, and the two were often mistaken for sisters. The easiest way to tell them apart appeared to be the shape of Julia's nose. When she was very young she had a particularly nasty fall, causing severe damage in the process. The local doctor had no real idea what to do about it and medical treatment was expensive anyway. The injury was patched up and Julia would have to be content with the cute little button nose that looked as though it were placed on her face as an afterthought.

Daisy Wilson, who was almost as famous as Charley's mother for her use of colourful language, would later become involved with a German baker from The Hill District. Her beau, Freddie Kittel, would usually come calling on a Friday with a bag of rolls and bread as a gift for Daisy and her family. Although the couple would never know a 'normal' married life, due in part to the reluctant Mr. Kittel, they did have children. With no father at home, Daisy had to be hard on her kids. A strict upbringing and strong work ethic seemed to work for the Wilson children, as they all went on to live good lives and make something of themselves. Charley's friend and protégé, Bobby Lippi, has nothing but respect for Daisy and what she did for her family.

> "Daisy was a fine woman. Her man was white and when he only showed up at weekends they all expected her to be like some of the other black women, free-and-easy for the rest of the week. But, there was nothing free and easy about that woman. She was tough and she was tough on them kids. They studied their books. They were educated. Daisy wasn't for bullshit."

> **Bobby Lippi**

Daisy's son, Freddie, discovered he had a talent for words early in his development and he later went on to become a Pulitzer Prize winning author. Using his mother's surname and his own middle name, Frederick August Kittel went on to write 'Ma Rainy's Black Bottom', 'Joe Turner's Come and Gone' and a tale about a black baseball player called 'Fences'. When interviewed for a biographical documentary televised on the South Bank Show in London in 1991, August Wilson was quite open about the influence that Charley Burley had on him as he was growing up.

"I know men like that, (Troy Maxon, the central character in 'Fences'). I think the closest, you know, to a man like that would be Charley Burley. I grew up without a father and he lived right across the street from me. He was a very strong male image for me in my life and the fact that he went and knocked people out only added to the intrigue and mystique of the male being conqueror."

August Wilson

Although Wilson has indicated that the retired baseball player from 'Fences' is based, to some extent, on his step-father he has also admitted that the experiences of Charley Burley are embodied in Troy.

"That's what being a man meant to me, to be like him. I wanted to grow up and dress like him, he wore those big Stetson hats, things of that sort, and I couldn't wait to be a man to be like Charley Burley. Everybody always called him 'Champ' and I thought he was the champ. I always wanted to do something so that if I walked down the street, I'd be a hero like Charley Burley.

August Wilson

Charley may have sought out male role models in the testosterone-laden sport of boxing, but he was always comfortable in the company of females. He would often spend time in the company of his mother, his sisters and their girlfriends. It was, after all, an environment to which he was accustomed. Conversely, a constantly full house may have impacted upon Charley's longing to spend time in the company of the person he was most comfortable with - himself.

Three weeks after his paid debut, he was back in the ring, this time at Duquesne Gardens, in the opening bout on an Elwood Rigby promotion. At the time Rigby was the subject of local boxing commission proceedings due to his involvement with fellow promoter Jake Mintz. It was alleged that Mintz had shown considerable favouritism towards Rigby and his fight cards in the city. It was not the first, nor the last time, that Mintz would gain attention for questionable operating procedures.

The Gardens, at the time, was the only indoor ice skating establishment in Western Pennsylvania. With a soda fountain, an upstairs ballroom, regular hockey league games and school skating sessions, the Duquesne Gardens on North Craig Street were very popular up in the Oakland district of the city. Between 1925 and 1930 the Pitt Pirates played their league matches there and although the venue had seen some troubled times and equally troubled owners, ex-lightweight champion of the world Benny Leonard amongst them, the facilities were enjoying something of a resurgence thanks in part to the boxing shows now being held there.

Charley's opponent for his second professional showing was 'Young' Ralph Gizzy of Donora, Pennsylvania, younger brother of the popular 'Battling' Gizzy, a seasoned veteran with a respectable record and a sturdy jaw. The bout with Gizzy was a much sterner test for Charley and he managed to give a fair showing of his promise. Charley didn't appear to struggle too much with the experienced Gizzy and after scoring a knockdown in the second round Charley "buffeted Gizzy around like a cork" but was apparently unable to land any further blows of significant power, walking away with a clear points decision. On the same bill that night was Billy Conn who was progressing nicely in the punch-for-pay ranks, beating another tough Pittsburgh fighter, the Chinese-American Ralph Chong over ten rounds. With this latest victory, (he now had a record of 29 wins with only six defeats and a draw), Conn's own fistic future was looking promising.

To close out 1936, and his first year as a pro, Charley was matched with former amateur victim Eddie Wirko on a four-bout card at the Moose Temple on November 9th. Wirko, who had lost on points to Charley the previous May, held a decision over Leo Sweeney as an amateur and was figured by promoter Jake Mintz to be a good test for Burley. A six-and-a-half pound weight disadvantage proved to be too much for Wirko who, after taking a severe body beating for the first four rounds, did not come out for the fifth. The crowd, who paid a total of $1,538, also saw another local favourite Fritzie Zivic of the city's famous fighting Zivic family, chalk up his 46th win in 66 professional fights, as he beat Gaston LeCadre over ten rounds.

With the holiday season approaching, Charley was hopeful of another bout and another payday. Although several promotions went ahead in Pittsburgh before the end of the year, right up to December 28th in fact, it was not possible to get him an opponent. Promoter Jake Mintz assured Chappy Goldstein that Charley would be active again as soon as 1937 was under way and, as promised, he matched Charley with previous opponent Ralph Gizzy in January at Oil City, just north of Pittsburgh.

With a party of about 50 Smoky City fans in tow, State boxing commissioner Dr. W. B. McClelland, Phil Goldstein, Charley and his stable mates, Johnny Birek and Whitey Schramm all rolled into town at around noon on the day of the fight. An estimated 700 local supporters turned out at the Knights of Columbus Auditorium for what was the first sign of local professional fight action for almost six years.

Featured as the semi-final bout of a four-fight card, the return with Gizzy turned out to be shortest bout of the night, and yet in the first round it looked like it would be the most entertaining as both Gizzy and Charley seemed willing to mix it up. From the way they handled themselves in the opening three minutes, Charley showed that he was the more experienced of the two and would probably have gained the decision had the fight gone the scheduled eight – round limit. But, 28 seconds into the second round it was all over, with Gizzy flat on his back. Those closest to the action thought that Gizzy was rendered unconscious more from hitting his head on the floor of the ring than from the blow struck by Charley. Of course that argument was academic, as Gizzy was out and Charley was now four for four with three knockouts. He was also the only winner from the group of visiting Pittsburgh fighters on the bill.

Local promoter Johnny Hahn was as impressed as anyone else present that night and, just over two weeks later, brought Charley back for a semi-final slot on a Monday night card at the same venue. The opponent was veteran Ray Collins who needed no introduction to the local fight fans. The Lake Erie fighter had met some top-notch performers in his time including Johnny Jadick, Tony Herrera, Stanley Dorfman, Wesley Ramey, and Sammy Mandell and while he had not fared so well against the better fighters, Collins was considered a worthy opponent for a raw and relatively inexperienced 19 year-old.

On the night, it was the greater experience of Collins, and little else, that kept him in the fight. While it lasted, he gave Charley Burley and the crowd a good run for their money, with his ring tactics often ranging from the sublime to the ridiculous. The latter in evidence when he missed Charley coming out of a clinch and grazed referee Joe Thomas on the cheek. But Collins took a fearful beating in the fourth round and looked on the way out, only to be saved by the bell, after which he required assistance to return to his corner. With his battered opponent unable to come out for the fifth session Charley added another stoppage victory to his record.

Charley was now five for five and despite his relative inexperience he was promoted to semi-final status for his next bout at McKeesport, just outside of Pittsburgh. Charley's talents were now starting to attract a substantial amount of ink in the local newspapers and at the Palisades Rink, in his first scheduled ten-round fight; he was acclaimed in the papers as 'the best-looking bet on the card'. Displaying 'classy boxing and sharp punching' Charley 'worked like a veteran' as he dropped opponent Johnny Folio twice en-route to an inside the distance win. The finish to the fight came with Folio on the receiving end of rights and lefts to the head and body. Referee Red Robinson rightfully stepped in and halted the uneven affair after one minute and 30 seconds of the fifth round. After the bout, Charley was signed to box Ray Gray, of Newcastle, Pennsylvania, in a six round bout at Motor Square Garden, on Liberty Avenue in Pittsburgh, the following Monday.

With just a long weekend to recover from the Folio bout, Charley went back to Pittsburgh to prepare for his next opponent. On the same card, at Motor Square Garden, would be a headliner featuring a fighter who would become one of the standout fighters of the era, the great Holman Williams.

Although there were three ten-round fights on the card at Motor Square Garden, the opening six-rounder was mooted beforehand as the one that might steal the show. Despite the galaxy of punchers like Red Bruce, Holman Williams and Frankie Misko, and gamesters like Al Gatchell, greatest interest was being shown in Charley Burley, who was pitting his seven knockouts in eight starts against Gray and his three knockouts in as many pro starts. The anticipated punching session was the opener of a Jake Mintz promotion.

Bobby Pacho, a wiry little New Yorker, who had made a good showing with Fritzie Zivic when previously in the city, was the feature of the card along with opponent Holman Williams. The Detroit fighter had shown his worth twice before in Pittsburgh and had scored two knockouts. In another ten-rounder Al Gatchell, Cleveland heavyweight, whose game showing in a bout with big Eddie Hogan the previous month made him a lot of friends, came back against 'Red' Bruce. In the first ten-rounder of the night Honeyboy Jones, a neighbour of Charley's on the Hill, tackled Eddie Misko, touted as middleweight champion of Michigan.

The crowd made the most noise during the Jones-Misko battle. 'Honeyboy' had Misko hurting from a crashing right-hand punch at the very end of the first in a slam-bang affair. A mere 20 seconds into the second round a hard right to the body finished off the Detroit fighter. Meanwhile classy Holman Williams held back the challenge of Bobby Pacho, winning a comfortable decision.

Charley Burley also had to be content with a win on points over Ray Gray who proved to be a real tough mug. Winning by the proverbial city block, Charley cut up his opponent about the eyes and mouth, but couldn't floor him despite having him very wobbly at the end of the fifth round. Charley was looking better with every outing, able to use both hands effectively, cool under fire and punching with power way beyond his weight class. The evening's entertainment netted promoter Jake Mintz $2,165.00 and he was extremely happy with the showing of all the fighters concerned.

For two contests in May of 1937 Charley continued to win handily in his encounters with local talent. Sammy Grippe of Ashtabula, Ohio lasted the distance in a rather dull affair in which he refused to lead and Charley refused to work up close. While southpaw Keith Goodballet attempted to confuse his opponent by switching from left to right leads, he was lucky to survive the first round and ultimately provided little opposition to Charley's smooth-flowing, though unorthodox, style. A sustained attack to head and body by Burley ended when the East Liverpool fighter was dropped by a right-hand punch in the second round. Up after a count of eight, Goodballet was in no position to defend himself and the referee called a halt with 20 seconds of the stanza remaining. Charley was already looking for a showdown with one of the city's bigger names, regardless of their experience or reputation.

Dandy Allen, a local area trainer of note, was now working with Charley on a regular basis. Allen was also acting as training advisor to John Henry Lewis while the light-heavyweight champion was under the management of Gus Greenlee. The handling of Lewis was one of Greenlee's rare forays into the fight game, although he did briefly attempt to manage Holman Williams when the welterweight star was in Pittsburgh. Big Gus was the main man in the numbers racket in Pittsburgh and the venture made him a small fortune.

Although the origin of the numbers game is rather vague, it is a gambling enterprise that grew in most major towns and cities across the United States from the earlier part of the 20th century. With pennies, nickels or dimes placed on the correct forecasting of a series of three

33

numbers, a large amount of money could be won. Bars, gyms, taxicab or Jitney joints, (Jitneys are basically unlicensed taxis), were often used as number stations where 'runners' would put down the bets of the local populace.

A percentage of the stake money would be used as prize money with other, various-sized percentages going to the runners, the number joint operators and of course the man himself. The winning numbers would be determined by the numbers worn by the first three horses over the finish line in a particular race or races at a certain track or from other sporting results or newsworthy events involving a sequence of numbers that could not be fixed or tampered with. Often no one would win, in which case the 'house' kept all of the stake money or allocated a part of it to a 'roll over' or pot, thus making the next prize even larger and more desirable.

The prospect of winning a large amount of money kept many of the poorer working classes playing the game for years on end, often without any kind of a win. One of Charley Burleys minor vices, besides the occasional cigar and the Lucky Strikes he smoked, was gambling on the numbers. Like most other people that played the game, he had his own set of numbers that he never changed and while the sequence 536 never won him a major pay-out during his younger years, sometime down the line a big win would land him in a rather sticky situation. Charley, like many thousands of others, placed his bets and waited for the big hit, while Gus Greenlee got bigger and richer from their hard-earned money.

The management of a fighter was hard enough, but the management of a black fighter, of which Pittsburgh had many, was a task that the streetwise numbers man didn't relish one bit. With the racketeer's involvement in the sport, Greenlee could do without any kind of outside pressure and the possible consequences for his numbers business. Despite his own ethnicity and his position in the community, it has been said that Big Gus rarely helped out a black fighter from his own neighbourhood. With his career rolling along and with eight knockouts from eleven fights Charley was matched with fast-stepping 'Irish' Mickey O'Brien. Mickey, from Braddock, just outside of Pittsburgh, had a reputation as a puncher and was considered a stern test for the young, lean-legged Burley. The papers were calling the bout the Hill boy's first big test, but Charley; ever sure of his abilities, figured he already had the fight won.

"I'll whip Mickey, and then I want the promoters to get busy and line up Billy Conn, Fritzie Zivic, or any others that are top-notch-ers. Do they think that I will ever get anywhere fighting set-ups all my life?"

Charley Burley

Charley was not speaking of a 'set-up' in the commonly accepted term of a dive or 'tank-job', but it was obvious that for the career of any young fighter to develop, he must be carefully matched. Charley Burley obviously had the talent, what he needed now was a real test of his true potential. Many ringsiders who had seen Charley fight locally were talking in an undertone about his chances with some of the bigger name and more experienced fighters in Pittsburgh. The only thing that kept them from coming out loud with it was the fact that he hadn't fought over the ten round distance yet. Even though Dandy Allen and Charley himself felt that he was ready, there were still some unanswered questions concerning Charley's stamina for a long, gruelling fight and his ability to take a punch. At Hickey Park, on a show that was held over for three days due to torrential rain, Charley attempted to answer some of the critics.

"Irish Mickey O'Brien, 146$^{1/2}$, of Braddock, spent a weary half hour trying to catch up with Charley Burley, local colored boy, in the 10-round semi-final, but the clever home boxer easily captured the unanimous decision. Using a left jab to pepper O'Brien's face, Burley experienced little difficulty during the first five rounds as he made Mickey miss time after time. O'Brien finally caught up with his dusky rival midway in the sixth round and seemed to have Burley worried with a rapid-fire attack by both hands. However, Burley resumed his fine ring work in the seventh, staved off Mickey's wild rushes and romped home an easy winner."

Pittsburgh Post Gazette

The word on Charley was starting to spread from Pittsburgh and the June 1937 issue of the highly respected Ring magazine, rated young Burley as the outstanding welterweight contender of the month. The word around the local gyms was that one of the big indoor attractions for that winter might well be Burley against Billy Conn, Fritzie Zivic, Teddy Yarosz or the veteran Bobby Pacho. The fact that Charley, with only 10 professional fights, was being touted as an opponent for the above-named fighters is the real testimony to his ability. Pacho had contested over 100 bouts, sharing the ring with such luminaries as Ceferino Garcia, Barney Ross, Tony Canzoneri, Glen Lee and Wesley Ramey. While Teddy Yarosz was a former middleweight champion of the world, Zivic had over 70 professional fights under his belt and Billy Conn was fast approaching 40 contests.

Charley was rapidly running out of local, similarly experienced talent, and Jake Mintz was starting to look further afield for quality opposition. A fight in Buffalo at the end of June had to be cancelled as Charley was experiencing trouble with his right hand and a bout for July 20th at Hickey Park against Remo Fernandez also had to be cancelled as Charley came up with a couple of broken ribs.

It was not too long however before Charley was back in action as Jake Mintz hurriedly put together a charity show at Hickey Park for August 9th. The show was for the benefit of the family of Johnny Page, the Chicago fighter who had recently died after being knocked out in the ninth round by Eddie Zivic at the same arena.

For the promotion Mintz brought back Los Angeles fighters Johnny 'Bandit' Romero and Remo Fernandez. The 'Bandit' was a decent fighter and had a good reputation in Pittsburgh after beating former national amateur middleweight champion Jimmie Clark on the same bill that Charley should have fought Fernandez. Substituting for the injured Burley on that night was John Henry Thomas, whom Fernandez beat comfortably with "a fine burst of speed and jabbing tactics." The California-based Mexican was certainly a much stiffer test than Charley's previous opposition and he was a respected fighter in his home state. After the bout Charley became a more respected fighter in his home state.

"Charley Burley, Pittsburgh's most promising battler since the day that Jackie Wilson first showed his class proved to all and sundry Monday night that he was of championship ability and should be given better spots and better opponents. Monday night Burley went to work like a master on the wiley Mexican, Remo Fernandez. He boxed him with all the finesse of a champ, paced himself like a racehorse and at the end of seven of the eight scheduled rounds had so completely cut the invader, the opposing seconds were forced to call a halt between rounds.

It has been a long time since local fans have been able to see a fast, shifty boxer with a punch who would go in and fight and fight hard.

Time-and-time-again Fernandez went to the ropes in an effort to outfight Burley there as he had done John Henry Thomas a few weeks previous. But the local boy was by far too smart for him and several times came close to ending matters with Fernandez backed up to the hemp. At one point the fans were forced to call to the California lad to stay away from the ropes and get on the run."

Pittsburgh Post Gazette

The local fight crowd thought that Charley was just the type of fighter that might bring a welterweight title to the city. They also felt that if the local promoters were smart they could begin to feature him in longer distances and with better opponents. Not that Fernandez was of inferior class, he had recently lost a close ten-round decision to the then unbeaten and highly-rated Eddie Booker in California and was no slouch in the ring.

Jake Mintz fooled no one with his claims for The Bandit's opponent, one Eddie Boyle of Cleveland. Boyle could neither defend himself nor throw a punch as Romero battered him about the Millvale Arena ring for a little over three rounds. Mercifully, Boyle's seconds came to his rescue after 55 seconds of the fourth round while their man was being counted over. A few months down the line Romero would break the 21 fight, unbeaten streak of Archie Moore in San Diego, winning over ten rounds. Eddie Zivic also made an appearance on the card losing to Charley Burns over 10 rounds. Strangely, Burns was Zivic's original opponent the night of the tragic meeting with Page.

Exactly two weeks later, Charley met Sammy Grippe for the second time in three months. The Post Gazette's Harvey Boyle saw it this way.

"It was a dull fight because Grippe declined to do anything but play safety-first, but even so took a bad lacing. Burley moved him back continually as Grippe was continually seeking cover. Burley managed to use his left regularly to the jaw and often swept a right across Grippe's unwilling chin."

Harvey Boyle, Pittsburgh Post Gazette

Around the middle of the 6th the referee called a halt with Grippe cut-up and defenceless. The return with Grippe was something of a backward step considering the class of opponent that Charley had beaten in Remo Fernandez and it appeared that Chappy Goldstein was beginning to experience problems in getting his charge more frequent bouts against increasingly experienced opponents. Charley must have found it difficult to motivate himself for run-of-the-mill local fighters and was urging his manager to look further afield.

The main problem for Goldstein was one of finances. Local promoters would only pay so much for each fighter on the bill, according to status and affinity with the crowd. The fight fans in Pittsburgh, as with the cauliflower cognoscenti of most other fight city's, such as New York, Chicago or Boston, always demanded the best for their dollar when it came to entertainment and they, like any other discerning fans, did not want to see uncompetitive matches or one-sided blowouts.

Finding fighters of sufficient calibre to provide exciting competition for the crowds in addition to developmental contests for Charley was difficult enough, even without the handicap of having to pay the going rate. Charley may have been content, for the time being at least, to fight on a regular basis for a smaller purse, but he also knew that he had to meet higher quality opponents in order to further his career. Darling of the Pittsburgh fight scene Fritzie Zivic, and his manager Luke Carney, informed anyone that would listen that they were quite happy to accommodate the Hill boy at any time and any venue in the city. They contended that it was Chappy Goldstein who was the barrier to the match that much of Pittsburgh wanted to see. For his part, Goldstein realised that he had a potential world-beater in Charley and he was not willing to risk a setback at this early stage of his development. Zivic was a veteran of over 70 bouts and had been a professional fighter for more than six years. He was also one of the most popular fighters in Pittsburgh.

'The Hill District Holocaust', as Charley was being called, wanted to prove that he was not only the best fighter on The Hill, but also the best in the city. While Charley was showing more interest in Zivic and Conn, Chappy Goldstein matched him with Eddie Dolan of Jamestown, New York. The Connecticut-born fighter was on a 13-bout unbeaten streak and looking to continue his success.

The fight at Hickey Park, which was on the undercard of Henry Armstrong's four-round knockout of Charley Burns, provided Charley with an opportunity to demonstrate that he was a class above the likes of Gizzy, Folio, Grippe and Dolan. On the night however, things did not go according to plan and Charley was on the wrong end of a decision for the first time in his professional career. The fans booed loudly during the bout, which was a rather dull affair, and they continued to jeer when the decision was announced. The contest was untidy and Charley apparently boxed as poorly as he had ever done. Neither fighter received much in the way of damage and with little to recommend a rematch, other than revenge for Charley, there was no talk of the two boys going at it again.

In terms of local standing Charley had been taken down a peg or two, and boasts about his ability to mix with the higher-rated fighters was put in doubt. Although his career had got off to a flying start, Charley had been temporarily grounded by this recent setback. An unbeaten record, for top-flight fighters at least, was something of a rarity, but Charley was surely disappointed with the loss of his perfect start, especially as he had been fighting on a professional basis for just under a year. A certain amount of strain was also beginning to show in the relationship between manager and fighter. Charley would not fight again for over four months but when he did, he was much happier. The following year, 1938, would be Charley's busiest year of fighting to date. It would also prove to be one of his unluckiest.

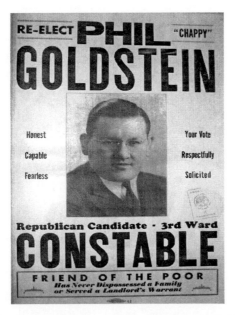

Charley's first manager Phil 'Chappy' Goldstein during his early days in local politics (circa 1938)

Chapter Three

The Pittsburgh Fight Club

At the beginning of 1938, Steve Cox, a fight promoter in the city, real-ised a personal ambition when he set up the 'Pittsburgh Fight Club'. The idea behind the venture was to hold a boxing event every week, with shows that would feature the City's up-and-coming fighters in action against each other and against imported pugilists. Mr. Cox figured that there was enough talent locally, each with good support, to justify such a proposal. He also felt that local fighters would welcome a regular pay-day, something that many of them had not been getting.

The plan was to feature these fighters in four-round bouts in what were hoped to be short, but exciting affairs, much like the recent show-ing at the Etna Elks amateur 'Diamond Belt' tournament. The crowd had really enjoyed that night's action and Mr. Cox and his matchmaker, Jack 'Butch' Hollister, reasoned to the press that the Pittsburgh fight fans would enjoy shorter, more action-packed professional fights as opposed to some of the long-winded eight – or ten-round affairs, which had recently left the paying customers baying for blood.

To secure the services of Pittsburgh's young talent Cox and Hollister approached local managers asking them to sign up and support the club. Johnny Ray, manager of Billy Conn, offered his own services and those of his novice fighters, including 'Mean' Irv Sarlin, Mt. Olive heavyweight protégé. Another of the local fighters to become involved with the club was Ralph Gizzy, who had recently experienced a change in fortune and was winning regularly.

The Duquesne Gardens in Oakland was chosen as the regular venue for the club's weekly fights. Zach Robinson, Mimmie DeMore, Casey Rodes, Rich Gregory and Charley Burley were among other newcomers to offer their services. This new promotional set-up appeared to make Phil Goldstein a happier manager, as Hollister and Cox were attempting to operate outside of the promotional net of local big wheel Jake Mintz and his connections further afield.

"Charles Burley, more often called the 'Hill District Holocaust', is

40

limbering up his siege guns and the heavy artillery in preparation for one of the busiest fight months he will have experienced since donning the mitts back in the amateur days.

The clever Burley has tentative bookings for practically four straight weeks, one of which may possibly be with an imported headliner. After been given the grand 'go-by' by local promoters for almost six months in which he challenged any welterweight in the land, Burley makes his first start of the New Year on Jack Hollister's all-star card on January 27th at Duquesne Garden in the feature attraction against an opponent to be named.

Burley has been working out at the Centre Avenue 'Y' sharpening his pet decrees of offence, a tripping left hook and a short right-hand that have reeked disaster to 14 of 15 worthy opponents. Those who know the fight game and have seen Burley in there, all are unanimous in their praise and agree that the 147 pound flash is pound-for-pound the equal of the best in his division."

Pittsburgh Press report

Although most reporters very rarely have all the details exactly right, often confusing the number of fights a boxer had contested or the spelling of opponents' names etc., it appears that several newspapers around this time in Charley Burley's career had the same number of recorded bouts. The most recent editions of Charley's records have his first bout of 1938 as number 14. However, cross-referencing of newspapers of the day indicate that between September 1936 and September 1937 Charley contested at least two more bouts than those shown on his present record. Reporter Bert P. Taggart, writing on Charley's progress in 1939, mentions Johnny Williams and Cleto Locatelli among Burleys knockout victims. Both names are missing from his record and written descriptions of any action have yet to be unearthed. Taggart did interview Charley, his manager and Jake Mintz for the article, but that does not mean that the bouts actually took place.

The first show of the Pittsburgh Fight Club on January 27th was a disappointment for the promoters, as the gate for the evening's entertainment totalled only $658.70. They refused to become too downhearted however, as the talent on display was equal to, if not better than, any recent offerings presented by other, more notable promoters. Instead,

41

they consoled themselves with the fact that the poor showing could have been accredited to an intervention of nature, with a heavy snowstorm hitting town barely an hour before fight time. The fledgling promoters felt this definitely kept many casual fight fans at home.

Despite numerous substitutions and switching of opponents, the crowd of around 1,000 was treated to some interesting encounters. All of the new boys won, with Rich Gregory showing the best form for a boy just out of the amateur ranks, as he dropped his hapless foe, Red West, three times in under two minutes for a first round stoppage win. Charley, despite fighting for the first time in over three months, scored the only clean knockout of the evening, putting away 'Tiger' Jackson of Kent, Ohio in the second round. Charley figured that $20 once a week would be OK if the opposition was going to be this easy and he signed up to fight previous victim Johnny Folio on the following week's show. In his second showing for the fight club, Charley was again victorious over the Virginian as Folio tasted the canvas in the second and third rounds and, despite a nine-pound weight advantage, could not match Charley for strength.

These cut-price shows were proving to be popular with the fans, although the attendance did not increase dramatically and remained at around 1,000. For this reason, it was decided that the next card would be moved upstairs into the smaller arena. The seating upstairs would comfortably accommodate an additional 400 paying customers should the need arise and would have the added bonus of moving them and the ring off the ice in the main arena.

Most of the fighters were pleased to be getting a regular weekly income and their names in the papers, so they signed up for the third weekly show. Charley easily out-pointed Carl Turner for a third consecutive win under Hollister and Cox's promotion and requested an opponent of higher standing for his next fight, leaving the promoters with a slight headache. They were determined to keep Charley as part of the fight club, but they knew that they would have to pay good money to get a rated guy in to keep him happy. After a frantic few days and a substantial amount of phone calls they came up with a fighter who was considered good enough to test anyone of limited professional experience.

Art Tate, a black fighter from Cleveland, Ohio, had been a good amateur in his hometown and had reportedly won many titles there. The most impressive thing about Mr. Tate though was the 31 victories on his record. Charley was shooting for win number 17 (or 19 if the press reports were accurate), and was determined to manoeuvre himself into a local showdown with Fritzie Zivic. The 'Lawrenceville Larruper' was rated as the tenth best welterweight in the world behind Ceferino Garcia, Jack Carroll, Gustave Eder, Saverio Turiello, Izzy Janazzo, Holman Williams, Cocoa Kid and Jimmy Leto all of whom were vying for a title shot against champion Barney Ross.

The Charley Burley versus Art Tate bout was extended a couple of rounds to six, with the promoters hopeful of an exciting affair. Eager to impress and always able to raise his game when he so desired, Charley was off the mark and into action before the echo from the first bell had died away.

> "Charley Burley, the pleasing local colored ring performer, added another scalp to his string last night by knocking out Art Tate, another colored boy who hails from Cleveland, in the second round of a scheduled six-rounder on the fight card at Duquesne Garden. The time of the knockout was listed as 1:22. It was evident from the start that Burley had too much on the ball or in his gloves for the Clevelander. He opened the knockout gate for Mr. Tate in the first round by dropping him for an eight-count. Tate weathered the following storm, but a volley of punches dropped him for the count early in the next stanza, this time to stay. He was 'out' fully a minute before he was revived by his seconds."

Pittsburgh Press

Again Charley had scored the only clean knockout of the night and again the crowd went home talking about his chances with Zivic or Conn. Charley's progress was seemingly still insufficient to light a fire under Phil Goldstein, who was not paying his charge the attention he deserved. The papers were now starting to feature 'The Hill District Holocaust' more often and in greater depth. It was apparent to most that Charley had the ability to go places and slowly, the good Constable was waking up to the fact. While keeping one eye on the weekly Pittsburgh Fight Club cards, Chappy Goldstein was casting the other over more highly-touted opposition for his man. The bout that the fans wanted was Burley against Zivic and eventually Goldstein relented. The press started to promote the fight from the moment it was announced and there was a genuine air of excitement about the build-up. One reporter told about the difficulties there had been in making the match.

"Promoter Jake Mintz announced last night that the battle between Fritzie Zivic and Charley Burley, scheduled for the Motor Square Garden next Monday night, has created more advance interest among the fans than any other boxing show he has staged this season. In fistic parlance Jake Mintz is a promoter and Chappy Goldstein manages a stable of boxers. In the minor judiciary both are bona fide constables, but for some time they've been at logger-heads over their fistic and political doings. Yesterday, however, they got their noggins together and agreed to let bygones be bygones. They shook hands, and to prove to each other that they really meant to forgive and forget the past, Goldstein finally agreed to allow Charley Burley, colored welterweight and ace of his stable, to meet Fritzie Zivic of the Strip, in a ten-round headline bout at Motor Square Garden a week from tonight."

Pittsburgh Press

It was also reported that previous attempts to match Charley Burley with Fritzie Zivic had run into obstacles of Constable Goldstein's making. However, he now knew that if his most promising prospect was to advance any in the fight game he would have to think a little bigger and co-operate with his least favourite promoter Jake Mintz, in addition to Zivic's manager; the very shrewd Luke Carney.

To many, the fight had been a long time coming and promoter Jake Mintz, a short, broken-nosed, willowy man of Jewish descent, had to dig deep into his pockets to get Goldstein to agree to terms, (which were not disclosed). The North Side promoter had been trying to get the talented Burley under his promotional umbrella since he first turned professional, but he was unable to persuade Goldstein to give him sole promotional rights over the promising up-and-comer. With such a big match, and with so many demands from both parties, Mintz was able to make some gains of his own. The date of the bout was set for March 21st 1938, and one condition of the fight was that Charley discontinued fighting for Cox and Hollister on their weekly shows at the Duquesne Gardens and trans-fer over to Jake Mintz and his Hickey Park promotions at Millvale on the North side of Pittsburgh. This proposal apparently suited Goldstein, as the $20 per week from the 'Fight Club' promotions was proving insuffi-cient financial reward to keep Charley on-track for his guaranteed $1,000 for the year, and he lost no time in signing the contract.

The press began to have a field day running stories during the build-up to the fight, and opinions differed as to how it would go. Just three months into the year the records of both fighters were comparable, Charley had won four out of four with two knockouts, while Zivic was three for three with one stoppage win to his credit. When it came down to overall experience however, Charley Burley was not in the same league as Fritzie Zivic.

The popular Pittsburgh fighter was of Croatian decent and was a member of what is probably the most famous family in the history of boxing. In all, five of the Zivic boys were fighters; Jack, Pete, Eddie and Joe all fought with varying degrees of success throughout the early part of the 20th century. Fritzie was the youngest and he had the longest career of any of the Zivics, campaigning from 1931 until 1949.

By the time he met Charley Burley for the first time, the 24 year-old Lawrenceville lad was a veteran of close to 80 fights and the evidence of his trade was there on his face for all of the world to see. Square-jawed with steely determination in his eyes, the flattened end of his bridge-less nose was a misformed blob in the middle of his face. Fritzie said that he owed the shape of his proboscis to Perfecto Lopez and a head-butting contest that they both engaged in one night in 1934. A 'doctor', and Fritzie used the term loosely, removed too much of the cartilage and Fritzie's next opponent, Phil Rios, pounded on it until it caved in.

It would not have been possible to mistake Zivic for anything other than a rough-and-tumble prizefighter and in addition to looking the part, he also had a reputation as being one of the dirtiest ring-men around. Relying on a well-stocked bag of tricks to gain control of a struggle within the ropes, butting, lacing, gouging, tripping, pinching and biting were all part of the Zivic repertoire, although he once said that he would never, ever, thumb anybody in the eyes because he wouldn't want someone to do that to him.

Billy Conn, who had beaten Fritzie over 10 rounds in 1936, often chided his fellow Pittsburgher for being a cry baby, claiming that Fritzie didn't mind too much doing unto you, but hollered like hell if you did it back to him. Despite these foul, though not always blatantly nasty, tactics Fritzie Zivic was a very popular fighter, especially in his hometown. Mostly because he was tough and usually gave his all, but also because he was a nice guy out of the ring. Up to the fight with Charley, Zivic had only once failed to go the distance and that had been four years previous when he was knocked out in three rounds by Laddie Tonelli in Chicago, a result he later reversed. Other victims of the popular Zivic included

Johnny Jadik, Bobby Pacho, Bobby Bland, Perfecto Lopez and Harry Dublinsky.

Jake Mintz was happy with the way tickets sales were going for the fight and he was confident of a sell-out crowd at the Motor Square Garden. Chappy Goldstein however, was not happy. While he must surely have had confidence in the best fighter in his stable, the experience and 'modus operandi' of Zivic left him a little worried. He had filed an objection to Dr. W. D. McClelland, chairman of the state athletic commission, concerning the tactics usually employed by Zivic and had not received a reply.

Dr. McClelland however, had gone on record to state that if Burley won and weighed within the welterweight limit of 147 pounds he would take Fritzie's place as contender to champion Barney Ross. This presented a further wrinkle in the contract negotiations, of which there had been many, as the two managers began to argue over the weight. Luke Carney demonstrated that he was far worldlier, in fight game terms, than Goldstein by negotiating for the fight to be contested at a maximum weight of one hundred and forty-nine pounds.

Zivic, who was training at the Lyceum under the guidance of brother Eddie, was weighing 152 pounds after a workout 10 days before the fight and was confident of making the limit without any undue stress. He was still in good shape following a March 10th knockout victory over Tommy Bland and the final stages of his preparation consisted chiefly of sparring to maintain his fighting edge. Fritzie rarely had trouble making weight anyway and his lean, muscular frame always had a look of knotted steel wire.

If Charley Burley was the victor in the local clash, but weighed 147 pounds he would not climb over Fritzie Zivic in the ratings. However, if the Lawrenceville lad won while weighing over the welterweight limit he would retain his top ten rating. In terms of the world ratings Luke Carney and his charge could not lose, provided Charley weighed over the limit come fight night.

The Burley camp were getting down to serious training at the Centre Avenue YMCA Sparring partners Ossie Harris and John Henry Thomas, in addition to the large crowds that watched Charley train, were given plenty to consider as the Hill boy was displaying some dynamic punching power. Ossie Harris, or 'Bulldog' as he was being called, was a recent graduate from the amateur ranks, where he too had lost a decision to local favourite Leo Sweeney. The solidly built African-American was a rough-house fighter, all crash and dash action with little finesse.

Although he did possess some boxing ability, 'awkward' might be the kindest way to describe him. In 1936, as a middleweight, 'Bulldog' had been a Pittsburgh representative at an inter-city show in Buffalo New York. On that occasion he came back with a winner's trophy to which he promptly added a senior Middle Atlantic crown and a Diamond Belt title. Several of the city's promoters felt that Harris didn't quite have what it took to be a solid professional and he was initially turned down by Jules Beck, Jake Mintz, Bill Drummer, Art Rooney and his co-promoter Barney McGinnley. Eventually Ossie got his start with Jimmy McGirr in McKeesport. For the moment though, he was learning the ways of the professional fight game by helping Charley Burley prepare for the most important bout of his short career. Before the fight, the odds were in favour of Zivic at 10-3 for the decision, though he was touted to stop Charley Burley inside six rounds. Never considered a murderous puncher by any standards, Zivic had recently hit a run of good form and appeared to be punching quite heavily. With four knockouts in his last nine victories, Fritzie's confidence, along with his punches, was booming. Charley Burley had never been off his feet in the ring so was not unduly worried about his opponent's punching power. He was, however, concerned with the tricks that might be employed to secure victory for Zivic. These fears were echoed by his manager, who felt that the Lawrenceville lad was possibly given an unfair advantage by the city's boxing officials.

> "Nobody can lick Zivic the way they let him fight here. If the referee makes him go according to the rules, Burley will be plenty good enough. But poor Tommy Bland [Fritzie's last opponent in Pittsburgh] never had a chance because that referee let Zivic pull things which should not be tolerated in any ring."

Phil 'Chappy' Goldstein

As the fight would prove, Goldstein's fears were well justified. All that Charley Burley wanted was a fair shake and an opportunity to display the talents that he felt would propel him to bigger and better things. On Saturday March 19th Charley had his final training session before the fight. Down at the gym he was interviewed by Wendell Smith of the Pittsburgh Courier who was attempting to get some inside information as to Charley's physical and mental condition.

> "Every night before I go to bed I ask God to help me with this fight

against Fritzie Zivic. A victory will mean everything to me. It will mean a chance to get out of the hole that I have been in most of my life. I know that he will help me and I know that I will win."

Charley Burley

The day of the fight came and Charley was quite relaxed after spending a quiet Sunday with Julia and his family. On the scales for the weigh-in, Charley received a shock as he weighed three-quarters of a pound over the welterweight limit. Fingers were pointed, as the members of the Burley camp were suspicious of gamesmanship. His weight had been below the welterweight limit during the final stages of his preparation and if Charley Burley did anything right – it was prepare.

"She [Julia] would chew his gum to take all the sweets out of it. Then he would chew it, so he wouldn't get the sugar. Now that sounds ridiculous, but when Charley was in training, you know."

Bobby Lippi

Zivic came in three-quarters of a pound under the stipulated weight and as it stood, a victory for the Hill boy would not elevate his status among the ranking welterweights. Zivic had nothing to lose except face, and he could always argue that he had underestimated Charley should he suffer a reversal. Similarly, Charley Burley had little to lose and much to gain, as he wasn't really expected to beat his veteran adversary. A win would merely reinforce his claim to be the best fighter in Pittsburgh and project him into the spotlight as a genuine contender.

That Monday night, at the Motor Square Garden on Liberty Avenue, the opening bell of the main event signalled the beginning of what many described as a torturous half-hour for the betting favourite. After a couple of rounds of tentative, range-finding jabs Charley Burley turned up the heat and his left-hand punches burned into Zivic's face with monotonous regularity. By the fourth round Zivic's face was glowing red from the rasping punches that Burley had continually stung him with and the Lawrenceville lad knew he had to do something soon to halt the runaway train from The Hill that was threatening to derail his own career. Wrestling and tripping tactics were subsequently employed and on three occasions Zivic spun his tormentor through the ropes, out of the ring and onto the apron. The first of these rule infractions would normally incur a finger-wagging from the referee, but the third time should have cost Fritzie on the scorecards, points that he could ill afford to lose. Yet, he escaped punishment for his actions just as he did when he decided that it was time to use his gloved fists for purposes other than punching. Referee Freddie Manstrean was eventually forced to warn Zivic for his illegal tactics, but several times he was blind-sided by the canny veteran and did not witness everything that transpired. The crowd, in an attempt to assist the referee in enforcing fairness, booed loudly when Zivic resorted to heeling and lacing.

In rounds, four and seven Charley was forced to hang on as Zivic attempted to wrestle, hold, and hit. Otherwise, his plan of punching, moving, and not allowing his opponent to settle proved to be very effective tactics. When Zivic attempted to level matters with a leaping left hook he was caught flush with a powerful right-hand counter that rocked him back on his heels. Come the tenth and final round, a cut, bruised and swollen-faced Fritzie Zivic had to be dragged up off his stool. Summoning up all of his undoubted courage, Fritzie charged into the fray in one last desperate attempt to salvage something from the fight. Charley Burley, displaying resolve beyond his years, dug in and met the flailing Zivic in the trenches. For almost the entire three minutes, both men stood toe-to-toe and winged in hooked and arcing punches, each one designed to settle matters before the final bell. Charley's seconds must have had palpitations, as they felt for sure that their man was far ahead. A gun-fight in the last round was not what they wanted to see.

When the final bell did ring, the crowd signalled long and loud its appreciation for both combatants. Then came the decision. Referee Freddie Manstrean voted for Burley seven rounds to two with one even, while judges Dr. George McBeth and Karl Koehn inexplicably cast for Zivic. The crowd of over 3,000 booed loudly, as a weary, but victorious, Zivic was practically carried from the ring. They continued to voice their displeasure for over five minutes afterwards. While the majority of those in attendance felt that Burley had won, the opinion of the newspaper reporters at ringside was as divided as that of the judges.

"Were you ever the victim of a mirage – of seeing something you felt was yours, only to reach out and discover that it had vanished into thin air? Or, have you ever had in your hands something, honestly earned, only to have someone, unappreciative of the effort in acquiring it, reach out and snatch it from you? If you have, you can commiserate with Charley Burley, Hill Negro fighter. Burley was magnificent in jabbing, stabbing and punching his way to a one-sided victory."

Regis Walsh, Pittsburgh Press

Walsh was not the only paid observer to the action who felt an injustice had been done.

"Charley entered the ring Monday night with a prayer on his lips and dynamite in his youthful fists, and gave Zivic one of the neatest boxing lessons the white boy ever received in his long ring career. The sepia slugger from the Hill district, out-slugged, out-boxed and out-gamed the highly-touted Fritzie before 3,000 fight-crazed fans. He won seven of the ten rounds in one of the most thrilling battles in Pittsburgh's fight history. But, when the fight was over, the weary hand of the badly-beaten Fritzie Zivic was raised as the victor."

Wendell Smith, Pittsburgh Courier

As was the case with the judges and the fans, there was also a difference of opinion amongst the press.

"Considering however, that Zivic has oodles of experience compared to the unknown colored boy, the latter made a very creditable showing, and in fact some of the fans hooted the decision, and the referee, Fred Manstrean, even cast his silent vote for Burley. How this latter conclusion could be reached is somewhat of a mystery in the light of how Burley, with one eye puffed up to the size of a nickel crockey, began sagging a little around the knees in the sixth round, appeared winded and fagged, and was groping around most of the time when the fighters got at close quarters."

Harvey Boyle, Pittsburgh Post Gazette

Boyle did give Charley some credit though, citing the fact that he managed to land "a right-hand stinger" to Zivic's jaw no fewer than ten times. Boyle felt that Zivic's superior experience gave him the edge, especially in the clinches when he "tossed and pulled him around so much that Burley did not know exactly where to catch on and meanwhile Zivic was punching to the body and cuffing that bad eye." Others felt that Charley had shown his veteran adversary too much respect and was a little lost when it came to the rough-house stuff.

> "He [Zivic] was the dirtiest fighter I ever met. He kept thumbing me, he gave me some black eyes."

Charley Burley

The fans, the press and not least Charley Burley, were all entitled to demanded a rematch. Jake Mintz had no qualms about staging a second meeting as the first had netted over $5,000 and money talked just as loud then as it does now. The main problem would be convincing Fritzie Zivic that, for the sake of his reputation, he would have to beat young Mr. Burley more convincingly.

Although he had met many black fighters during his busy career, up to the fight with Charley Burley, Fritzie Zivic had never contested a match in front of his home fans with a fighter of African-American descent. Typical of his nature, Charley made no bones about his defeat at the hands of the more experienced Zivic. He had lost the official decision and even if he thought he had won, he merely accepted the result and moved on. He couldn't change the outcome, but he could try to turn it around next time he and Fritzie met in the ring.

Luke Carney would not entertain talk of a rematch until the dust had settled on the first encounter or until his charge had met Remo Fernandez in Detroit. When Zivic had had a chance to perform against a previous stoppage victim of Charley's and his performance monitored and judged by his pilot, then maybe they could all sit down again and discuss terms. For his part, Goldstein was adamant that there should be an immediate rematch and he would not think of matching Charley with anyone but Zivic. Negotiations and promises of a second fight kept things pretty much wrapped up for over two months and consequently Charley remained inactive while Zivic honoured a previous commitment against the aforementioned Remo Fernandez. While the experienced Mexican struggled to last into the seventh round with Charley, Fritzie

51

Zivic had to be content with a points victory over ten rounds.

On May 31st 1938 Henry Armstrong, who at the time was also world featherweight champion, jumped up two weight divisions and took the world welterweight title from Chicago's Barney Ross in what was the Windy City fighter's final bout. With that victory, Armstrong became the first black welterweight champion since Young Jack Thompson seven years earlier. By July of the same year Hammerin' Hank had also won the Lightweight title from Lou Ambers, becoming the only fighter in boxing history to hold three world titles at different weights simultaneously. It has been argued that if it had not been for some suspect judging, he would also have taken the world middleweight title from Ceferino Garcia in March, 1940.

Charley continued to remain in shape should a second fight with Zivic materialise. Meanwhile Luke Carney signed Fritzie to meet Petey Mike in Brooklyn in May. A knockout victory for the experienced Lawrenceville fighter left the way open for negotiations on a rematch. In the meantime, feeling that the fight all of Pittsburgh wanted to see might not be soon forthcoming, Chappy Goldstein decided that he had to keep Charley active. For June 1st on a bill featuring Sammy Angott, Charley Burley was matched with welterweight Mike Barto. The New Kensington fighter had been campaigning for a number of years and could also count Zivic as a points decision conqueror, having lost to him over twelve rounds in 1935. After making the match, and just a few days before that contest went ahead, Goldstein, Carney and Zivic were approached by Jake Mintz who had a proposition for them. The promoter had a free date at Hickey Park and was frantically putting a bill together to fill the gap. This lit a fire under Goldstein and Carney, with all parties coming to an agreement in double-quick time.

Zivic's manager, with one eye on the welterweight crown, realised that while his fighter was still ranked one of the top-ten welterweights in the world by the powers that be, in the hearts and minds of the Pittsburgh fight fans he was only second best until he could prove otherwise. He took up Mintz's offer for the Hickey Park date and relished the opportunity to set the boxing fans straight as to who was the best fighter in the city.

In order to present his side of the argument, Charley Burley first had to attend to a prior engagement. Before seeing Mike Barto floored once in the second round and three times in the fourth, the small crowd at Hickey Park observed an occurrence that was as new to each and every one of them as it was to Charley Burley. In his only moment of success in the fight, Mike Barto hit Charley Burley with a left hook that forced the local fighter to touch down with one knee. There was no count as the contact with the canvas had been for the briefest time, but there was, if only for an instant, some added interest to the proceedings. Sadly for him, Barto's chance for what would have been a shock win evaporated in about as much time as it took Charley to recoil off the canvas. By the fourth round it was over. A right cross and a right uppercut accounted for two nine - counts, while a right hand to the heart scored a third, forcing the referee to call a halt

Ecstatic at the prospect of gaining revenge over Zivic, Charley went straight back to the gym. He had no intention of letting Fritzie or Luke Carney get the better of him again, in the ring or on the scales. In fact, for the Barto fight, Charley's training had been going so well that he weighed just over 142 pounds.

After the first encounter Charley admitted that he may have given his conqueror too much respect, but he was determined not to be so shy of mixing it with Fritzie from the off the second time around. In the gym Charley and his trainer Dandy Allen began working on a strategy that would enable him to defeat the thick-skulled Zivic, while removing the risk of causing any further damage to Charley's already aching fists. In the gym these new techniques were drilled and drilled until they became second nature. In subsequent sparring sessions they were practised with equal tenacity and resulted in at least one sparring partner per day calling it quits after feeling the effects.

While Charley grew in confidence with each passing day, Fritzie Zivic undoubtedly became more anxious. He was ranked as high as he had ever been in his career and he knew that if he kept on winning he would eventually receive a shot at the title. What must have bothered Fritzie was the fact that not too many observers felt that he had really won in the first meeting with Charley. A defeat in what was his eighth year as a pro, to a local fighter who, on the world scene, was unranked at the weight, would surely spell the end for the last of the fighting Zivics.

Jake Mintz had promised that the winner of the fight would be matched with a ranked contender in the near future so as to strengthen their claim to a title shot. Career-wise this was a crossroads fight for Zivic and any thoughts of defeat at the hands of the young Charley Burley could not be entertained. It was win or bust for the Lawrenceville lad.

On fight night, the atmosphere at Hickey Park in Millvale was palpable. The crowd, who had paid close to $5,000 gross to see the action, were mainly pro-Zivic and this was reflected in the betting odds at ring-

53

side. After saying his customary pre-fight prayer in the dressing room, Charley made his way to the ring to await his opponent. As Zivic entered the ring to a cacophony of cheers, whistles and shouts, Charley's seconds removed his green silk robe as he skipped and jigged around nervously in his corner. At centre of the ring referee Red Robinson gave the fighters their final instructions. In an oratory that almost rivalled the Gettysburgh Address, Robinson warned both fighters against the use of foul tactics.

The speech was a total waste of time as far as Zivic and the referee were concerned, because as soon as the first round got under way Charley Burley looked as though he was going to be the victim of a vicious mugging. Zivic chased down Charley in an attempted to close the gap between them and on the occasions when he was successful, he resorted to the tactics that had brought him victory the last time the two had met. These same tactics prevented Charley from being as effective as he might have been in the first couple of rounds, but the Hill fighter, via skilful employment of the jab, began to put some space between himself and the wildcat in front of him. In the fourth round, once he found some room to punch, Charley brought out his secret weapon, a weapon that had been so carefully honed in the gym.

"Right hands to the heart. Charley hurt his hands on his head. You know they X-rayed Fritzie Zivic's head and found out that his skull was extra-thick and Charley fixed him with them right shots."

Bobby Lippi

From the moment that first body shot landed, the course of the fight changed and Zivic must have known he was a beaten man. The tactic proved so successful that Fritzie turned from fighter to dancer and not the fleet-footed, ring-circling style of dancer, he wanted to dance with Charley Burley the way couples dance to the last record of the night, up close, hugging and clinging. Surprisingly referee Robinson allowed the employment of these tactics by the Lawrenceville veteran and it was undoubtedly the official's leniency that allowed Zivic to remain in the fight. Although his rough-housing had enabled him to edge the fifth and ninth rounds, Fritzie Zivic was well beaten come the final bell. He had very little left for the last round and Charley put the final seal on the matter by giving an outstanding display of box-fighting. After the bell to end the final round, and a thrilling contest, a hush fell over the crowd. Burley appeared to have done enough to receive the decision, but would the judges recognise his efforts and superior skill this time around? After the cards were tallied, the unanimous decision in favour of the Hill fighter was greeted with rapturous applause as even the pro-Zivic crowd acknowledged that the better man had won.

Zivic was written off by sports writers in the following days' newspapers as being washed up and finished as a world class fighter, yet Fritzie Zivic had more heart and determination than anyone could have imagined as he would later go on to prove the press and the public wrong. Charley was pleased at getting a just decision for his efforts and he had proven that he was the better of the two fighters.

While the press wrote off Charley's vanquished opponent, they wrote about the 'Hill District Holocaust' in glowing terms, even going so far as to speculate on his chances with the new world welterweight champion Henry Armstrong.

"Sure, I'll fight Henry Armstrong, I'll fight anybody."

Charley Burley

According to Bobby Lippi, Charley not only had the ultimate realisation of who and what he was, he also had the mindset of a great fighter. The kind of attitude that all the great fighters possess. Bobby firmly believes that this 'mindset' and this sense of self or identity that Charley possessed, was evident in most black fighters. He argues that most of the white fighters just didn't think or feel the same way.

"There's a mindset that you got to have. You've got to have that mindset that nobody can whip you until they whip you and even then you don't believe it! There's a meanness in a prizefighter. The average person out there isn't mean, a prizefighter has got that meanness. And I don't give a damn what made them mean, its there or it isn't, and it never leaves. I don't mean vicious, where you'll bite the other guy's ear, maybe 'mean' is not the right word, but you cannot be whipped! It is not allowed."

Bobby Lippi

Bobby may be Italian by ancestry, but he has spent most of his life in black communities and he views people as essentially the same, (as in no one is better than anyone else), but with certain differences, especially African-Americans and their own 'mindset'.

> "It's that determination and maybe desire, you know? And the blacks are taking over football now, but now they're kicking the shit out of each other! It's there. That 'will to win'. If you're gonna be a winner, the attitude is 'I'm not a nigger! I'm a man and I don't give a shit who the best black man is, I'm better than he is!' They develop this attitude, 'I'm a man'. Where as white people, they're full of shit! They don't have that attitude. They think that because they got a few stinking dollars in their pocket, they got the late model car or they're in charge of the loan office at the bank their attitude is 'go fuck yourself'. It gives them a superior attitude with absolutely nothing to back it up except their position or their authority."

Bobby Lippi

In an attempt to capitalise on his success over Fritzie Zivic, Chappy Goldstein looked towards the East Coast and a number of rated fighters who might be willing to take on Charley Burley in Pittsburgh, or anywhere else for that matter. Eventually he reached an agreement with Chris Dundee for his ranked welterweight Phil Furr to come to Hickey Park and meet Charley on a Jake Mintz promotion in July. The North-side based promoter was experiencing some problems of his own in regards to getting a headliner for the upcoming show. Boxing commissioner McClelland and Ray Foutts, manager of former middleweight champion Teddy Yarosz, had some personal differences and could not even agree to disagree over the terms and conditions for Mintz's proposed Yarosz versus Billy Conn fight.

Since losing his crown in 1935 to Babe Risko in Pittsburgh the tough Yarosz had met Billy Conn twice, losing back to back decisions to Johnny Ray's man in 1937. A third meeting between the two would draw a good crowd in Pittsburgh as both were hometown fighters and Mintz wanted to put Conn, Yarosz, Burley and possibly Zivic on an 'all-star' card at Hickey Park. The headache for Mintz was that Fritzie was in New York looking to rebuild his flagging career on the back of the two knockout wins he had scored since his defeat by Charley Burley, so he was out as an attraction.

56

This coupled with the bickering over the Yarosz-Conn battle was making life difficult for the promoter. With Burley and Furr signed for July 11th Jake Mintz attempted to reconcile commissioner and manager for a joint headliner. Unfortunately, this proved to be impossible given the time frame that the promoter had to work in. However, he continued to work for the second fight for later in July as two headline shows in as many weeks would suit him fine because he would then have two potential sell-outs.

The problems between Foutts and McClelland appear to have been the result of dealings between the manager and another Pittsburgh promoter Elwood Rigby. In order to make the match between Teddy Yarosz, managed by Fouts, and Billy Conn, the promoter had to make certain financial concessions. So as not to upset Conn and Johnny Ray, Elwood Rigby agreed to pay Yarosz the greater cut of the purse, so long as he took some of that payment in tickets for the fight. While this was not against commission regulations, for some reason it upset McClelland and he was determined to stamp his authority on the situation by being uncooperative with Fouts. The local press felt that Dr. McClelland was acting like a 'little Hitler' with his ruling of the local boxing commission.

Come the day of the Burley and Furr fight Dr. John E. McClenehan called Mintz to throw a stethoscope in the works and add to the promoter's woes. Charley had developed a painful rash on his chest and the doctor informed all concerned that the Hill fighter would be out of action for at least two weeks. Stricken with panic, Jake Mintz called Fritzie Zivic in New York and asked him to step in for Charley against Phil Furr. Never one to look a gift horse in the mouth, Fritzie seized upon the opportunity to upstage his local rival and immediately returned to Pittsburgh. Mintz, relieved that he didn't have to cancel altogether, moved the sell-out show to the following night. So, while Charley Burley recovered from a case of shingles Fritzie Zivic capitalised on his misfortune by punching poor Phil Furr from pillar to post in a little under three rounds of one-sided action.

The Lawrenceville lad was back and looking impressive with three fights and three knockouts since his losing effort against Charley. Zivic's latest win, against a fighter who had been the distance with Izzy Janazzo and Barney Ross, was most impressive and he now had his boxing career back on track. While Zivic continued his knockout streak against Joe Lemieux in Newark on August 2nd, Charley attempted to get back into title contention by facing the experienced California-based Cuban, Leon Zorrita, over ten rounds at Hickey Park the very same night.

Despite his recent illness and the gulf in experience - Zorrita had contested close to 70 bouts - Charley stopped the fast punching Cuban in six rounds. A trip to the canvas and an assault from Burley's fists (that referee Al Greyber referred to as "Lewis machine gun-like"), forced the stoppage just over two minutes into the round. Zorrita's acting manager, Pittsburgh promoter 'Apples' Meyers, was not too happy with the referee's actions and protested loudly. Referee Greyber defended himself by arguing that it may have only taken one more punch for a disaster. Greyber had an unusual amount of compassion for injured fighters and was always a 'safety first' type of a referee.

A former fighter himself, Al Greyber had not only first-hand experience of the savagery that could occur in a boxing ring – he had once opposed the legendary Harry Greb – he had also experienced the horrors of war in Europe. It is possible that these life experiences made him the boxing referee he was. Overall, Charley's victory was an impressive one and he looked forward to the promised showing in New York, an incentive that Jake Mintz had added during the build-up to the Zorrita fight.

Unfortunately for professional fighters, what a promoter says and what a promoter does, occupy two opposite ends of the spectrum. Hopeful of exposure in a higher class, and more hopeful of the money that went with that exposure, Charley was looking forward to the East Coast trip. New York was the place to fight, be it the world famous Madison Square Garden or St. Nick's Arena, any boxer worth his salt wanted to fight there and Charley Burley definitely knew his worth, even if he was a little shy about verbalising it. Charley started to make plans concerning the trip. Maybe he would visit with Irving Jenkins, Frank Payton, Bernard Danchik or Dorothy Tucker, some of his team-mates from the ill-fated trip to Spain. Whatever he decided to do, he was going to make the most of his trip. His promoter however, had other plans for him.

Charley Burley around the time of his fights with local rival Fritzie Zivic.

Chapter Four

A Title Shot

Jake Mintz, with the recent deal involving the Fritzie Zivic fight, now had promotional rights to the hottest fighter in Pittsburgh and was looking for a way to project Charley into the world spotlight. After failed negotiations to bring several of the top-rated welterweights to town to fight Burley at Hickey Park, Mintz was forced to consider other avenues. Never very friendly towards each other 'Chappy' Goldstein and the promoter were allowing personal animosity to interfere with the progress of Charley Burley. Several opponents were suggested, but the constable of the ward refused them all.

In an attempt to distance himself from Jake Mintz - and possibly strengthen his own position - Goldstein sought the assistance of his old manager Lou Brown. The New York-based manager, along with trainer Jimmy Bronson, had handled Chappy during his fighting days and was now a useful contact in the city. Mr. Brown not only had the relevant personality traits to survive in the wheeling-dealing world of professional boxing, he also had the experience and the contacts. If Goldstein could get Charley some action in New York, he wouldn't have to rely on Jake Mintz to keep his boy busy. In the meantime, the Northside promoter had signed up the services of the 'coloured' welterweight champion of the world, Louis 'Cocoa Kid' Hardwick and had scheduled a championship match between the 'Kid' and Charley Burley for Hickey Park in August. According to the record books, Cocoa Kid, (aka Louis Hardwick), was born in January 1913 in Puerto Rico. Fight manager and Ring magazine columnist Jersey Jones claimed that Cocoa Kid travelled from Cuba with Kid Chocolate in 1928 to get fights in the United States. A study of Kid Chocolate's fights in the USA at that time reveals that at least two other Cuban fighters were on the undercards; they were Juan Cepero and Baby Face Quintera. Kid Chocolate was eventually deported to Cuba for failure to renew his visitor status and was active there before returning to America at a later date. Baby Face Quintera also returned to Cuba (evidenced by recorded fights there in the early 1930s), but (as yet) there is no trace of Cepero in Cuba after 1929. The notion that Cepero changed his name to Louis Hardwick and claimed Puerto Rican nationality is given further weight by the fact that Cepero boxed in December 1929 (in New York), then apparently disappeared, while Hardwick (as Cocoa Kid), has his first fight in January 1930. Early photos of Cocoa Kid also show a similarity in personal style and appearance to the Cuban Bon-Bon. Was Cocoa Kid sufficiently influenced by Kid Chocolate to take his name as well as his look? Hardwick is an unusual name for a Puerto Rican national, although the area he claimed to be from, Mayaguez, is predominantly white. Press reports from the New York Times in December 1929 describe Cepero as being similar in build to Panama Al Brown. The reporter could well be describing Cocoa Kid who was also tall and rangy for a lightweight (though he would mature into the heavier classes as he aged).

It is an interesting theory that is supported by a number of boxing historians and it does hold some water. However, eminent boxing historian Luckett V. Davis insists that, while the confusion is understandable, there is no truth to the rumour that Juan Cepero and Cocoa Kid are the same person. Davis insists that Louis Hardwick is Cocoa Kid and that he fought prior to 1930 as Lou Hardwick. However, the only Lou Hardwick of the time was a black fighter from the south who was described in one report as 'the Atlanta Negro' and in another as favouring a slugging style. Further speculation is caused by the fact that Cocoa Kid referred to himself as either Louis Hardwick, Louis Arroyo or Louis Humberto depending on which newspaper reporter he was speaking to. If he were a legitimate Puerto Rican immigrant to the United States, why the different names? Former lightweight contender Wesley Ramey defeated Cocoa Kid in 1933 and often used him as a sparring partner. His son - Wesley Ramey Jnr. - remembers that, to the best of his knowledge, Cocoa Kid was a Cuban fighter. A photograph of Cepero or Lou Hardwick may help put an end to the speculation, but until then it is an interesting story.

Whatever his origin, Louis Hardwick was based in Hartford, Connecticut and, as Cocoa Kid, was high-class operator. He had beaten Jack Portney, Werther Arcelli, Pancho Villa, Andre Jessurun and Teddy Loder. He had also met Lou Ambers, losing over ten rounds and had a loss and a draw versus Kid Azteca. Amongst his more widely known opponents was the slick-boxing Holman Williams, against whom Cocoa Kid (up to 1938), had four wins in five meetings. The fifth, and most recent, meeting between Holman Williams and Cocoa Kid, held in New Orleans June 11th 1937, had been for the belt that now adorned the Kid's waist.

"The famous gold belt, emblematic of the colored welterweight championships, which is being contested for next Monday night at Hickey Park Bowl, between Cocoa Kid, champion and Charley Burley of Pittsburgh, arrived in Pittsburgh yesterday and was placed on display in a store window on downtown Fifth Avenue.

The belt has an interesting history. It was donated by the Ring magazine to the winner of the fight between Cocoa Kid and Holman Williams at New Orleans, 1937. Cocoa Kid won the title and belt. He defended the belt against Sonny Jones, Canadian welterweight champion, at Holyoke, Mass, November 15th, 1937. Cocoa won the fight by knocking out Jones in six rounds

The contracts for the fight state the winner will hold the belt and the colored 147 pound championship

And Charley Burley is determined that the belt will stay right here in Pittsburgh.

The fight is over the 15 round route and the weight is 147 pounds, the official welterweight poundage for titular matches. Burley will have his hands full. The Cocoa Kid has a great K. O. record to his credit as well as a long string of decision, wins over great fighters."

The Monessen Daily Independent

It appears that the belt contested by Cocoa Kid and Charley Burley was not the one described in the press prior to the fight as the existing belt contains the names of Crescent City fight promoter, Marty Burke and Lew Raymond (at the time promoting out of Pittsburgh). This version may well have been commissioned for the winner as there is no reference to the Ring magazine on this belt. The version referred to in the press report - and its fate - remains a mystery.

Burke, who had been promoting in his hometown for a number of years, was one of the outstanding middleweights of his day. Fighting between 1918 and 1929 Marty Burke took on just about anyone at or over his own weight, fighting the likes of Gene Tunney, George Chip, Harry Greb, Carl Morris, Billy Miske and 'Young' Stribling. He also acted as a regular sparring partner for Jack Dempsey. Although not always success-ful against some of the better middleweight and heavyweight fighters of his time, Burke was held in high esteem by fight game aficionados and was now doing very well for himself as a boxing promoter with a reputa-tion for giving the fans their money's worth.

By the time Cocoa Kid signed to fight Charley Burley, the belt that was emblematic of the 'coloured championship' was redundant, as Henry Armstrong was the reigning world welterweight champion. Still, Jake Mintz figured that the added attraction of a 'world' title fight on his bill for August 22nd would only add to the clamour for tickets. The rest of the bill featured local talent in abundance with the semi-final showcas-ing the talents of Freddie Lenn, fast-climbing South Side middleweight, against Bill Battles of East Liberty. Freddie Lenn was an ex-marine and was beginning to show some good form since turning professional.

As an added incentive promoter Jake Mintz promised the winner of that contest an engagement for the following week against another local up-and-comer, former collegian Billy Soose. Although Charley was highly rated by the Pittsburgh fight fans, though possibly not liked by as many due to his convincing defeat of Fritzie Zivic, most thought that the experienced 'champion' would be too good for him.

With such an important fight in what was only his third year as a profes-sional boxer, and with the prospect of the money that would surely follow such a high profile match, Charley knew that he had to make an impression. Many lessons had been learned from the first encounter with Zivic and Charley was determined not to make the same mistakes again. He knew that he had to go all out from the first bell, and that his usual tactics of starting somewhat slow and gauging the other fellow's worth might not be applica-ble against an experienced fighter such as Cocoa Kid.

Four days before the fight and after completing another session under the watchful eye of trainer Dandy Allen, Charley felt compelled to go and visit his manager. His left hand had been bothering him for some time and Chappy Goldstein was shocked when he discovered the extent of the damage. The middle finger of Charley's hand was grotesquely swol-len, and so stiff that it could not be bent. Goldstein called his co-manager in New York to seek advice as to a method of treatment. Brown, who had yet to see Charley Burley fight, gave his advice over the telephone and then made plans to travel to Pittsburgh to check on his progress. Upon his arrival in the smoky city, Brown discovered a panic-stricken Goldstein and a concerned Charley Burley.

If the promoter of the event had been party to the same information as the Burley camp, then he would undoubtedly have been overcome with panic. The condition of the finger had worsened so much that it could not be bent to fit inside a boxing glove. Aware that treatment for the injury would prove to be expensive, especially if it deteriorated or required long-term attention, Chappy Goldstein called upon the services of Dr. Morris Foster. The good doctor supplied medical advice and treatment without payment under the agreement that he would gain a stake in the fighter's career.

On the day of the fight the finger had improved very little, despite vigorous treatment and there was talk of a postponement. Charley wouldn't hear of it. He had suffered setbacks before and knew that he had to build on recent successes in order to enforce his argument for a title shot. The fight went ahead as scheduled and while he was still very concerned about his injury and its long-term implications to his career; Charley hurled leather at his opponent as if everything were fine with the tools of his trade. A whipping left hook caught the defending champion on the chin early in the second round and sprawled him on the canvas. Showing the maturity that comes with close to 1,000 rounds of professional fighting, the Kid took a nine count before rising to resume battle. In the fourth the champion stunned Charley with a right-hand blow to the head and his more telling work won him the round. Round eleven may have been the Kid's most effective round as he backed Charley up several times with a two-fisted, attack catching him with hooks to the head and stomach. With Charley apparently ahead in the scoring, the crowd began to wonder if the Hill boy had what it took to go the championship distance of 15 rounds as he was again put on the defensive by the Kid's sheer volume of punches.

Overall, Charley had an argument for the first round, which consisted of tentative boxing by both parties. The second, fifth, ninth and tenth were also scored for the challenger while the third, fourth, eleventh, twelfth and thirteenth rounds could have gone to the defending champion. When the bell to start the fourteenth round rang out, the bout was evenly balanced, and although Cocoa Kid had been coming on strong he was now beginning to show the effects of Charley's heavy blows, with his right eye completely closed and his left looking to follow suit. Both fighters knew they had to put up a grandstand finish. A storming 14th round showing by the challenger, in which he had the champion staggering on several occasions, swung the bout back in his favour. By the time the fifteenth and final round got under way the crowd, who had paid a total of $3,457.00 to witness the evening's events, were convinced they had seen one of the greatest fights in recent times, title or no.

Charley attempted to cement the win by putting up a display of non-stop punching for the final three minutes, though at times he appeared over-anxious for the knockout and missed more than he landed. The two fighters were overjoyed to hear the final bell of an exhausting bout. The crowd roared their approval of both contestants before settling down into an almost eerie hush to await the judges' verdict. When the unanimous decision of referee Al Greyber and judges Willie Davis and Karl Koehn was announced, Louis Cocoa Kid walked across the ring and handed his championship belt to the new 'Coloured' Welterweight Champion of the World, Charley Burley.

Besides an exciting headline bout, the crowd at Hickey Park also got to see an extremely entertaining under-card. The 'South Side Marine' Freddie Lenn outlasted Bill Battles in an exciting slam-bang affair that saw both men close to a stoppage defeat on several occasions. As promised by the promoter, the winner fought Billy Soose the following week in a meeting of two local unbeaten young middleweights. Soose extended his run to eight wins with four knockouts with a ten-round decision over Lenn who would continue to fight for several years with varying amounts of success. When his boxing career came to an end, Freddie Lenn became a very successful coach, eventually working with the United States boxing team for the 1968 Olympic games in Tokyo.

Charley now had in his possession a championship belt. It may not have had the rich, jewel-encrusted lustre of the 'real' world's welterweight championship buckle, but none-the-less, it was his and he could rightfully have his name inscribed upon it. Sadly, the inscriptions 'Won by Louis 'Kid' Cocoa 1937' and 'Won by Charley Burley 1938' were the only two testimonies etched upon the brass and steel buckle, as this version of the 'coloured welterweight championship of the world' was never contested again.

Just two weeks after the encounter with Cocoa Kid, Charley fought Boston-based Italian Werther Arcelli in Pittsburgh, winning the bout by virtue of a first-round knockout. The fight itself is notable for one reason only as Charley inflicted further damage upon his left hand, damaging the third metacarpal, (middle knuckle), of his powerful left. A hand that had jolted, stung, frustrated and knocked down most of Charley's opponents was so badly injured as to affect future performances and also plague him for some time. Despite this fact, Charley was matched against the fast-developing Billy Soose for a show that would act as a fund-raiser for the Allegheny County Council disabled veterans' association.

Since beating Freddie Lenn the young middleweight had scored two knockouts, against Charley Weise and Babe Risko, and had lost one on points over ten rounds to Johnny Duca. In what was still his first year as a professional fighter the record of Billy Soose, up to that point, stood at ten wins from eleven contests with six knockouts. The youngster from Farrell, Pennsylvania was being pushed by his manager Paul Moss, who apparently wanted to get as much as was possible out of the talented Soose before the college boy's undoubted smarts told him that fighting was a mug's game. As a Penn State alumni Billy Soose had the brain, dedication and application to graduate with degrees in biology and mathematics. It was probably his affinity with numbers that helped Soose realise that a promising white fighter could earn serious money if matched and promoted successfully.

After making the match, Paul Moss became concerned for his charge as more and more people started to fill him in on the talented Charley Burley. He enlisted the help of trainer Ray Arcel to prepare Soose for what appeared, with each passing day and each piece of information, to be a mammoth task. Even though Charley Burley was the younger of the two fighters by some two years, the trainer thought that Moss was some kind of a nut for matching the new boy with a fighter who Ray Arcel thought was one of the best around. Joe Louis included.

Ray Arcel was often used as a 'fire fighter' by concerned managers, frequently coming in to work with a fighter just a few weeks before a big fight, as was the case with Billy Soose. Arcel had learned the game from the bottom up, working in the small fight clubs in his adopted home of New York. Initially fighting for a few bucks himself, the Indiana-born Arcel gained insights to the fight game from some of the greatest old-time trainers around. In later years he would be brought in to try and help a dozen members of Joe Louis' 'bum-of-the-month club' in their quest for boxing immortality. He and his fighter lost out every time, but Arcel stuck at it and eventually he came up with a win over Louis at the 13th time of asking in the form of Ezzard Charles. Arcel worked with nineteen world champions, from Benny Leonard to Roberto Duran and he rated Charley Burley as one of the greatest he ever saw.

Dandy Allen was again in charge of Charley's preparation for the fight, with Charley's pal from the Hill, Bobby McKnight, assisting. As part of the build-up for the fight, both fighters visited the veterans' hospital in Aspinwall for the usual run of publicity photographs and interviews. It appears that both Charley and Billy Soose were happy to be helping such a worthy cause as the veterans' drive to fund a camping trip for children of the ex-servicemen.

Charley had recently been rated as high as number three in the country's welterweight rankings and was determined to build upon his recent ring success. Billy Soose, on the other hand, was being touted as one of the best young middleweight prospects around by many of the New York sports writers. Although it was still early in his career, the fight with Billy Soose was already shaping up to be something of a crossroads fight for Charley. If he was to gain recognition as a legitimate contender for Henry Armstrong's title then he had to keep winning. Based purely on the weight alone, a match featuring an up-and-coming welterweight against a much-fancied young middleweight, one would be inclined to favour the naturally heavier fighter.

Ray Arcel, wary of Charley Burley's punching power, advised Soose not to mix it with the Hill fighter if he wanted to stay in the fight. Arcel warned the young middleweight that to his heavy-handed opponent he was nothing, just another obstacle to be taken out. With these warnings ringing in his ears, Billy Soose went out into the ring at the Motor Square Garden in Pittsburgh on that chilly Monday night and did his utmost to avoid any kind of punch that was hurled in the direction of his young, undented chin.

"Charley Burley, local Negro boxer, a right good welterweight, invaded the middleweight division last night and served warning that he is ready to challenge for top honors.

Building himself up from a normal 147-pounder to 1521/2 pounds, Charley pasted Billy Soose of Farrell, 1563/4, with everything but Aunt Minnie's dresser to easily win the decision.

At the outset, it appeared as if Burley would stop his opponent in a hurry. He started out jabbing Billy, who is much taller and rangier, and then varied his attack, employing an assortment of left-hooks and right smashes to the body and head that hurt. Soose, however, recovered rapidly and belted Charley with a pip of a right to the chin a moment before the bell rang ending the first round..."

Jimmy Miller, Pittsburgh Sun-Telegraph

The "Pip of a right" landed by Soose was arguably the only fleeting success that the Farrell boy would have as he again damaged the hand that had only recently undergone extensive rebuilding. As it was, Charley shook-off any effects of the punch and continued to force the action from that point on.

> "Craftily Burley had laid his plan of attack - a sweeping offence which almost took Billy off his feet in the first tree rounds. And then - failing to bowl game Billy over - Charley showed that he knows his way around by unceasingly dogging Soose every minute of the strenuous half-hour, seldom letting the Farrell kid, who needs plenty of swinging room with his long arms, get far enough away to put necessary leverage into his wallops. But Burley stayed on top of Soose, even in the fourth, which Soose won, and in the fifth, in which he got an even break, to wilt the fighting morale of the kid who was staking energy and ambition against experience and a rugged fighting style."

> **Harvey Boyle, Pittsburgh Post Gazette**

It was only in the last couple of sessions that Soose let fly with a few more punches but, despite the late rally, the young Farrell fighter dropped a wide ten-round decision to Charley who took eight from ten rounds with one being even.

> "Burley took the lead at the outset and was the master of the situation throughout, with Soose making a dying rally in the last two rounds when his punch was gone. It was not so much the fact that Burley won as the manner in which he won that left an impression. As in all of his recent bouts, he stepped into his opponents with confidence and kept forcing the issue with straight and hooked lefts, rights to the head and body and even uppercuts. He never gave Soose a chance to get set and discounted the latter's advantages in height, weight and reach in the first minute of fighting...

> ...If Soose had been able to fight as well as he was able to assimilate punishment and remain erect it might have been a close fight. As it was, he was outclassed by a young fighter who undoubtedly is going to become one of the game's leading middleweights."

> **Harry Keck, Pittsburgh Sun-Telegraph**

After the fight, the mood in both dressing rooms was as different as night and day. Soose sobbed in his room, bitterly disappointed with his performance. In the victor's dressing room there was pandemonium. Chappy Goldstein was pacing up and down the wooden floor, waving his arms and becoming almost as excited as he had when he had slung Charley's silk robe into the lap of Courier reporter Wendell Smith at ringside as the contest got under way. "See, see, I told you guys Charley would win," he was heard to shout over the noise.

> "Charley's such a fine boy it would have broken my heart had he not come through tonight. Why, his heart and soul were in the fight. It's all he lived for. Some said he was overmatched in this fight. Well, I guess he proved our contentions tonight, didn't he."

> **Dr. Morris Foster, Co-manager of Charley Burley**

Writing in his 'Time Out' column, Wendell Smith of the Pittsburgh Courier described the good doctor as, "just a little fellow, but his heart is as big as a bass drum." The reporter also praised Foster for coming to Charley's rescue when he was in financial need and helping him when he needed it most. Charley himself was happy to have come through another stern test with comparative ease. As he sat on the table with a big towel draped around his waist and as his friend Bobby McKnight administered the traditional post-fight rub down, he was his usual magnanimous self when interviewed by Wendell Smith.

> "Billy Soose is a fine fellow. He fought hard and clean, but I guess this was just my night. I am going to New York soon and maybe the folks on the Hill will be real proud of me if I ever get a crack at the title."

> **Charley Burley**

The New York trip had been arranged to coincide with Henry Armstrong's welterweight title defence against Ceferino Garcia at Madison Square Garden on November 25th. It was hoped that the combined efforts of Goldstein, Foster and Brown might persuade Armstrong's manager, Eddie Meade, to give Charley a shot at the crown.

69

While the party prepared for the trip, telegrams of congratulations poured in commending Charley on a fantastic performance against an opponent who was five pounds heavier and, more importantly, a much more fancied fighter. Amongst the plaudits and bouquets came a challenge for Charley from ranked middleweight Glen Lee and his management. The New York middleweight was rated in the top ten and had met some good-quality opposition. Among his most notable opponents up to that point were: Solly Kreiger, whom he had beaten over ten rounds, Ceferino Garcia (a win each in two ten-round fights), and also Young Corbett III, to whom he lost over ten.

Although Charley and his management were more interested in pursuing the welterweight title, which was closer to his natural weight, (at the time he was walking around at about 155 pounds), they would entertain any middleweight as long as the money was right.

The win over Soose and the acclaim from the fight game and press gave the Burley camp a high that they had not previously experienced. However, their euphoric mood was soon blown away by the grim reality of Charley's worsening hand condition. X-rays taken after the Soose victory revealed that, in addition to the bone chips floating around the same troublesome area, the bone was also cracked. Preliminary treatment would consist of placing a cast over the hand to allow the break to heal, but Goldstein, Foster and Brown were informed that surgery would be required to mend the additional damage.

Although things were definitely on the up for the Hill District Holocaust, and there were plenty of good offers coming their way, it was decided that Charley would concentrate on fighting welterweights only for the time being.

Charley knew he could knock out any fighter he could get a belt at, regardless of weight, but the slugging required to hurt the heavier boys was having a detrimental effect upon his hands. During the fight with Billy Soose Charley was constantly loading up on his punches, grunting out loud as he threw, in an attempt to make an impression upon the rock-jawed middleweight, (Soose was never stopped in his entire professional career). For the sake of Charley's hands, such slugging could not continue and would not be required in most cases, providing the opposition was not too big and heavy.

In Manhattan, Goldstein and his charge did the rounds of gyms and newspapers spreading the word on the man they thought was Pittsburgh's greatest fighter in many years. 'Dangerous' Dan Parker, of the famous New York Daily Mirror, personally congratulated Charley

70

on his latest victory over such a highly regarded opponent. Lofty praise indeed from a man who was feared throughout all of boxing. One word from Parker could ruin a highly rated or regarded fighter. The opposite was also true, as the powerful scribe could build up any kind of tomato-can into a fighter of world-class reputation.

Just prior to the commencement of the Armstrong versus Garcia bout, and immediately before the live radio broadcast of the fight went on the air, Charley was introduced to the crowd at Madison Square Garden. Standing in the ring that night Charley must have felt that he had finally arrived on the world scene. Called "one of the outstanding contenders" and "one who will be seen in action in New York soon", Charley left the ring to rousing applause.

After Henry Armstrong had defeated Ceferino Garcia over 15 rounds in defence of the title that Charley so badly wanted, Chappy Goldstein approached Hammerin' Hank's manager Eddie Meade to discuss the possibility of a title challenge. Meade informed Goldstein that Armstrong would probably be relinquishing the title as fighting the heavier men was placing an undue strain on his fighter who was a natural lightweight.

Benny Leonard, former lightweight king, who was a friend of Meade and of Armstrong, had also suggested that Henry give up the title to concentrate on the lightweights. If Armstrong gave up the championship belt, then Charley was in an ideal position to capture a shot at the vacant title, as he was now rated in second place behind Ralph Zanelli of Providence. If Armstrong decided to hold on to the crown, then Charley would have to keep winning to add weight to his argument for a title fight.

With his hand still in a cast, where it remained until the middle of December, and his ranking position assured over the holiday period, Charley Burley looked back on an event-filled and successful 1938. He had recently become married to his first, and only, true love, Julia Taylor and was very happy. He was also hopeful of continued success in the last year of the decade, but before 1939 was over Charley must have wondered what gods he had offended and what he would have to do to get his boxing career back on track.

(Left) The championship belt that was emblematic of the 'Colored' king of the welterweights. This version was won by Cocoa Kid (above) in a bout with Holman Williams in 1937 and won by Charley Burley against Cocoa Kid in 1938.

Chapter Five

Don't Say Zivic, Say Burley

With Henry Armstrong atop the world's welterweights, the Pittsburgh dailies were banging on about a title fight for Fritzie Zivic. But, just as Zivic had his supporters amongst the boxing writers, so too did Charley Burley. Wendell Smith, whose sporting fame would spread beyond the pages of the city's black weekly Pittsburgh Courier, was obviously one of Charley's greatest boosters.

> "Charley Burley, not Fritzie Zivic is Pittsburgh's best welter. Scaling the ladder of fistic fame with an amazing burst of speed, Charley Burley, Pittsburgh's sensational welterweight socker, awaits the year with vivid dreams and cherished hopes of getting a crack at the welterweight crown, now adorning the capable brow of Henry Armstrong."

> **Wendell Smith, Pittsburgh Courier**

Smith described Charley as, "a dreamy-looking kid, who acts and fights similar to Joe Louis." Charley may have been flattered by the comparison, but he knew he was not Joe Louis, he was Charley Burley, and he wanted a crack at the title, regardless of who was called champ.

By the second week of 1939, Henry Armstrong had made another defence of the title that his management had insisted he was giving up. By defeating Baby Arizmendi over ten rounds, on January 10th, Hammerin' Hank took his successful welterweight defences to three. With there being no sign of Armstrong giving up the belt, Charley's management decided that he must strengthen his claim for a shot at the champion. To this end, they signed to meet the highly regarded Jordan 'Sonny' Jones of British Columbia.

Jones, who was rated by the NBA as second-best welterweight to Henry Armstrong, was also hopeful of a title fight. All he needed to do to retain his standing among the leading welterweights was to beat Charley Burley. Unbeaten as an amateur, the Canadian had engaged in close to 100 fights in seven years as a professional. Always willing to travel, Jones had competed in all of the main cities in his home country as well as Seattle, Holyoke and New York. In a tour of the UK, he had tasted defeat only once in twelve outings. Losing in the eleventh round via a foul to Jake Kilrain in Glasgow. Among his more notable opponents were Andrea Jessurun, Ernie Roderick and Eddie Dolan with whom he earned a draw.

The Charley Burley and Sonny Jones fight, along with the one eight-round and two six-round prelims, was to take place on the usual Monday night slot at the Motor Square Garden. However Jake Mintz graciously moved the card to the Tuesday to avoid a clash with the Etna Elks Amateur Diamond Belt tournament that was also taking place.

With the press in overdrive to promote the fight, Jake Mintz, through his contacts in New York, was able to raise the profile of the fight even further. To the winner of the bout would go a place on the under-card of the Joe Louis and John Henry Lewis world heavyweight title fight at Madison Square Garden on January 25th.

Jones, dressed rather sharply in a tailored suit, was considered rather good-looking by one of the Pittsburgh Courier's female reporters and it is unlikely that her opinion changed after the Canadian stripped for the scales and displayed his lithe, olive-coloured physique as he posed with Charley for the pre-fight photographs. The press took to referring to the Canadian as a 'mulatto', from the word mule, in order to describe his mixed parentage. An unfortunate tag at best, but the reporters obviously didn't realise that Charley Burley, the local hero in the upcoming pro-ceedings, also had one parent who was black and one who was white.

With his frizzy red hair receding rather rapidly up his forehead, Sonny Jones' face had an elongated, egg-shaped appearance, which made him look older than his years. The Canadian looked as though he might hold an advantage in the weight, especially when observing his large, broad shoulders, but when he stepped onto the scales, he was close to three pounds lighter than Charley. The visiting fighter was also slightly shorter and was at a disadvantage in the reach stakes. Still, Sonny Jones defi-nitely looked the part and if his record, and his boastings, were anything to go by, Charley Burley would not be having things his own way.

"Last 'Chewsday,' one Sonny Jones, fair and rugged from the Canadian shores, dashed into our offices and said he would pound the proverbial 'stuffins' out of our very own, mild-mannered, glove-slinging, win-weav-ing, clever-boxing Charlie Burley. I visualized my pockets jammed with shekels from the 'weaklings' of old Smoketown who would dare wager against the hometown boy."

Pittsburgh Press

The bout itself proved to be an exciting affair with Jones shaking Charley on a couple of occasions, especially in the third round when it looked as though he was badly hurt from a crunching right-hand punch to the head. The shot rocked Charley so badly that he appeared not to have recovered from its effects when, at the bell to end the session, he went to sit in the wrong corner. From the first though, it was apparent that the hometown fighter wasn't prepared to take any chances as he got off to an unusually fast start, rocking the Canadian with a solid left hook in the opening session, one of many powerful shots that drew blood from the outset.

Local 'ring worm' Sammie Milai, sitting at ringside, felt Charley was "starting too fast." However, the local fighter was able to sustain his early burst of non-stop aggression. Aside from the brief moment of success in the third, Jones was playing catch-up right up to round six when things began to heat up and he appeared to have found a second gear. Displaying superior body punching, Jones started to catch Burley with some hurtful-looking punches to the midsection as his short hooks scored repeatedly.

Just as the bout was getting interesting, and it looked as though Charley might have his work cut out for him, he turned the fight on its head. A smashing right shook Jones to the soles of his boots and, despite the pain that shot up Charley's arm like a thousand hot needles, an immediate follow-up right dropped the Canadian to the canvas.

As Charley headed for a neutral corner, the roar of the local fans resounding in his ears, Jones rolled over then sprang to his feet, his face a gory mask of blood. Regis Welsh of the Pittsburgh Post Gazette felt that Jones had fallen to the canvas after missing with a wild shot following the exchange of punches that resulted in the cut eye. Whatever the cause of the trip to the canvas, the gash to the eye was deep and wide and the blood was flowing freely. Charley, sensing an opportunity, tore into his injured opponent with both hands and the Canadian appeared defence-less as smashing shots to the head forced the referee Red Robinson to call a halt with just over a minute of the round remaining. Robinson, an ex-fighter and an experienced and respected third man, knew that there was absolutely no way that the Canadian could continue and he led the crestfallen fighter back to his concerned seconds.

Charley practically skipped back to his corner, as his delighted handlers pounced into the ring. Spinning around to face all sides of the audience the victor acknowledged the cheers of the partisan crowd, a broad smile threatening to break out across his relieved-looking face. It had looked for a moment as though the course of the fight may change as the battling Canadian fought gamely to regain some momentum, but like a true champion and despite the throbbing pain in his fists, Charley administered the finishing blow at precisely the right moment.

"Good breaks have been few and far between since the likable Negro lad, Charley Burley, first pulled on boxing gloves. He battled his way through almost a hundred amateur bouts before he decided that what he was doing was worth being paid for. Then, when he decided to turn pro, it was uphill all the way - four rounders with tough kids; six rounders with tougher kids - finally main events with the toughest.

Never once did he whimper - he fought them as they came, developing all the while until he reached the point where national recognition beckoned to him. He fought and beat Fritzie Zivic when everyone else was backing away from the Lawrenceville mauler; he fought and beat Billy Soose when the Farrell lad looked like the greatest prospect here in years.

So by the law and averages of compensation- that good break he got last night should not be begrudged him. But the many who saw it felt that Burley would have been in plenty of trouble before the termination of the scheduled 12 rounds had not one of his right-hand smashes cut a gaping gash over Jones' left eye."

Regis M. Welsh, Pittsburgh Post-Gazette

A break he may have received, but that break came at a price. Yet again the hands that had put paid to close on 100 opponents and had pounded out thousands of rounds at a punch bag were literally beginning to crack under the strain. Charley's style had never allowed him to take it easy when delivering a punch to the target. He loaded up on everything that he threw, each punch designed to have maximum effect and now he was paying for it. The promised showing on the Joe Louis-John Henry Lewis title showdown had to be cancelled as Charley headed for the operating theatre and surgery on his hands. Bobby Lippi and Julia Burley remember that serious reconstruction took place.

"What did he have put in there (Julie), was it sheep bones? These here [middle knuckle]. Sheep bones or some other kind of bones, but it didn't stop him. He had no fear of injury. And the amount of times after a fight he'd fill up a bucket with ice because them hands would be swollen. And he'd never complain! You'd never hear him saying ooh, this hurts or that hurts."

Bobby Lippi

With bone-graft surgery required for the left hand and some minor repairs to the right, Charley would remain inactive for over five months. During this period of rest the top-ten ranking welterweights remained active. In the intervening period Fritzie Zivic put together a fine run of eight wins from nine contests, his only defeat coming at the hands of Kenny LaSalle, a reversal that Zivic later avenged. Some of his more notable wins during this period came against Jackie Burke, Bobby Britton and a weight-weakened Eddie Booker, with the West Coast fighter being forced to lose close to ten pounds to secure the fight with Zivic in New York. Henry Armstrong successfully defended the welterweight title four times and Cocoa Kid and Holman Williams each had six bouts apiece.

As a result of his inactivity, Charley disappeared from the rankings. With his career going nowhere fast and faced with a long period of rehabilitation, Charley's young, tormented mind had to wrestle with the possibility of premature retirement from boxing at the age of 21. Things were so bad in fact that when Charley filed an application for a social security account number on May 29th of that year he listed himself as unemployed.

If he was to get back into the ratings and press for a world title fight Charley would have to get back into action soon and against quality opposition. The chief concern had to be whether or not his hands would hold up to the punishment he would have to inflict on them while getting into fighting shape and when punching the heads and bodies of the boxing world's toughest welterweights. A rubber match with Fritzie Zivic would have been an ideal bout for Charley at this juncture, but making such a match, or any other high-profile fight for Burley, was proving problematic for Chappy Goldstein. He wrote to Harvey Boyle of the Pittsburgh Post-Gazette in order to appraise him, and the local fight fans, of the present situation.

"In regard to the article in your column last week belabouring certain fight managers who will let their boys fight out of town for a fourth of the money they receive here, I am heartily in accord with your views. These same managers demand the equivalent of a mortgage of the fight club, the promoter's right eye and a piece of their fighter's opponent.

I am referring particularly to Luke Carney and the reason it is so hard to make a match that the local boxing fans want and should have, to-wit, Charley Burley and Fritzie Zivic. It is not surprising that Luke, who, by the way, is rapidly getting the reputation of being able to get a fighter more fights for less money than any other manager in the country, should be so unreasonable in his demands.

The real reason that Luke Carney quivers every time he hears Charley Burley's name is he remembers last June 13th when Fritzie Zivic received the worst beating of his career at the hands of Charley Burley. In all fairness to Fritzie, I am reliably informed that he wants the opportunity to fight the 'rubber match' against Charley. Therefore it is not a case of the fighter being scared, it's his manager, Luke, who gets the jitters and high blood pressure every time he hears the name of Burley mentioned as an opponent for Zivic.

Charley has always given his best, never been in a bad fight, has won all his fights on his own merit and has yet to be censored for foul fighting. It is about time that the local boxing scribes and fans got behind a lad that is a credit to his profession and clean sportsmanship and is willing to meet any or all claimants for the chance of fighting Henry Armstrong.

In line with this policy I have signed a blanket contract with Ray Fouts for any of these three opponents - Fritzie Zivic, Ceferino Garcia or Glen Lee. This proves that we mean business! We don't want to go around the country beating pushovers and setups to bolster our claim for the right to a crack at the welterweight crown. Do Luke Carney and Fritzie Zivic feel the same? I wonder."

Chappy Goldstein

In order to regain some of the lost ground, Charley's management decided to put him in with a ranked fighter immediately upon his return to competition, a move that Chappy Goldstein would regret. Besides managing Charley, Goldstein was spending an increasing amount of time and energy stirring up trouble on the Hill as the recently appointed Constable of the 3rd Ward and his already shaky relationship with his star attraction was beginning to crumble. Pairing Charley with the tough veteran Jimmy Leto was a gamble that Goldstein could ill afford to lose and his judgment was questioned by most of the Pittsburgh fight fraternity.

Jimmy Leto, an Italian-American who originally hailed from Bayonne, New Jersey, had been a ranked contender for a number of years. A better than average puncher, Leto had put blemishes on the records of many an aspiring welterweight. In two meetings with 'Cocoa' Kid he had won twice, he had also beaten Fritzie Zivic, the experienced Harry Dublinsky, Steve Halaiko, and Andrea Jessurun. At the time of the first meeting with Burley, Leto was based in Hartford, Connecticut and was being guided by Lou Viscusi, who would later go on to manage world champions Willie Pep and Bob Foster.

Charley had reportedly recovered from the hand surgery that he was forced to undergo after the Sonny Jones victory and was said to be in tremendous condition. Fitness however, is one thing. Being ready to fight as far as timing and reflexes are concerned is another. Nagging doubts over his ability to punch with the usual awesome power must also have affected Charley as he started very tentatively against the Hartford hooker. The constant bobbing and weaving of Leto, coupled with a decent body attack, enabled him to garner an early and decisive lead. In a bout that saw him regain punching confidence and some degree of timing a little too late in the proceedings, Charley dropped a split, ten-round decision to the grizzled veteran with judge 'Wee' Willie Davies casting for the local fighter.

Disappointed at the result, but determined to improve upon it next time around, Charley went straight back to training. Spurned on by some negative press and whisperings amongst the Pittsburgh fight fans as to his real ability, Charley set himself a quite daunting regime while the people at the money end went into negotiations with Lou Viscusi for a return bout with Leto.

Luke Carney had witnessed Charley's latest performance and wanted to make a third match with his man Zivic. Carney had used the excuse of Fritzie not having recovered from the flu the last time the two had met and now felt that the time was right for a decider. Carney himself was not one of Charley's biggest fans and thought that the Hill boy was overrated. To Carney's, and much of the Pittsburgh fight crowd's way of thinking, Charley Burley had yet to prove himself. Sure, he had beaten Billy Soose, Cocoa Kid, Sonny Jones and the fight fans own 'blue-eyed favourite' Fritzie Zivic, but what had he proven? Soose was talented, there was no disputing that, but he was a relative newcomer. Cocoa Kid and Sonny Jones had taken part in over 200 bouts between them and were considered veterans and possibly on the slide, and of course, illness had prevented Zivic from putting his welterweight rival firmly in his place.

Carney reasoned that Burley had been beaten by most other ranked fighters that he had faced, Eddie Dolan, Jimmy Leto and Zivic in particular, although all three had been close decisions. Convinced that the time was right to propel his charge towards a title fight, Luke Carney signed for a Fritzie Zivic-Charley Burley rubber match, convinced that the "coffee-coloured upstart" would be firmly put in his place. Carney's sentiments seemed to be echoed by a large proportion of the Smoky City's fight fans most of whom were white. While the bulk of Pittsburgh's pugilists were of African-American descent the reverse was true of the fans and, of course, the reporters. One exception to this was at the historical black newspaper the Pittsburgh Courier. The weekly was founded, owned and operated by Robert L. Vann, a prominent member of the city's black population.

Wendell Smith was one of the Courier's best reporters at the time Charley Burley was attempting to forge his way up the welterweight rankings. Smith had reported on Charley's adventures in Spain for the Courier and was highlighting his successes among the professional fighters in the city. Famous in later years for helping with the integration of Jackie Robinson from the Negro leagues of baseball into the Brooklyn Dodgers, Smith usually told it as it was. He saw Charley Burley as possibly the best fighter to come out of Pittsburgh in the city's long and colourful history.

Although he was the favourite, in terms of appeal, Fritzie Zivic found himself to be the underdog in the betting prior to the fight. The Pittsburgh fans may have outwardly expressed support for the Lawrenceville fighter, but when it came to money, they were as shrewd as the next punter. Burley may have been the better fighter but that didn't mean he had to be the most popular, even if the odds on him of 3-1 signalled otherwise.

With the disputes between himself and Phil Goldstein becoming more frequent, Charley was now in a rather tricky situation. Despite his tender years and relative inexperience in the professional fight game, this third fight with Zivic was a make or break situation for Charley Burley. A second loss to the Lawrenceville lad, in addition to the recent defeat to Jimmy Leto, would be disastrous for Charley's world title aspirations. While a win would not only put his career firmly back on track, it would also amplify the causes of the disputes between fighter and manager.

Charley's appraisal of the whole situation was that the good constable just wasn't doing enough for him and his career. He may be the reigning 'coloured' welterweight champion of the world, but he knew that the title was little more than a token as the current welterweight champion was Henry Armstrong and if Hammerin' Hank could get a title shot then, Charley figured, so could he. Unfortunately, talent was not the only prerequisite for a title challenge and still isn't today. Connections were what counted and, despite having the New York connection with his own former manager, it appears that Goldstein just did not have the connections, the personality or the smarts required to push Charley's career in the right direction.

This was highlighted again during the negotiations for the third Zivic fight when the purses were discussed. Teddy Yarosz was to be the top-priced fighter on the bill and received $2,500 with his opponent, Al Gainer, getting $1,250. Zivic got $2,250 while Charley Burley received significantly less, netting $1,650 for his troubles. The rest of the purse money was divided up as $1,500 to Sammy Angott, $900 to Petey Sarron and $100 each for the four boys who made up the supporting six-rounders. As both Pittsburgh fighters were the headliners for the show there should at least have been purse parity, but Zivic was the bigger name and the most popular fighter, he was also white and it was the white fighters who commanded the better bargaining power. To make matters worse, Jake Mintz was pressuring Goldstein to sign Charley Burley over to him and his promotional stable and was frequently putting a flea in Charley's ear over it.

In addition to promoting, Mintz - a former fighter and now a constable of the ward - was also looking to dabble in the management market. He had bought Hickey Park, an outdoor bowl, at a sheriff's sale and proceeded to assert himself as the town's biggest promoter. Aided by fellow entrepreneur Jack Laken, Mintz staged carnivals every Monday night and postponed a show only because of poor weather. "Every Monday night, crowd or no crowd", was Mintz's dictum.

His boxing background naturally led him to promote the sport he had once participated in and he soon started to branch out beyond the confines of Pittsburgh. His connections to Mike Jacobs and the 20th Century Sporting Club, under whose 'farm system' he now promoted, enabled him to bring some of the bigger name fighters to town. The same connections, Mintz reasoned, would ensure the right kind of career-advancing fights for the Hill District Holocaust. The kind of matches that would get him noticed and would practically guarantee a world title fight. Such matchmaking and promotion, however, would come at a price and Charley would probably have to become involved in 'business' fights in order to pay his way. In the meantime, Charley naively consoled himself with the fact that if he kept on beating the rated fighters, eventually his demands for a title shot would be heard.

Just over a week before Charley stepped into the ring against Zivic for the most important fight of his career to date, Chappy Goldstein walked into the offices of the Pittsburgh Courier and gave reporter Wendell Smith an exclusive.

> "I am going to sell Burley's contract, because we cannot see things the same way anymore. There was a time when I could tell him things for his own good, but now he has grown too big for me and when a fighter gets too big for his manger it is time they should call everything off. I won't handle a fighter who won't listen to advice that is intended for his welfare."

> **Chappy Goldstein**

It appeared that Goldstein was willing to take $5,000 for Charley's contract. Burley, as a commodity, was definitely appreciating as Gus Greenlee had offered Goldstein $500 for the Hill fighter's contract less than two year before. Whether Charley would have fared any better as a Greenlee fighter is open to debate. It is doubtful that 'Big Gus' could have done any more than Goldstein under the circumstances. Another report at the time indicated that fighter and manager no longer got along and it was also stated that they didn't talk, but had taken to shouting when within earshot of each other. Wendell Smith of the Courier expanded on the issue;

> "If Phil follows up his threat and decides to let Charley go his own way, it will mean that Burley will find the fistic road much harder to travel than he has in the past.

We must give Phil Goldstein credit for handling Burley on the up-and-up ever since he took over his contract. An important figure in fistic politics, Goldstein has been able to secure Burley more top purses, with the possible exception of John Henry, while slinging leather in local rings than any other sepia boxer has received.

And behind the outer crust is a story that casts a poor light on Burley, who, it appears, has been difficult to manage for some time. Not long ago we warned that Burley was slipping from the sacred path by refusing to stay on the right side of the tracks. Perhaps this is the result!"

Wendell Smith, Pittsburgh Courier

A key factor with regard to the management of Charley Burley at the time was that Chappy Goldstein had been elected to the post of 'Constable of the 3rd Ward' in the Hill District in January 1938, after the previous post-holder, James Lovoula, was elected Alderman. Goldstein was aligned to the one-time 'boss of the Strip' Pat O'Malley (at the time a politician for the same district of Pittsburgh), who was in direct competition with Thomas M. Geary - who also happened to be the Police Magistrate and was the boss of the police force responsible for the Hill. To say that the O'Malleys and the Gearys could not get along is putting it mildly. To add further fuel to the fire Chappy Goldstein, after his appointment to the position by the court, set about cleaning up the Hill District in gang-buster fashion. He claimed in the local press that vice and gambling were running 'wide-open' and that he was shutting down at least 30 clubs. The initial success that he and his deputies had ruffled quite a few feathers and raised many questions concerning the effectiveness of the police on the Hill. With 39 arrests in 40 days and many gambling a prostitution rackets closed-down Goldstein seemed good on his promise to "Mop-up the 3rd Ward" but he was embarrassing the local police in the process.

The fact that Alderman Lovoula, Goldstein's predecessor, was also aligned to the Gearys and the police made the situation potentially worse for Goldstein's position and popularity. The last straw appeared to be when the good constable and his officers raided the Ameritas Club on the Hill in April of 1938. The club was well known as a political and social headquarters for Geary and his associates and the raid by Goldstein quickly descended into farce. Believing that certain individuals were "Feloniously gambling for drinks" inside the establishment on Wylie Avenue, Goldstein, Mark O'Malley (brother of Pat and a constable of the 2nd Ward), and their three deputies served a warrant on the proprietor, James Spangard. Goldstein apparently became enraged enough to draw his gun and fire several shots into the ceiling when Spangard laughed in his face as he ripped-up the papers. The police, by then not Goldstein's biggest fans, were called to break up the ensuing fisticuffs and the constables and their deputies were arrested for breach of the peace, while Spangler, his brother and a waiter at the club were taken to Mercy Hospital to have their wounds tended.

Remanded without bail, Goldstein and his party threatened to have the arresting police officers arrested. Bail was sought in rapid order from presiding Justice of the Peace, Margaret Morgan, who decided that all should be freed pending further investigation.

Hostilities again broke out when, after an appeal hearing in front of the sitting judge to resolve who had the right to arrest whom, a scuffle broke out on the corner of Fifth and Grant Street. Frank Mazza, an off-duty police officer in plain clothes, whose brother had just been arrested by the constable, approached Goldstein. Mazza, who was reported to be wielding a blackjack at the time, told Goldstein; "I swear Chappy that you've got your neck in a noose this time, and you won't get it out." Again Goldstein demonstrated that he was not beyond using a gun instead of his fists when called for, as he reached for his sidearm. A local barber ran out of his shop to diffuse the situation, but the mutual resentment rumbled on.

The situation escalated to a more serious level when a bomb was found planted in a baby carriage in the hallway of Pat O'Malley's apartment. It appeared that the Geary's (the chief suspects in the bomb incident), were not going to be easily put-off in the battle for control of the 2nd and 3rd Wards. This was again evidenced when a petition was raised to have Goldstein ousted as constable. Chappy's argument was that due process meant that objections could and should have been raised when he was first proposed for the position. Despite the numerous signatures obtained by supporters of the Geary's - a list that included many businesses on the Hill - Goldstein could not be relieved of his duties unless found negligent and so he stayed.

It is likely that this series of events caused several problems for Charley Burley as he had friends in the police department and on the Hill. The fact that his manager was trying to clean-up Charley's own community in such a strong-armed fashion meant that the boy from the Hill was stuck in the middle. Risking alienation from his manager or from his friends and neighbours Charley had to come down on one side or the other. The 'sacred path', as Wendell Smith put it, may not have been for Charley Burley as, like it or not, he was from 'the other side of the tracks'. Goldstein's antics must have caused several people to have a word in Charley's ear and it appears that when Charley listened to them instead of his crusading manager, things got worse and the resulting ill feelings bubbled under the surface right up to the match with Jimmy Leto and immediately prior to the rubber match with Zivic.

Wendell Smith, possibly considering where his loyalties should lie as the preeminent sports writer for the black Pittsburgh Courier, attempted to rally support for Charley amongst the city's largest black community:

> "Young Charley Burley, the Tan Terror of the Hill, is in a mood that causes us to feel for the welfare of 'Ole Fritzie Zivic, the peanut vendor of the Strip, and at the same time issues a warning to all those who will be sitting in the first three rows at Forbes Field Monday night.
>
> It seems that 'Charley the Clipper' has been 'done' wrong of late and it has transformed him from a passive, conservative boxer into a dynamic, vicious slugger who is determined to get even with those he feels have been mistreating him.
>
> Fortunately, the transformation has come about just before the Zivic affair. It means that Mr. Zivic is in for a bad evening. One that promises to be just as unfavorable as was the night he last met Burley. Which, if you will recall, was just short of 'moider'.
>
> Within the last month the ties that bind the Tan Terror and manager Phil Goldstein have been strained no little. In fact some claim that the only ties between them are the dollar ones they presented each other at Christmas time. The spirit, Yuletide and all, between the two has gone.
>
> 'Charley the Clipper' claims that 'Chappy' has been going about the Hill telling little white lies about him. He also states that if it doesn't cease soon, Chappy's family will be shedding tears and patting him in the face with a spade.

When Charley climbs through the ropes on Monday night he will not be ushered in by Goldstein. It will be the first time since he quit fighting for medals and started demanding means of exchange for his efforts, that Burley has not had the advantage of Goldstein in his corner.

Added to this loss, Burley has been training without the services of Dandy Allen, who has been his trainer for the last two years. It seems that Burley and Dandy have also had some words. Words that cannot be published.

So when Charley climbs through the ropes to meet Zivic in this most important fight, he will be somewhat of an orphan. But he swears that he will be in top form and give Fritzie the works.

Zivic will have a cheering section from the Strip that is something to hear. They are behind Fritzie to a man and will be there to encourage him on to victory. In carrying out their job, there is no doubt that they will issue numerous slurs and catcalls in our Charley's direction.

For some reason, the Hill has been slow to take to Burley. He has been a great fighter. He is still a great fighter. A boy who came pounding his way out of the streets and up the welterweight ladder like a rocket, Charley has never had the support due him.

A move is now underway to rally fans Monday night in the Hill district together and form a cheering section for Burley, Monday night. Burley is a clean-cut Negro boy trying to get someplace in this tough world. He must be encouraged. He must know that, despite the fact that he has had a few troubles; the fans on the Hill are behind him all the way.

The current whisper that 'Charley is great' should develop into a deafening roar Monday night. It's up to you!"

Wendell Smith, Pittsburgh Courier

For the Burley-Zivic match the agreed upon weight was the upper limit for the welterweight division - 147 pounds. With Burley coming in over 149 - and Zivic at 145 - Luke Carney tried to have the match called off. The local commission suggested that he take Burley's forfeit in compensation and, after much persuading, Carney agreed to the penalty. Zivic, to his credit, told matchmaker Ray Foutts that he would fight Burley whether Carney agreed or not.

On the night of the rubber match with Zivic, at Forbes Field in the Oakland area of Pittsburgh, Charley - as Wendell Smith indicated - found himself without the usual services of Dandy Allen. While Chappy Goldstein chose to let his actions speak louder than his words, for the time being at least, by sitting in the crowd, the experienced Allen chose to work across the ring from Charley in the corner of Zivic.

With his estranged manager distancing himself from the evening's proceedings and his trainer offering advice to the opposition on how to beat him, Charley was facing a psychological battle even before the first bell had rung out. Throughout the build-up to the fight, Goldstein had been heard to nag and insult Charley and anyone else that fancied an earful. Whether this was a product of the frustrating atmosphere under which he was trying to operate, or simply a character flaw, it is not known, but Goldstein was successfully managing to push himself further away from Charley Burley.

The third Burley versus Zivic bout was classed as being significant enough to require the services of top-class referee Arthur Donovan, who had officiated at many world title fights over the years, predominantly in his home city of New York. Many of the fight fans anticipated seeing Donovan in action in the feature bout as they watched both Teddy Yarosz and Sammy Angott win over the ten-round distance. The Yarosz-Gainer fight was something of a dreary contest with Gainer showing little appetite for mixing it up with the former middleweight champion.

With the arrival of the contestants, for what golden-tongued announcer Joe Tucker called "the feature attraction of the evening", came a surprise for the crowd. In Charley Burley's corner, in place of the erstwhile Dandy Allen, was the recently retired former light-heavyweight champion of the world John Henry Lewis. Lewis had been assisting with preparations for the fight by sparring and offering advice to Charley, but no one expected him to work the corner. Also assisting in the corner for what had become more of a grudge match between various members of the Burley camp, was Charley's pal, Bobby McKnight.

While the third meeting between the city's two best welterweights may have been billed as the feature attraction of the night, it most definitely failed to feature anything resembling an evenly contested boxing match. Through no fault of his own, Charley found himself in one of the dullest fights of his career. Zivic didn't get anywhere near his tormentor, as Charley repeated the prescription administered during their second meeting. Even with Dandy Allen, who knew Charley Burley's ability and style as well as anyone else present that night, unable to inspire or instruct Fritzie sufficiently, the bout slipped round by round away from Zivic.

Sticking to a well rehearsed gameplan, Charley employed the left lead to devastating effect Charley baffled his opponent with straight lefts, left uppercuts and left hooks, all delivered in what sometimes appeared to be one blurring motion. The right hand was used sparingly, but when it was employed, it rocked Zivic every time.

"He [John Henry Lewis] didn't want me to use the right unless I was sure that I could beat him to the punch. I was doing exactly what I was told for a reason."

Charley Burley

While Charley's attacks were accurate and effective, Zivic's were not. Frustrated at his inability to mount a successful attack the tormented veteran began to hold and wrestle at every opportunity. By round five the crowd were gaining more enjoyment from watching referee Arthur Donovan and his curious habit of wiping his hands on his shirt each and every time he had to break the two boys from a clinch. By round seven the crowd began booing Zivic and his tactics, urging him to fight more. When their moaning fell upon deaf ears many of them began heading for the exit. At the end of the ten rounds Charley had won by such a wide margin that one wag reported that Zivic was so far behind that a telescope would be needed to see him.

The tactics decided upon by John Henry Lewis and the rest of the Burley camp had worked well and even referee Arthur Donovan, who was the third man in the ring during some of the greatest fights in boxing history, was impressed with the young Hill fighter's performance.

"I'm saying that, on what I have seen tonight, he's the only man entitled to a shot at Henry Armstrong, with the management he'd need from the corner he'd be capable of beating Armstrong."

Arthur Donovan

Lester Bromberg, the veteran boxing writer, was ringside covering the fight for the New York World Telegram. He was also impressed by Charley's almost exclusive use of the left hand, especially how it was used so effectively against such an old hand as Fritzie Zivic. Bromberg made a mental note to tally the number of right hands thrown by the victor and counted six. After the recent injury worries Charley's left hand appeared to be capable of standing up to sustained work and to this end, he looked to set the record straight with the last man to beat him, Jimmy Leto. The rematch was staged just over two months after the initial meeting and this time Charley made no mistakes as he outworked the veteran over ten rounds. The bout was a slow one for the fans who apparently cheered the loudest when the card indicating the tenth and final round was paraded around the ring.

"Leto spent three-quarters of the time backing up and one fourth leaning against the ropes or in one of the corners.

What fighting was done out in the open was done by Burley, but he queered most of his part by holding on like an octopus every time the fighters got into a clinch.

Burley might have done better with an opponent who was willing to stand his ground."

Harvey Boyle, Pittsburgh Post-Gazette

With Goldstein now acting as something of a part - time manager, but stubbornly refusing to let go of the greatest fighter he had ever been connected with, Charley was matched infrequently for what remained of their time together. It would be two months before Charley was back in action again. The belligerent Chappy Goldstein grudgingly returned to corner duties for the 90 seconds it took Charley to dispose of his next opponent at the Moose Temple in Pittsburgh. Mickey Makar, an Irishman from Bayonne, New Jersey, had a win over Jimmy Leto and was given a puncher's chance against Charley, who's recent form had not won him many admirers in the press. Starting in determined mood, Charley soon connected with a right hand that ended the fight. A punch that, according to one reporter at ringside, "might have knocked out Joe Louis."

For his final fight of 1939 Charley, with Goldstein still in tow, headed off to New Orleans for a contest against Holman Williams. The Detroit fighter is often regarded as one of the greatest fighters never to challenge for a world title. With a career lasting from 1932 to 1947, Pensacola-born Williams engaged in around 144 professional fights, although it has been said that he competed in close to 300 contests. Born in 1915 and turning to the professional ranks at the age of 17, Holman Williams boxed some of the biggest names of the 1930s and 1940s. His career as a fighter is very similar to that of Charley Burley's in that he was avoided to a certain extent by some of the top-class white fighters.

What made Williams and Burley different as fighters was punching power. While more than half of the victories on Charley's record came via the short route, Williams once went close to two years and 20 fights without stopping an opponent. This was due largely to the terrible damage he inflicted upon his hands during the earlier stages of his boxing career. For his first two years in the professional game, the Detroit-based fighter had a fifty-percent knockout ratio and his hands were broken several times during his career. It appears that as he progressed in the fight game his hands could no longer take the punishment inflicted by heavy punching and that ratio soon dropped. Williams developed his style at Detroit's Brewster Center just as Joe Louis was coming through and helped the Brown Bomber prepare for bouts many times. At one point Louis actually took over the management of Holman Williams with, it has to be said, varying amounts of success. In an interview with Sam Green in the August 1946 edition of The Boxing News, Williams recalled the early days of the Brown Bomber's career.

"When I was coaching the novices at Brewster Recreation Center about 15 years ago, Joe was in the class, but he didn't make much of an impression on me. The only reason I noticed him was that he was the biggest kid we had. He must've weighed about 155 then. Most of the others were a skinny lot.

Joe got the decision and we gave him a little red ribbon with the word 'Champion' in gilt letters. I doubt that he was any prouder the night he stopped Jim Braddock in Chicago for the heavyweight title."

Holman Williams

Williams describes Carter as: "the only kid at Brewster in those days who was close to Joe's weight." It was Louis' spirit that tipped Williams off as to his potential.

> "So they fought three or four times and Joe always was the winner. They gave the crowd action. I remember one night they fell through the ropes and kept right on punching outside the ring. I wasn't sure of Joe until that night he fought Johnny Miller. You remember Miller, of course – a tough, hard-hitting guy who was Michigan State AAU champion of his class. Miller knocked Joe down nine times in three rounds, but Joe was on his feet at the finish. I knew then he had something."

Holman Williams

Eddie Futch, one of boxing's all-time greatest trainers, was also around at the time, making himself available as a trainer and corner man. The legendary trainer has often cited Holman Williams and Charley Burley as the two greatest fighters he ever had the privilege to see and was quoted as saying that he would rather watch Holman Williams shadow box than watch most other fighters in action.

> "Holman Williams was a great boxer, but he never got the recognition because he wasn't a puncher. He had the finesse of a Ray Robinson, but no punch."

Eddie Futch

The world-famous trainer of champions initially became aware of Charley Burley when he was an amateur fighter himself in 1936. Holman Williams was in the gym in Detroit talking about a fight he had fought in Pittsburgh. What had stuck in his mind most was not the two-round victory over one Roger Shea, but the young welterweight with whom he had sparred. Williams knew then that Charley Burley would be something special and he told many boxing people in Detroit about the classy young Pittsburgher. According to Futch, Joe Louis and Jack Blackburn were also fans of the young Charley Burley.

The 15-round contest between Burley and Williams was the first of what proved to be an exciting series between the two technicians. The fight was billed as being for the 'Colored' championship held by Burley,

91

but if the belt was not at stake and the bout had been contested over the ten round distance Charley may have gained the victory. As it turned out, he had his more experienced foe on the canvas three times in the fourth round and pressed for the victory against the slippery Williams during the following two stanzas. To his credit, Holman hung in there and seized the opportunity for victory when Charley, a mile ahead after nine rounds, injured his shoulder. Williams was able to come back against a one-handed opponent and grabbed a close decision after 15 eventful rounds. Local promoter Louis Messina may have provided a belt for the new champion as the belt Cocoa Kid won from Williams, which Burley took from the Connecticut fighter, remains the property of the Burley family to this day.

Again, bad luck cost Charley in the ring, but he would be afforded the opportunity to gain revenge over the classy Michigan fighter in the future. For the moment though, it was Holman Williams who had the upper hand. In addition to the shoulder injury, the loss - and the subsequent slip in the ratings - Charley appeared to have injured his hand. Fortunately it was not too long before he was back in the ring, but that didn't stop Chappy Goldstein venting his frustration at his charge's predicament (with regard to his rating by the NBA and his injuries) to Harry Keck of the Pittsburgh Post Gazette. At the end of the year Goldstein had received a letter containing the latest rankings from the National Boxing Association. Zivic, Holman Williams, Charley Burley and Pedro Montanez were listed as the contenders for Henry Armstrong's title.

"Where do they get this stuff? Burley has beaten Zivic three times; although he got the decision only twice, and he can beat him any time they put it on the line. Montanez is a lightweight - he's fighting Lou ambers for the 135-pound title. In his last bout, Burley all but knocked out Williams in New Orleans before he hurt his right shoulder and had to fight the last 11 rounds of their 15 round bout with one hand. He had Holman down three times in the fourth and then pulled his arm out yanking him back into the ring. Any place else they would have stopped the bout to keep Williams from getting killed in that fourth round. The fans were getting up to leave, thinking it was all over.

Burley is going to fight someone here on Christmas or New Year's Day and you'll see how good he is. All we want is a shot at the title. Those guys the NBA ranks with Charley are a dime a dozen and we'll prove it. Then we'd like to get Armstrong. It's about time Charley was getting a real break. His hands are good again and his shoulder's ok and all he's waiting for is a title shot."

Chappy Goldstein

If Goldstein wanted recognition for his fighter as the best welterweight in world he went about accomplishing this task in a very strange manner. The bouts he thought he may have lined up for Christmas 1939 or New Years Day 1940 failed to materialise and a little over two months later Charley was back in action against tough Chicago middleweight Nate Bolden in Pittsburgh. Bolden, who had recently lost to Teddy Yarosz, also in Pittsburgh, was good enough to have beaten Tony Zale in two of four meetings. He would also go on to defeat Honeyboy Jones, Joe Sutka, Jake LaMotta and the murderous-punching Curtis 'Hatchetman' Sheppard among many others. He was also, for what it was worth, the reigning 'Colored Middleweight Champion'. With Billy Soose versus Georgie Abrams and local lad Ossie 'Bulldog' Harris also on the bill promoters Rooney, McGinley and Fouts expected a decent turnout for the Gardens.

Soose was out for revenge against Abrams (having dropped an eight-round decision to him the previous year), but again came unstuck against the Washington fighter, despite having his opponent on the canvas twice in the first round. It appeared to certain sections of the press that Soose lacked the finishing touch and seemed to have "...no enthusiasm for the game."

For the Burley - Bolden fight a compromise weight of 156 was agreed, making it a 'championship' fight. Charley came in at 155, while Bolden was just a pound heavier. Nate, who acted as a spoiler in order to nullify Burley's attacks, complained of a cold while the fans just complained. They didn't really like what they saw and voiced their displeasure throughout. The press, by-and-large, appeared to be with the paying public as they could find little in the way of excitement to write about. Charley was partially vindicated in the reports as he at least tried to make a go of it.

"Burley hit him at will with both fists and might have knocked him out if Nate had opened up and fought. Charley has been in several such spots here in which his opponent has made a bad fight of

93

it, damaging Charley's reputation as well as his own. Incidentally, Charley is moving up into the middleweight class where he may get a better class of opposition."

Jimmy Miller, Pittsburgh Sun-Telegraph

Indeed, in its April 1940 ratings, the Ring magazine had dropped Charley from its welterweight rankings, but he had yet to make an appearance in the middleweight division. With the year off to a winning start Charley travelled down to New Orleans for a bout with the up-and-coming Baby Kid Chocolate. The 20 year-old had beaten Philly's Gene Buffalo, had lost to Phil Furr and was being highly touted around New Orleans. Living up to this reputation, Chocolate made a good go of it against Charley Burley in their April 12th match. He shook Charley on a couple of occasions before succumbing to a fast left-right combination that dropped him for a count and forced the intervention of his seconds.

Two weeks later, and still in the Crescent City, Charley opposed full-time car-washer and garage attendant Sammy Edwards. Edwards had been a case of third time lucky for the promoter Paul Jones as the original opponent, Jimmy Jones of Boston, pulled out of the scheduled ten-rounder before Texan Willie Nyland also refused the fight. The Houston fighter's apprehension appeared well-founded as his substitute was dropped in the first round for a count of nine before a heavy body-blow put paid to his 'efforts' in the second.

While Charley and Chappy Goldstein were in New Orleans the Pittsburgh police were in one of Goldstein's old haunts on the Strip breaking up an illeagal numbers joint. The address was linked to a Chappy and a number of other local 'businessmen', but all in Pittsburgh were denying knowledge of the racket being run from there. It appear that the police were awaiting Goldtein's return so as to place him under arrest but, before that could happen, an associate of all concerned - Fred Martin of 5th Avenue - took the fall for the operation and Chappy was no longer being sought. Whilst it could be reasoned that the whole episode was engineered by certain sections of the police department in order to get back at the former Constable of the Ward the episode appeared to place further strain on his relationship with Charley.

Despite the relatively poor showing of his recent opposition, Charley was at least listed amongst the middleweight elite for May. Though his appearance there looked to be short-lived as, with his next fight, he looked capable of making the welterweight limit with ease. Next up for him was a 10-rounder against Al Weill's fighter Carl Dell in Holyoke, Massachusetts. It appears that the local boxing fraternity were looking forward to having a fighter of Charley's class in town. One writer's pre-fight report harked back to the day when Chappy Goldstein was in his prime.

"Good fighters being scarce in this day and age and when boxing in this section needs a couple of shots in the arm, it is pleasing to note that Charley Burley, the Pittsburgh Negro, finally is to make an appearance in the Valley Arena ring Monday night against Carl Dell of New York. Much has been written of Burley and said of Burley, many efforts have been made to get him into a Holyoke ring. Now all he has to do is live up to all the good things that have been written about him. He shouldn't have too much trouble doing this, judging from his the record that is his background through his comparatively short but very successful boxing career.

From a technical standpoint, the appearance of Burley is the big thing for it will give the good boxing followers of Western Massachusetts a chance to look at a really good boy and they haven't had many chances of this sort of late for boxing is in the doldrums, for why we don't know, although your answer is just as good as ours on this one. But there's another angle to Burley's appearance that is good news. This is that Phil Goldstein is coming along to handle Burley's efforts against Dell.

The younger generation of fight followers who are used to going to the Holyoke battle pit Monday nights for their fistic enjoyment know of Goldstein only by hearsay. The older fight fan remembers him as a very pleasing featherweight in the days when the valley arena was first blooming. Goldstein never won any world's championships but the old-timers recall him as a good featherweight, a little rough but always certain to give the crowd a run for its money.

In fact, for the general good of boxing there should be more Goldsteins today. Phil wasn't against cutting a few corners when he was in the ring. His theory was that it was every man for himself and if he could get away with anything that was going to help Phil Goldstein win a fight, he was going to do it. And then, too, he always had the crowd in mind, for we know of repeated instances where he went out of his way to put on a good show. He had the right idea too, that the crowd was entitled to be pleased. Boxing could stand a lot of Goldsteins today; then it wouldn't be in the state that it is in."

Vic Wall, Springfield Mass, Union

Charley would certainly have to go some to live up to his handlers advance notices, as the fans would have been expecting great things of him. He did not disappoint and was able to raise the pace and turn up the heat on his opponent just when it was needed most.

> "Dell was the aggressor in the early part of the match which developed some bad feelings over Carl's head tactics and clinching. For the most part the pair concentrated on body attack, but Dell's (Arturo) 'Godoy' style of boxing up and down on an elevator, tended to dull the performance.
>
> Burley started late after Dell had carried the fight to him in the first two rounds. Once Dell [sic] pegged punches to Dell's stomach in the third, the New Yorker buckled and fought defensively with bobbing and weaving tactics.
>
> Burley took Dell's best punches and countered with heavy right uppercuts. Most of the way the Pittsburgher proved a better boxer as he weaved in and out of Dell's punches.
>
> For five rounds the bout was close, but from the sixth out Burley clearly demonstrated his superiority and the eight and ninth had Dell wobbly on the ropes. Burley's efforts to finish the New Yorker failed because he was over anxious and rusty after the layoff."

Holyoke Daily Transcript and Telegram

Charley proved that the weight-making problems alluded to in the press were unfounded as he came in a 147$^{1/2}$ for this latest victory. As it stood, he may well have been better off concentrating his efforts on the lighter division, as the middleweight division was a muddle when it came to a monarch. While Charley was making headway amongst the world's welterweights, both Ceferino Garcia and Al Hostak claimed that they were the rightful middleweight champion. Garcia's claim arose out of the fact that he had defeated Fred Apostoli for the title that the San Franciscan had won from Marcel Thil in September 1937. While Hostak's claim was that he had defeated Freddie Steele for the NBA New York World middleweight title in July 1938. Hostak had subsequently lost and regained the 'championship' in two battles with Solly Kreiger of Brooklyn in 1938 and 1939.

By the time Charley Burley signed to fight the highly ranked Georgie Abrams in Pittsburgh in July 1940, Garcia had been relieved of the 'world' title by Ken Overlin and Hostak had again lost his grip on the NBA title via a 13th round TKO on July 19th, 1940 to Tony Zale of Gary, Indianna. In his last bout before winning the title, Zale had stopped Baby Kid Chocolate in four rounds - two rounds longer than it took a 149 pound Charley Burley. In his first fight after becoming middleweight champion Zale lost over ten rounds to Billy Soose. It appears that while he may have been floating between the two weight categories, Charley was equally at home in either as three of his last six victories had been at the higher weight.

The bout with Abrams was significant in that both fighters were looking to get into the championship mix alongside Zale and Overlin. A more logical bout for the winner would have been a return go with fast-rising Billy Soose who had recently beaten Overlin in a non-title fight. Overlin's manager, Chris Dundee, was of the opinion that Soose should beat Abrams before getting a title shot. That would indeed be a tall order for Billy as he had lost to Abrams both times they had met. If styles made fights then the bout between Charley and Abrams would be guaranteed to pull the fans in.

"Abrams is a wild, windmill type of the Greb order while Burley, straight up, hard puncher is a pretty sound boxer and is a better hitter than Abrams, although he does not score as often. The fight offers such a big opportunity for both that it would not be surprising if they cut lose hard enough that the thing would terminate inside the limit."

The Pittsburgh Press

Charley entered the ring at his heaviest ever, coming in at 156 pounds, just beating his previous mark of 155 for the Nate Bolden fight. Abrams meanwhile came in at 161. The Pittsburgh Post Gazette felt that Charley, despite the disadvantage in the weight, would "not be on the short end." That assertion was justified as far as the action was concerned but not, as it would turn out, for the result rendered by the officials. Concerned that he may be hampered by warnings that cost him the first and second rounds, Charley moved up a gear for the middle five rounds.

> "Abrams took a right to the jaw to start the fifth, found his head bobbing from Burley's jabs, and although he came back with punches, Burley gave him three for one.
>
> Burley's best round was the seventh when he crashed in a series of blows to the body and head that had his opponent groping and holding, and the eighth was just a breeze for the confident Burley who handled Abrams with the greatest of ease.
>
> Abrams best time came when the bell started the ninth, at which time he charged into Burley with a clean left hook to the jaw, his best blow of the night, and one that caused Burley to seek cover in the clinch. From then until the finish Abrams found the range better than he had all night, although Burley, while a little tired, connected with his right. But Burley lost ground toward the finish where he seemed to have the fight completely on his side before the ninth."

Harvey Boyle, Pittsburgh Post-Gazette

Boyle also indicated that the only visible harm done to both fighters in what was "a fast, if rough, fight, most of the way." was slight damage to the eyes. The 'windmill' style of Abrams didn't appear to be enough of an offensive once he sampled Charley's power in the first round. From that point on he was described as "too cautious" for much of the bout. At the conclusion of the ten rounds Judge Chick Rogers went for Burley, while Johnny Fundy somehow thought Abrams deserved the nod. Charley gave Abrams the gift of round one due to the low blow and Georgie deserved round two - foul or no. Rounds three to nine were, by all accounts, the local fighter's by some distance. Jimmy Miller of the Sun-Telegraph felt that Abrams came back in the final two as Charley "... appeared listless and hardly able to get off a solid punch in these two rounds." With the balance of the rounds in Charley's favour by six to four, the decision of Fundy was surprising. Equally surprising was the decision of referee Buck McTiernan who sat on the fence and voted the bout even. Thus the official decision was a draw. There was some talk of the two fighters doing it again in order to determine a challenger for Billy Soose. Sadly, this never happened and both Burley and Abrams were left out in the cold while the mess that was the middleweight division was unravelled by other managers, promoters and fighters.

While Charley Burley may have felt hard done by, as far as a world title was concerned, a thought should also be spared for Georgie Abrams. The tough Washington scrapper fought many of the better fighters of the day and was an unlucky loser in his only shot at the middleweight title. The largely forgotten-about Abrams, as solid a pro as there ever was, beat Billy Soose in three out of three meetings. He also beat Teddy Yarosz, Jimmy Jones, Phil Furr, Vincent Pimpinella, Ernie Vigh, Joe Sutka, Cocoa Kid, Anton Raadik and Jimmy Leto. Abrams' only chance for glory came in November 1941 when he opposed Tony Zale for the vacant middleweight title in New York. The older and more experienced Indiana fighter came away with a 15-round victory and the crown.

The fact that their July 1940 meeting was declared a draw must have rankled with Charley, especially as the superiority of neither fighter was officially established, yet Abrams went on to contest the middleweight championship with Tony Zale.

Under yet another promotion by Jake Mintz, Charley won as he pleased against the respected Kenny LaSalle at Hickey Park over ten rounds.

"Burley hit his veteran and sturdy opponent with everything but the bucket, but not once did LaSalle ever bend or duck or in any way show any signs of distress. While the affair was no part of an even contest from the first bell to the last the fans satisfied a morbid curiosity as to how many punches a human being could take and still keep his feet and head.

Burley hooked to the body almost as often as he cared to and found his opponent's jaw wide open for clean cracking right hands, yet while one round after another through the whole 10, the visitor from the wide open spaces, where men are men, never asked for a quarter. In fact, to prove his imperviousness to punishment, LaSalle gave a sort of cowboy yell to signalize the start of the tenth round and with the finish in sight, put on a little punching show himself. He caught Burley with four or five pretty good hooks to the jaw.

While it was a one-sided victory for Burley, it was an over par round for the Pittsburgher as LaSalle took some prestige away from Burley's power. However, with LaSalle used as a sort of measuring rod locally,

99

Burley came out with a little extra honor in view of the old rivalry between him and another local boy Fritzie Zivic...

...Burley left no doubt as to his superiority over the former Texan. In fact, the only thing that held the crowd through the 10 rounds was to have settled whether LaSalle could stand up under the sort of attack Burley handed out over the 10 rounds."

Harvey Boyle, Pittsburgh Post Gazette

The winner was promised first crack at Fritzie Zivic once Zivic had met Sammy Angott, reigning lightweight champion, at Forbes Field the following week. Fritzie won that one, but ignored the pleas of Jake Mintz for a guaranteed sell-out against Charley, instead concentrating on securing a world title fight with Henry Armstrong. Charley stated that, as he had beaten Zivic twice, it should be him in with Armstrong for the title. Harry Keck of the Sun-Telegraph felt that, on their respective performances against the tough Texan, Charley Burley had proven himself the better fighter.

At ringside for the Burley-LaSalle bout had been the fast rising middleweight prospect Jimmy Bivins, who hurled down a challenge to whoever won. While the support of the press may have boosted Charley Burley over Fritzie Zivic as the better welterweight (on his showing against LaSalle at least), at no time during this period did they promote Charley as one of the better middleweights. In fact, Ring magazine, in its annual ratings, did not rank Charley Burley in the higher division until the end of 1942.

The challenge of the young Jimmy Bivins was taken up in September of 1940 and the event put Charley back a step or two, despite the fact that he was still a welterweight and Bivins was, at the time, a middleweight. The official weights were $160^{1/2}$ for Bivins and 153 for Charley Burley. Regis Walsh of the Pittsburgh Press claimed that Burley was thirteen pounds lighter than Bivins come fight time. This number proved unlucky for Charley, as Bivins was a little too big and clever for him.

"Burley won the first round, a fairly close one, but lost in the ensuing three rounds, in which Bivins shellacked him with rights to the head to go out in front. In the third, Bivins' long rights to the head completely befuddled the local scrapper and left him wide open for a portside attack that almost dropped him.

Burley, although he lost the round, came close to flooring Bivins in the fourth with a left hook to the body. It was a short, savage blow and it forced the Clevelander to hold.

Burley left-handed Bivins plenty in the fifth, to win the round, but his efforts again died out and Bivins steamed back to annex the following three sessions. He visibly hurt Burley with a left and right to the head in the seventh. The fifth round was even, with Bivins holding the early advantage and Burley closing fast. The final round went to the Hill scrapper when, for the first time in the bout, he fought as he knew how. Burley beat back Bivins at every turn in the last round with a two-fisted attack and staggered him with a looping right shortly before the bell."

Jimmy Miller, Pittsburgh Sun-Telegraph

Miller also stated that it takes a good fighter to beat Charley Burley. History would prove that Bivins was undoubtedly that.

In a 1996 interview with Robert Cassidy, for the Ring magazine, Bivins recounted his own memories of the Burley fight.

"At the time I fought him he was raising Cain and I was an up-and-comer. But I wasn't afraid. He was a known fighter and I fooled him. He was smart, but he didn't take me as a great fighter because I was just coming up. Charley was fast, just as fast as I was. I just got in there and out-boxed him. I had a good jab and I used it."

Jimmy Bivins

With a career spanning from 1940-1955 Bivins suffered from the same career damaging attacks of pride and integrity as did Charley Burley. In his first year as a professional, the talented Clevelander beat Nate Bolden, Joe Sutka, Anton Christoforidis, Charley Burley and the veteran Homer Jackson. One glance at his record will show that Bivins beat some of the greatest fighters of his day and the 'Duration' heavyweight champion tag was scant reward for a career that should be revered and talked about far more than it is at present. When Joe Louis returned to championship action in 1946 it should have been Jimmy Bivins and not Billy Conn in the opposite corner, as the fight game owed him at least that much.

Once, when told he would have far more success at gaining a championship fight if he 'played ball', Bivins answered, "Hell, I'm a fighter not a ball player." While he may have done a little business and gone easy on a fighter or two along the way just to get a payday, he refused to go into the tank in order to further his career.

On October 4th 1940 a pivotal moment in the career of Charley Burley occurred as Fritzie Zivic relieved Henry Armstrong of the welterweight championship belt by way of a 15-round decision in New York. Somehow, Zivic got to fight for the title, despite the fact that he was rated behind Charley in the welterweight division at the time. Whilst two-time victim Fritzie Zivic was lording it up as the new welterweight champion of the world, Charley had to be content with a bout against 'Irish' Eddie Pierce of Dublin at an arena that Zivic owned in Lawrenceville.

> "As for Irish Eddie pierce, highly touted by Diamond [the manager who provided three of the fighters on the card for local promoter Bill Brummond], it is a good thing he is Irish, else he never would have been able to stand up under the punishment Charlie Burley dealt out to him throughout 10 one-sided rounds. Burley, 150, giving away seven pounds, was guilty of near mayhem as he battered the nigh defenseless Pierce about. Charley became so energetic in trying to score an early kayo, after hitting Pierce on the chin seven times in the first round, that he wore himself out, lost his punching class and let the thing develop into a messy affair. Pierce was gradually turned into a gory sight, staggering about, foolishly game until the finish, seldom, if ever, landing a clean blow."

Regis M. Walsh, Pittsburgh Post-Gazette

It appears that the fighters drafted in to face local opposition did not generate nearly enough excitement for the local fans.

> "Once again it was proved you can't fool the local fistic fans, for they stayed away in droves. The gate was a new low for this town. The gross was only $446 and the net $379.10.
>
> Pierce, who once was a fairly good fighter, could not get out of his own way, but he stood up under Burley's barrage of socks like a bomb shelter.
>
> It was a workout and nothing else for the local miller, who hit Pierce

with a wide assortment of punches, opening cuts under both eyes and drawing blood from the left ear. Burley was unmarked."

Jimmy Miller, Pittsburgh Sun-Telegraph

Ray M. Todd, in the January 1941 edition of the Ring magazine reported that "Burley hit the veteran with everything but the water bucket."

A bout with ranked contender Saverio Turiello in Washington was signed for November. A win against the respected Italian would no doubt boost Charley's stock a few points. However, the fickle hand of fate again left its prints upon the proceedings as Turiello was forced to withdraw. Scampering around for a replacement promoter Joe Turner and matchmaker Gabe Menendez came up with middleweight Vince Pimpinella from New York.

The bout was an apparently dull affair, with the only action coming in the ninth round when both contestants went at it in what was described as a "whirlwind of punching". Both fighters thought that they would give it their all for the final round. Unfortunately for them, and the crowd, both had miscounted and they still had one stanza to decide. Charley walked away with a unanimous ten-round decision as Pimpinella, possibly by virtue of his extra weight (close to 20 pounds by some accounts), managed to struggle through to the end.

The bout with Piminella was not only Charley's last payday for 1940 it was also his last under the management of Chappy Goldstein. The split was devestating for Charley Burley in a number of ways, but most telling was the total lack of activity. After the split with Golstein at the end of the year it appeared that none of the local promoters would use him and it would be five months before the dust settled and Charley's new manager could tout him for fights in Pittsburgh. The new management team would be something of a surprise to some and would effectively end Charley's title aspirations in the welterweight division.

"When he [Zivic] was in the money, he sold a bill of goods to one of my managers. He convinced him that he could do for me as my manager! And for very little dough he had my contract. Sam Silverman [a local attorney at the time] was on record, but Fritzie was my real manager. He promised me a shot at Freddie Cochrane for the title. Never got it, though."

Charley Burley

103

Since he had turned professional four years earlier, Charley had fought close to 85% of his fights in Pittsburgh. Under the management of Zivic and Carney he would fight just over 30% of the time at home. Whether the 'road warrior' scenario was a result of Zivic wanting Charley out of the local picture or more a result of the local promoters not wanting to use him is anyone's guess.

With the realisation that he would be highly unlikely to gain a title shot at welterweight, and with recent victories over middleweights Babe Synnott and Eddie Ellis, Charley looked to consolidate his position as a ranked contender in the heavier weight class. In May of 1941 previous victim Billy Soose won the middleweight championship of the world from Ken Overlin in the first televised bout promoted by Mike Jacobs. With two of his previous victims sitting pretty atop the world's welterweights and middleweights, Charley Burley was matched with former sparring partner Ossie 'Bulldog' Harris.

"A fighter so good that he is shunned by all the big name boys in his division, is the case of Charley Burley, classy colored welterweight who meets Ossie Harris in the feature bout on Hickey Park's opening show next Monday night. Burley's record sparkles with victories over well-known fighters, yet in the past year and a half he has found it quite difficult to get matches, because no one wants to meet him. It got to a point at one stage where Burley was thinking about quitting, but he decided to change his mind and remain in the game he knows best. Well - known fighters are still avoiding him like the plague, as witness the case when Ernie Vigh, New York middleweight, who would have had a handsome weight advantage over Burley, turned down a chance to meet him on the All-Star card at Forbes Field last Monday."

Pittsburgh Newspaper Report

Despite an advantage in weight and a proven knockout punch, the New Jersey-based Hungarian was unwilling to mix it with Charley, so the match with Harris was made instead. A certain amount of professional rivalry existed between Charley and his former training partner, for very good reason now that Charley was officially campaigning as a middleweight, yet Ossie Harris still had to be goaded into the fight by Jake Mintz.

"Harris said he was forced into the match by the promoter and his manager. He was told that if he turned down the match his fistic career in Pittsburgh would be finished."

Wendell Smith, Pittsburgh Courier

With thinly-disguised threats with regards to how the number of ring appearances might suddenly diminish should he refuse to co-operate, the normally likeable Harris was forced to accept the fight and also to promote a genuine rivalry between himself and Charley by mouthing off to the press. Although he had been stopped by Fritzie Zivic, in a brave piece of matchmaking by his manager the previous year, Bulldog Harris had beaten some good fighters and was mixing in very high company despite being in only his second year as a professional.

The rivalry had reached such a point come the night of the fight, that the normally quiet and reserved betting favourite popped his head around his rival's dressing room door and said, "Let's get this beating over with." Possibly recalling a recent sparring session when he had tried to upstage Charley in front of a gym full of fighters, but had been knocked cold for his trouble, Harris quickly adopted a rearguard action once the fight got under way. For much of the eight and a bit rounds of ensuing 'action' Ossie remained in self-preservation mode and refused to become involved in a fight.

Charley initially took it easy and manoeuvred Ossie around the ring, stinging him with shots at will. The crowd became restless and began to hurl abuse at the Bulldog and his safety first-approach. Spurred on by the crowd, either through guilt at stinking out the place or even bravado, Ossie changed his tactics and finally launched an attack. Relieved at his opponent's decision to make a fight of it, Charley reciprocated and promptly dumped Harris on his back. After struggling to his feet, Ossie was dropped again for the full count.

Some of the crowd thought that the fight was fixed because the two fighters were friends and the excitement had been limited to the couple of knockdowns in what proved to be the final round. The fact was that Harris was not in Charley Burley's class and may have been safer as a bouncer on the door of his mother's cathouse up on the Hill.

Philadelphia promoter Phil Glassman signed Charley for a fight at the Philadelphia Gardens for the end of June. The spot was for a preliminary showing on the under-card of Cocoa Kid versus Johnny Barbera.

105

"It's because he's never shown here before (the supporting role). Also, it's hard to get a top-notcher to fight him, because they consider him a spoiler. Most of the time he has to give away weight, upto 15 pounds, to get the match. I got somebody almost even with him for next Monday's card, Pedro Tomez."

Phil Glassman

For reasons unknown, the fight with Tomez never materialised, but promoter Glassman assured Charley of a place on his next promotion in Philadelphia. Three weeks later than initially promised, Charley returned to the city of brotherly love and the Philadelphia Gardens for a ten-round supporting bout on the undercard of Fritzie Zivic versus Johnny Barbera.

"Gene Buffalo was knocked out in his fight with Charley Burley. Buffalo was down in the second round and the fifth round. He was down twice in the fifth and the referee stopped the fight. Burley showed class - and a punch."

Lansing McCurley, Philadelphia Daily News

Local historian Chuck Hassom describes Young Gene Buffalo as a Philadelphia boxing legend. He was the nephew of the original Gene Buffalo and was a perpetual motion buzz saw. Locally he was known as "the black Harry Greb." Buffalo fought from 1934 to 1950, engaging in bouts all over the country and meeting the very best of his day. He scored wins over Fritzie Zivic, Andre Jessurun, Tony Cisco, Bobby Jones and Ted Lowry amongst others. He also boxed Holman Williams, Shorty Hogue, Jose Basora and Cocoa Kid

"In his most famous fight he tried to trick Ray Robinson. They were scheduled to fight a non-title fight at Scranton in '49 and Buffalo came in at 146 and Ray's title was on the line. An infuriated Ray demolished Gene in the first round."

Chuck Hassom

Charley was beginning to get into the swing of contesting around one fight a month and while he may have been keeping busy and earning

106

some money, he was basically just marking time. There was definitely no way that he was going to get a shot at the welterweight title while Fritzie Zivic had control of his boxing career and ranked middleweights, according to his new management, were nowhere to be seen.

It is difficult not to admire Zivic's business acumen, as he was essentially protecting his years of investment in the fight game and was determined to enjoy his role as champion. Newspapers began to consult him on upcoming fights and he was invited to speak at various dinner functions and other social events.

Being the only welterweight in Pittsburgh as far as the media were concerned may have been good for Fritzie Zivic and his fans, but it was definitely no good to Charley Burley, his career aspirations, or his pride. How the Pittsburgh fight crowd responded to such blatant gamesmanship by the local hero is difficult to gauge. The action by Zivic and his manager could be likened to Ray Robinson buying out LaMotta's contract after LaMotta's sole victory over his arch-rival, or even Willie Pep buying up Sandy Saddler.

When Zivic lost the title to Freddie Cochrane at the end of July 1941, Charley realised that he would be pushed further down the line of challengers, as Zivic looked to re-establish his career among the welterweights and hopefully get himself a second shot at the crown. In July Charley returned to Pittsburgh and Hickey Park for a curiously dull fight with Otto Blackwell. To say that Charley put up a poor performance against the Homestead fighter would be an understatement. Charley appeared to go through the motions, though he handled his adversary with ease.

"Because Burley does not fancy pouring it on or because he is out of practice, he seemed to be pacing himself rather slowly, but in every round he jabbed often enough with his left and came through with a one-two or a right cross to give Blackwell a rather tough night.

The fight was anything but spectacular, as Burley had no trouble tying his man up on the inside, when he wanted to, and blocked most of the leads that Blackwell tried to land at long-range."

Harvey Boyle, Pittsburgh Post Gazette

The most noteworthy feature of the match was that it was to be Charley Burley's last fight in Pittsburgh for the remainder of his contractual agreement with Zivic and Luke Carney. The fact that he was being blatantly messed around must have begun to irk him somewhat. No matter what he wanted for the development of his own career, Charley was being shunted away from the limelight and while this may not have been a new experience for him, the blatant mismanagement, coupled with his recurring hand problems, would have been extremely frustrating.

For what was to be his second, and final, appearance in Philadelphia, Charley fought tough Chilean Antonio Fenandez at the Convention Hall in the supporting bout to Ray Robinson – Marty Servo. Sugar Ray beat Servo over ten rounds to take his tally to twenty-five unbeaten, with Servo being only one of five fighters to last the distance.

"Antonio Fernandez 150$^{1/4}$ pound Chilean, gave Charley Burley, colored Pittsburgher, a furious scrap for eight rounds in the semi-wind-up, then faded out to lose the decision. Burley's strong finish saved him from an impending upset. He weighed 149."

Matt Ring, Philadelphia Bulletin

After beating Fernandez, Charley agreed to a bout in Minneapolis. A five knockdown, second-round knockout of Ted Morrison may not have set the boxing world alight, but it did introduce Charley to a crowd that was very appreciative of his talents. Hooking up for the first time with local promoter Tommy O'Loughlin for a fight at the Armoury, Charley felt that the Twin City's had something to offer him. If he could escape from his contract with Fritzie Zivic and distance himself from Pittsburgh and its love affair with the popular fighter, then he could possibly make a fresh start. However, events of a more global nature intervened.

"We got there [Minneapolis] on Saturday, on Sunday war broke out."

Charley Burley

When the United States were forced into WWII by the Japanese attack on Pearl Harbour in December, Charley was called to the draft and despite being a sound physical specimen to look at, was deemed unfit for the military, being classified 4F, due to a perforated eardrum.

If Charley had known the effect the war would have upon his career, he may have retired from the fight game there and then. Practically all of the reigning world champions of the day were either called up or enlisted, most important amongst them as far as Charley Burley was concerned were Tony Zale at middleweight and Freddie Cochrane at welterweight. This resulted in their titles becoming frozen for the duration of the hostilities with Germany and her allies.

Chapter Six

Tommy Takes Charge

The town of Eau Claire, Wisconsin is a small town and many of the locals would probably tell you that nothing much ever really happens there. At the end of 1941 things were not much different and probably a lot less exciting for the town's few thousand inhabitants. In order to raise money for food to feed the local poor and hungry over the holiday season Mayor Donald Barnes organised a charity boxing event to be held at the city auditorium.

"Charley Burley, Pittsburgh colored scrapper, knocked out Jerry Hayes, Milwaukee, in the fourth round of their scheduled 10-round main bout of Mayor G. Donald Barnes' charity fight card at the city auditorium here last night.

A crowd of approximately 800 saw the show with net proceeds slated to bring Christmas cheer to the needy.

Hayes, also colored, proved no match for the more experienced Burley but demonstrated a high degree of grit and courage. A slashing solar-plexus [punch], landed by Burley in the first round hurled Hayes to the canvas for a count of nine. He was down at the bell, the result of a similar blow, at the end of the second round. In the third Hayes was knocked down early but jumped up quickly and later took another count of nine. He was down for the third time in the round when the bell clanged.

Another solar plexus [punch] from his opponent's mauling right ended the battle after one minute and 14 seconds of the fourth round. Fans lauded Hayes' gameness in fighting on in the face of certain defeat."

Eau Claire Wisconsin Press report

Promoters, officials, equipment suppliers and just about everyone else connected with the event gave their services for free. The fighters were paid a nominal amount, reported as being, ".. less than their usual fee." Charley was apparently happy to lend his support to the event, but his main focus remained a title shot. In an interview with Joe Hendrickson of the Minneapolis Star, under the banner of 'Charley Burley is Tired of Being Kicked Around' the transplanted Pittsburgh let his thoughts be known.

"I hope I can get the fights I deserve. Every fellow that received the verdict over me, except Zivic, refused to give me another fight. They were awarded disputed decisions in the first place and have stayed clear since. Lately it has got so tough to get fights that I have made up my mind I would fight anyone from welterweight to light heavyweight. I'd like to fight Tony Zale, I'd like Tony Martin. I would enjoy meeting Bob Montgomery or Ray Robinson. Zivic too. Anybody. And that Charley Parham, bring him on."

Charley Burley

Charley had closed just the door on a frustrating year under the 'management' of Luke Carney and Fritzie Zivic. With a new guide, Bobby Eaton, and a new year to look forward to, Charley was desperate to move forward with his career.

For his first fight of 1942, Charley was matched with the rugged West Coast middleweight Shorty Hogue. A San Diego native, Hogue was installed at number six in the world middleweight rankings by the NBA prior to the match with Charley. He had won a combined 142 out of 144 starts as an amateur and professional and had been a Detroit Golden Gloves champion.

Hogue had won the California State middleweight championship from Eddie Booker and had split two ten-round decisions with Lloyd Marshall the previous year. Shorty also had three victories over Archie Moore. Promoter Tommy O'Loughlin had secured the services of Hogue after a frantic hunt to replace previous foe Charley Parham, who was pulled out of the scheduled match at the Minneapolis armoury. The popular black middleweight's management felt that he wasn't quite ready for someone of Charley Burleys calibre, although the Milwaukee native had knocked out Don Epernson on the undercard of Charley's bout with Ted Morrison to take his tally to 28 knock-outs in 30 fights.

111

Other rated fighters that had been contacted to step in as a replacement had been Fritzie Zivic, Mike Kaplan, Holman Williams, Izzy Janazzo, Sammy Secreet, Young Kid McCoy, Ceferino Garcia, Coley Welch, Steve Belloise, Antonio Fernandez and Fred Apostoli. Newspapers were divided as to which fighter had the real advantage for the upcoming bout. In terms of pure boxing skill, it had to be Burley. Yet, the free swinging and aggressive Hogue had a good record, having only lost two out of thirty-two fights. Shorty also had the reputation of having a very solid chin, as he had never failed to finish a fight. Hogue, and his veteran manager Tom Jones, had supreme confidence in gaining a knock-out victory.

Jones had been in the game for many years and had handled some great fighters including Jess Willard, Ad Wolgast, Stanley Ketchel and Billy Papke. Charley's latest 'manager', Bobby Eaton, could not lay claim to such an impressive track record and while Charley Burley was probably the greatest fighter Eaton would ever have any connection with, the veteran Tom Jones boasted that he had never had a bad fighter.

Although Charley would have many 'managers' down the years, it appears that certain individuals were only acting the part and very few of them actually had names and signatures on contracts.

"I bought Charley from Zivic for $500. Fritzie promised me he would sell him to me when he lost the welter-weight title."

Tommy O'Loughlin

Confidence was high in the Hogue camp as they left for Minneapolis barely an hour after agreeing terms. Both fighters were training at Potts gym and were managing at least an hour in the afternoons for sparring or boxing drills. On average, Hogue was getting in around six rounds of sparring, two with each of his three sparring partners, Jimmy Collins, Johnny Simpson and Wally Holm. Charley, training later in the day, was doing about ten rounds with seven different partners. His work was carried out under the observation of trainer Larry Amadee. The learned Amadee had the 'honour' of being one of the first black trainers to second a white fighter in the deep south when he handled Quentin 'Baby' Breese for a bout in New Orleans. Both Joe Louis and John Henry Lewis had also gained plenty from Amadee's adept tuition.

Willard 'Big Boy' Hogue (above left) and Willis 'Shorty' Hogue.
World ranked contenders who fought the cream of the West Coast
welterweights, middleweights and light-heavyweights. Both would
die under tragic circumstances.

The Burley versus Hogue bout was given extra spice when Tommy O'Loughlin announced that the winner would get a shot at Tony Zale later that winter. The response from Sam Pian and Art Winch, co-managers of Zale in Chicago, was that Zale had commitments up to and including the end of February, but they would contemplate a match for March. As for the fight between Burley and Shorty Hogue, that proved to be an exciting encounter for the Armoury crowd.

"Burleys punches were so spitfire, Hogue didn't have a chance to see them. A left jab that operated like a trip-hammer and a right cross that was plain deadly gave the much slower Hogue a brutal beating. Get the picture, Hogue slowly advancing, throwing heavy roundhouse hooks as the faster Burley sniped with his jab and crossed with his right.

First Hogue's face reddened. Then his left eye puffed shut. Soon blood appeared under his eye and nose. Finally, his good-looking Irish-Indian face was punched lop-sided. Occasionally Hogue did

113

jar Burley and frequently during the in-fighting Shorty's 12 or 13 pound weight advantage made the going a bit rough for the Negro. However, only courage and toughness kept Hogue going round after round. Then in the tenth, a fast left caught Hogue and dropped him for six. A left and a right put Shorty down for keeps after he arose and tried to retreat.

That was the most courage and best boxing the Armoury ring has seen. The 2,000 fans who paid $1,400 to watch know now why Burley is the most feared welterweight in the game today. He has everything, and promoter Tommy O'Loughlin has a job trying to find his next foe."

Joe Hendrickson, Minneapolis Star

Perhaps the most horrified witness to the carnage in the ring that night was Hogue's wife who, possibly fearing the inevitable shellacking her husband received when he struggled up for the first time, screamed at the referee to stop it after the first knockdown. One reporter wrote that the left hook and right hand that finished the fight were so fast as to appear simultaneously.

"They say the punch you don't see is the one that puts you away. Well, I don't' recall seeing that one."

Shorty Hogue

After the knockout, Shorty Hogue remained motionless in the ring for what must have seemed an eternity to his spouse. When he did recover she encouraged him to call-it-a-day, but the teak-tough Hogue fought on with disastrous results.

Just two weeks after the victory over Shorty Hogue, Charley was back in the same ring to face Jackie Burke. Billed from Ogden, Utah, the rough and tough Burke was a decent fighter who always gave his best and had previously been ten rounds with Holman Williams and had contested a draw with Eddie Booker. He was no match for Charley however and was he was knocked to the canvas six times in all as his conqueror swept him aside in under five rounds.

114

For his next two bouts Charley would have to travel to the West Coast of America, to San Diego, a place he would later call home. It was in San Diego that Charley first met and worked with a man who would remain a life-long friend. A.J. 'Blackie' Nelson was a lightweight amateur champion who worked with many famous West Coast fighters.

> "When I was younger I went to work the oil fields, my hair was coal black and everybody in the oil fields, you know, they got a nickname for somebody, either 'Shorty' or 'Toughy' or 'Blackie' or 'Red' or something you know. And that name stuck with them."

> **A.J. 'Blackie' Nelson**

When several of the top-notch West Coast fighters required speed work, they usually employed Blackie as a sparring partner. Fighting purely as an amateur, Nelson went to the ring 138 times, he won 129, (76 KO's), with only 9 defeats. Fighters such as Lloyd Marshall and Eddie Booker paid for his services at various times, as did former middleweight champion Fred Apostoli and Manuel Ortiz. Blackie remembers the high esteem in which these fighters were held and how that the two greatest fighters he ever had the privilege to see at work were Charley Burley and Eddie Booker.

> "They called them the 'Murderers' Row', you know. There was Lloyd, there was Charley and there was Jack Chase. There was another guy that not too many people are familiar with and he could have beat 90% or 95% of these fighters today, a guy called Eddie Booker."

> **Blackie Nelson**

Two weeks after the Jackie Burke fight, Charley scored a fourth-round TKO over violin-toting Milo Theodorescu at the San Diego Coliseum, with referee John Perry coming to the rescue of the brave Rumanian middleweight at 2:45 of the round. Rocky Graziano, in his autobiography, 'Somebody Up There Likes Me', remembers that Milo couldn't play a note on the violin and it was just a part of his image. The following week

115

Charley met 'Big Boy' Hogue at the same venue. The papers and promoters built this fight into something of a grudge match, with the emphasis being on revenge for the Hogue family. Each of the twins had a habit of challenging any fighter that got the better of the other in the ring. In his previous outing, against Bobby Birch at middleweight, 'Big Boy' had been stopped in the second round due to a cut eye. Psyched up at the prospect of revenge for Shorty, Big Boy Hogue told the local sports press that the day of the bout, Friday 13th, would be extremely unlucky for his opponent. The common consensus around San Diego was that Big Boy was the better of the two Hogue brothers when it came to boxing skills, while Shorty was the more aggressive and game of the two.

> "Shorty was kinda like Vinnie Pazienza, his style, you know. Not a great boxer, but a tough cookie."

> **Blackie Nelson**

Despite a disadvantage in the weight stakes of around ten pounds Charley was favoured in the betting at 3-1 the day of the fight. Those odds proved to be justified as Charley dropped Big Boy for a nine count in the first and scored a sixth round TKO over his opponent at the Coliseum, thus completing a double over the Hogue brothers. Shorty Hogue may have been the more aggressive of the two fighting brothers and he may also have had the better chin, but recently it had started to let him down. In October 1942, nine months after he had lost to Charley, Shorty acted as a late substitute for his brother against Archie Moore.

Blackie Nelson recalled that Big Boy was in town on the day of his proposed match with Moore when he cut his leg on the ripped and rusted fender of a parked car and a long, deep gash in his leg helped Willard to the realisation that he would not be able to meet Moore in San Diego that night. As was typical of the twins recklessness and bravado Shorty bravely (and undoubtedly foolishly) volunteered to take his place. If nothing else the Hogue brothers were tough (there was an older brother who was a rodeo rider) but an afternoon of drinking and womanising is no way to prepare for a fighter of Archie Moore's calibre.

Archie did not complain about the late replacement as he was out for revenge over Shorty since he had lost to him over ten rounds in January of the previous year. Acting as a drunken and ill-prepared substitute for his stricken brother, Shorty managed to last into the second round but took a fearful beating doing so.

116

Well and truly on the slide since his KO defeats at the hands of Burley, then Eddie Booker and now Moore, Shorty Hogue was definitely finished as a world-class fighter. He never really knew how to take care of himself and more recent preparation for fights had consisted of getting drunk and sampling the local night-life. In his last nine fights Shorty Hogue was knocked out seven times and 1942 turned out to be his last year as a fighter. Too many beatings in street fights and an increasing number of beatings in the ring against top-flight fighters accelerated the sad demise of the San Diego middleweight. Years later, according to Blackie Nelson, he was in a sanatorium in Los Angeles, totally unaware of who or where he was. It has been suggested by some that Charley Burley ruined a lot of fighters. In the case of Shorty Hogue, this statement was never more true, nor more tragic.

Back in Minneapolis Charley stayed in shape working out at the gym and by always doing his roadwork. He would occasionally go hunting for relaxation purposes. Julia actually bagged herself a goose on one trip, but wasn't enamoured with the whole hunting thing and decided to leave that to Charley. Mostly they would fish or ice-skate. Charley was good on the ice and Julia herself was amazed at the fantastic balance that Charley displayed when skating. Sometimes he would just slide around on the ice in his shoes. While Minneapolis may have been fantastic for winter sports and other sub-zero pursuits, one disadvantage of road running there, as opposed to Pittsburgh, was the lack of hills. Outside of the city, the snowbound files and icy lakes were not something that too many city-dwellers would be familiar with.

"I had never seen such wide-open spaces just covered with snow. I was from the city I'd never seen so much snow, it was a sight."

Julia Burley

The twin City's of Minneapolis and St. Paul could boast close to a dozen lakes between them. In the winter, the frozen lakes and the endless white snowdrifts covering the almost level terrain, made conditions ideal for the annual 'Winterfest'. The absence of hill work did not seem to affect Charley's training regime too much. He could still carry his usual two half-bricks with him on the road, one for each hand as he ran along, and he was able to complete ten rounds quite easily when required to do so. In fact, in all of his bouts in Minneapolis, seven in all, Charley was only taken the distance on one occasion, the other six were all stoppage victories.

The man that lasted the full ten rounds had already beaten Charley over 15 rounds, in December 1939. When Charley was signed to fight Holman Williams at the Armoury in February, the local fans were in for a treat. In the bout before this second meeting with Charley, Williams had out-pointed 'Cocoa' Kid, beating him for only the second time in seven meetings. For Charley's Minneapolis fans the bout with Holman Williams would prove to be a master class in the art of boxing. For ten rounds the contest ebbed and flowed with both fighters claiming boxing supremacy at various stages throughout the battle. The crowd and the press were full of admiration for both men, marvelling at the neat defensive work of Williams and the determination that Burley displayed in attempting to prove himself the better man.

"Charley Burley continued his winning streak by defeating Holman Williams of Detroit by a clear margin in their 10-round fight at the Minneapolis Armoury Thursday night.

If you were among those present as the Minneapolis welterweight whipped his Negro rival, then you saw one of the finest exhibitions of scientific boxing and sharp, punishing hitting witnessed in the twin City's in many years. The best in fact since Mike and Tommy Gibbons, Jock Malone, Billy Wells, Tommy Loughran and Sammy Mandell displayed their fistic wares.

Burley, boxing beautifully and lashing out with rapier-like fists incessantly for the full 10 rounds dominated the fight so clearly against the cunning and fast moving Williams, that Charley won the unanimous decision from referee Johnny Sokol and judges, Johnny DeOtis and Brit Gorman.

It was a fight in which Williams didn't dare make a single mistake, otherwise he would have been knocked out by the aggressive and determined Burley."

George A. Barton, Minneapolis Morning Tribune

The ninth round in particular showed evidence of this, as a jolting right from Charley drove Holman back to the ropes where he was punished severely with numerous body shots. The crowd showed their appreciation for the visiting fighter and his defensive skills as he survived until the bell ended the penultimate round. At the end of ten crackling rounds of championship-calibre boxing, the victory for Charley was a clear-cut one. Although there was only a quarter of a pound in it, with Charley the heavier at 148 pounds, the winner was by far the stronger of the two. Williams had been beaten for the first time in a nineteen-bout streak that went back to September 1940, when he had dropped a ten-round decision to Izzy Janazzo in Washington. In fact, with this loss to Charley Burley, he was on the losing side of a decision for only the third time since 1939 and only his third loss in 40 fights.

Charley was beginning to put together a streak of his own and was now unbeaten in 15 fights. He had ten stoppages during this period and had stopped six-straight before the meeting with Williams. He was now at number three in the world ratings and his stock had risen considerably following this victory over another rated fighter. The problem for Tommy O'Loughlin was exactly the same one experienced by 'Chappy' Goldstein, as finding willing opponents who were also of a sufficiently high ranking, regardless of their weight, was already posing quite a conundrum for the Twin City's promoter. Impressed by Charley's recent displays under his promotion, O'Loughlin was making noises about a world welterweight title challenge. With the backing of a group of Minneapolis sportsmen O'Loughlin was ready to offer the reigning champion, Freddie Cochrane, $25,000 to defend his belt in Minneapolis. The 26 year-old Cochrane from Elizabeth, New Jersey had won the title the previous year (1941), by out-pointing Fritzie Zivic in Newark, New Jersey. Since then he had fought, and won, two ten-round non-title fights against Lew Jenkins and Bobby Britton. If Tommy O'Loughlin thought that $25,000 would tempt Freddie into a title defence in Minneapolis then he, and his backers, were sadly mistaken. Cochrane was a connected fighter and certain individuals had control of where, when and most importantly whom he fought. Taking a new tack, Charley offered his services, free of charge, if Freddie Cochrane would meet him in a world title fight for the war fund. Charley and his management figured that the prospect of raising money for a good cause may prove appealing to the champion and he may be tempted into a defence. However, this tactic also proved fruitless.

"That's the way it goes, on and on. I do everything I can to get in there with the other challengers to prove my right to the title fight, but they stay away from me and I have to be satisfied with a high NBA ranking and nothing else. They leave me out in the cold all the time."

Charley Burley

Cochrane, who was one of the least active champions in the history of the welterweight division, would hold the championship for five years with only two official title fights, one when he won the title in 1941 and one when he lost it in 1946. In Cochrane's defence it should be mentioned that he was inactive from 1943-44 due to his service in the navy and he, like most other champions of the time (with one or two exceptions), had little say in who they fought. This however is no real excuse for his four years, two either side of his national service, of championship inactivity. During the time that he was world welterweight champion and active, Freddie had thirteen fights, including the one and only defence of his title, a four-round KO defeat by Marty Servo. In the other fights that he took part in, he lost to Garvey Young, (in a navy benefit fight), and Fritzie Zivic, both on points. He also won six by KO in 1945 and in the same year was twice knocked out by Rocky Graziano.

Speaking of Graziano, Freddie Cochrane's successor as world champion, Marty Servo was also knocked out by Rocky in a non-title fight in 1946. In fact, Servo was no more an active champion than Freddie Cochrane. After winning the title in February 1946 Servo, a New York State native, had only three bouts before announcing his retirement in September that same year, the fight with Graziano and two exhibitions. It was the fight with Graziano that led to Servo's decision to retire. He had received a terrific beating that night and his nose was very badly damaged. This injury forced him to quit the ring.

Increasingly frustrated with the situation, Tommy O'Loughlin wired Johnny Ray, manager of Billy Conn, an offer for a guaranteed $7,500 plus 35% of the gate for the light-heavyweight to meet Charley in Minneapolis. This would have worked out as a $10,000 plus pay day for the 'Pittsburgh Kid' and while it was good money for a non-title fight, it was peanuts compared to the $70,000 Conn had earned for extending Joe Louis the previous year. Although many thought him crazy, Tommy O'Loughlin could explain the method behind his apparent madness.

"It's just a shot in the dark with a little strategy behind it. You see, Mike Jacobs controls most of the eastern fighters by one means or another and he has had a lot to do with preventing good middleweights and welterweights from coming here to fight Burley. So, why not go in with a challenge to his favourite heavyweight? It will be a lot of fun for Burley and me to have Conn turn down the fight. Maybe we could make enough noise about a welterweight challenging the great Conn – and meaning it – so that Jacobs will decide to send out a few good men in Burley's class to try to take the heat off. It's fun anyway and if Conn should accept, it would be alright with Burley. Conn wouldn't fight him anyway."

Tommy O'Loughlin

Conn, who had recently beaten Tony Zale on points, was attempting to secure a rematch with Joe Louis and his management had no intention of risking the big money and such a prestigious fight against Burley.

"Art Rooney, [boxing promoter and owner of the Steelers football team], tried the best he could to get them two guys signed up. At one time he thought that he had the whole thing worked out. Johnny Ray, he was smart and there was no way that he was going to let Billy Conn fight Charley Burley. And that would have been the best fight that this city had ever had. That's the way Art Rooney was looking at it, the two top fighters. Johnny Ray knew that Charley would have beat him (Conn)."

Bobby Lippi

While the fight fans in Pittsburgh would have packed out any local stadium many times over to see such a match between two of its native sons, the fans in Minneapolis were also growing fond of Charley Burley after his recent performances there. His adopted town desperately wanted to stage a high-profile fight with him as the feature. Charley was also fond of the Twin City's. He was seeing more action there under Tommy O'Loughlin than he had in Pittsburgh under Zivic and Carney. Re-locating to the 'last of the eastern City's' had not been too difficult. Drawing parallels with Pittsburgh, Charley, Julie's and Angie's new home was also predominantly a mill town, (flour in place of steel), and had its own global industry – like Heinz of Pittsburgh – with Minnesota Mining and

121

Manufacture, (3M). The location has since been described by one mayor as 'solid, unpretentious and wholesome', the kind of tag that one may have pinned on Charley Burley. The fact that it was also a religious, bible oriented, catholic place would also have suited Charley and made him feel more at home. Once quoted as saying "You don't have to go to church to be good people", Charley not only carried a bible with him on the road and to the fights but, according to Bobby Lippi and Julia Burley, he read from its pages every single day. In a 1981 interview in the Pittsburgh Post Gazette, Charley told how he used to get down on his knees and pray for a title shot.

Realising that many of the top contenders were ducking their new star, a special meeting of the local boxing commission agreed that it would waive all rules in the books pertaining to weight. Usually a weight difference of more than ten pounds, except in the heavyweight division, prevented a bout from taking place. With all of the evidence before them, the boxing commission must have realised that they were taking something of a risk in this matter. Conn, being sufficiently trained to be in top condition, would have weighed about 170 pounds. Charley was hovering around 150 and, at the time, usually found his best weight to be about two pounds under that. The difference in weight would have been more than double that which was previously allowed.

While the offer of a guaranteed $10,000 may have been sweet music to the ears of many a contender, it was plain deafening to Conn and his management. In a letter to Nat Fleischer, editor of the Ring magazine, Tommy O'Loughlin vented his frustration.

"Dear Nat,

I wrote to you from the coast and asked about the front cover of your magazine for Burley, but so far haven't heard anything. I'd appreciate hearing from you if the page is available. On top of that we want to go along and take out a manager's address for the next issue. Burley fought Williams here last Thursday and it was sensational all the way, as Williams can really box, and he did everything known in the book to keep from getting knocked out by Charley, and the cash customers liked it very much. I'm having a tough time getting anybody to fight the fellow, and I'm offering good money. I offered Fritzie Zivic $4,000, with an option 35% after he was beaten in Chicago the other night; Garcia wouldn't come in with Burley for

$3,500 and points; Steve Belloise's manager hung up on me when I called long distance for the match. What the hell does a man have to do to get them to fight? You offer them 50% and still they wouldn't take it.

Everyone is broke and hollering, but still they will not fight him for good money. This is no bull, I really made the offer, and today I wired Conn offering him $10,000 to fight Burley and can't get an answer from Johnny Ray.

The Minnesota State Athletic Commission gave me dispensation to make matches for Burley in any weight including heavyweights. What the hell is the fight game for if they won't fight for money? I'm going to try light-heavyweights, and if I run out of them, I'll go into the heavyweights. What is the difference? Burley will stiffen most of the heavyweights anyway. Anyone he can get a belt at he will knock out.

When I was on the coast Burley fought Big Boy Hogue and knocked him out in the sixth. But never made the wire as they kept it off. But I have the clippings of the fight. Too bad they push good fighters around, as he would be a sensation in your city. But they keep hollering about no fighters. Its all bull Nat. Let me hear from you, and keep your eye on Burley, as you will hear lots more about the fellow soon, in fast company. Don't pass this fellow up, as he has the goods to deliver."

Tommy O'Loughlin

While O'Loughlin waited patiently on Cochrane or Conn, another local fighter's name was thrown up as a potential opponent for Charley, that of ranked middleweight Tony Martin. The Milwaukee-born Italian-American had turned professional around four months before Charley in 1936 and had a very respectable record. He had won 48 of 60 with 23 via KO and 6 draws. He had beaten fighters of high calibre including Remo Fernandez, 'Cocoa' Kid, Ernie Vigh, Dick Demeray and Coley Welch. He had been stopped only once in his career thus far and that had been against Tony Zale in 1941. Charley's reaction to a proposed meeting with Martin was typical of his mood at the time.

"He's a good fighter and he'll outweigh me six or seven pounds, but I'll let him have the money if he'll just give me the fight. Give me just enough to live on until the next fight and he can have the rest."

Charley Burley

As it transpired, the bout with Martin would not come off and Charley would be forced to make other, more drastic, concessions in his bid for recognition.

Tommy O'Loughlin (above left) with one of his fighters Perfecto Lopez. O'Loughlin was instrumental in moving Charley to California in order to further his career.

Chapter Seven

The Giant Killer

Previous to a ten rounds points victory over Tony Zale in February 1942, Billy Conn had fought a heavyweight by the name of J.D. Turner down in Missouri. Tommy O'Loughlin hit upon the idea of bringing the giant Texan into town for a fight with Charley. The Minneapolis promoter had been ringside that night in St. Louis and had the opportunity to speak to the former light-heavyweight champion before the fight. Conn felt that, despite the difference in weight of about forty pounds, he would stop the two hundred and twenty-pound Turner inside of four rounds. True, Turner could be stopped; he had been knocked out by Abe Simon, who was a whopping two hundred and sixty-pound, but what made Conn think that he could stop someone as big as Turner? After all, Conn had only managed to halt a dozen out of seventy previous opponents! Despite his supreme confidence, Conn had to settle for a hard fought, but clear points win over Turner. At face value O'Loughlin was taking a risk with his hottest promotional item, but in reality it was Turner who had the most to lose and the least to gain. Charley had lost to heavier fighters before and it would be no disgrace to lose to someone who outweighed him by close to 70 pounds. O'Loughlin felt however, that Charley was in little danger of being hurt, as it had been next to impossible for previous opponents to tag him with a clean, hard shot.

Izzy Kline, Turner's manager, was happy to get his charge such a high profile match, but J.D. was not as enthusiastic about the proposition. Once the fight had been signed he began to have doubts about how the outcome might affect his reputation. He felt that he would look bad beating up on such a small guy and thought that losing to a much smaller man would be a nightmare for his career prospects. The date of the bout between Turner and Burley was set for March 13th, 1942.

While he could never be considered a world-beater by any stretch of the imagination, Turner was a capable boxer and had a victory over Neville Beech, a rated heavyweight at the time. The boxing press also considered Turner a better prospect than Paul Hartneck (a Tommy O'Loughlin fighter) and Jim Robinson, two popular heavyweight fighters of the day. As a 'sweetener', big J.D. was promised a match with Bob Pastor should he defeat Burley. Pastor's management, it seemed, also had the same idea as Tommy O'Loughlin in regards to previous opponents of Conn's.

Turner and his management arrived in Minneapolis at 8am Saturday morning, six days before the fight, and scheduled a training session at Potts gym for 1pm the same day. Watching J.D. being put through his paces, many felt that his sheer size would make things dangerous for Charley. Along with the weight advantage the Texan would also enjoy an advantage in height of six inches. Surprisingly, with Charley having a 75 inch reach (huge for a welterweight and pretty good for a middleweight), there would be no advantage in that department for either man.

The old maxim of 'a good big 'un will always beat a good little 'un,' was quoted often. One problem with this statement was just how big and good did a man have to be to beat the likes of Charley Burley? The local press concede the fact that Turner was indeed bigger, but argued that Burley hit harder than the heavyweight and was the better fighter by a long way.

Charley's main concerns were with the rules regarding holding and hitting and the size of the gloves to be used. If a guy the size of Turner gets a hold on you and is allowed to punch away, he could, Charley figured, do a lot of damage to any fighter his weight. The local boxing commission laws stated that 6oz gloves should be used by welterweight fighters and 8oz gloves by heavyweights. How then, would that rule be applied to this fight? Charley hoped that he would be allowed to use the lighter gloves, while Turner would be required to wear the heavier ones. The commission decided that, in accordance with the rules, when two fighters from different weight categories meet in the ring, the glove size would be determined by the heavier fighter. Therefore, both men would wear 8oz gloves. Besides the glove issue, Charley expressed his concern in the Minneapolis Daily Times with the enforcing of the rules in the ring.

"I've noticed that referees around here don't strictly enforce the rule against holding a man with one hand while hitting him with the other. It's just as much a foul as hitting below the belt. All I'm asking is that the rules be enforced."

Charley Burley

As the day of the fight drew near, there were many opinions being expressed in the media as to what effect this type of 'novelty' fight would have upon the sport.

"It is more from Charley Burley's own attitude, than from any ability we have to analyse the fight, that we can expect him to beat big Jay Turner tonight. There isn't much basis for making dope. Who can guess what will happen when a great 140-pound fighter goes against a fair sort of 220-pound fighter.

How can the little fellow possibly hurt the big fellow? How can the big fellow fail to get a destructive punch home somewhere through ten rounds? But Charley is so sure of himself, speaks of ways and means with such confidence that we are compelled to take his word for it. He must know what he is about and the rest of us must be content to wait until tonight to find out."

Dick Callum, Minneapolis Times

All Charley and his management wanted was a break. If Charley should beat Turner the plan was to wire Mike Jacobs in New York and offer Charley's services free-of-charge on the upcoming, 'Carnival of Champions' which was being promoted by Jacobs to raise funds for the 'families of General MacArthur's troops'. The $100-a-plate benefit was to feature reigning welterweight champion of the world Freddie 'Red' Cochrane and Charley desperately wanted to be the fighter in the opposite corner for that event. There was however, the not so small problem of a Texas heavyweight to deal with before any further plans could be made. In a further attempt to lighten matters the press staged a publicity stunt and ran a picture of Charley, together with a huge grizzly bear kitted-out in boxing attire. When one scribe echoed the concerns of the Minneapolis fight fans in wondering, "...what little Burley can do to bring him [Turner] down." Charley's reply was simply, "They'll find out Friday night."

On the night of the fight Charley knew that he couldn't afford to swap punches with a fighter as huge as J.D. One moment's lapse in concentration could put a severe dent in his plans and possibly finish his career. Employing his speed and heavy punching to good effect, Charley out-manoeuvred his opponent while stinging him repeatedly with a spear-like jab. These tactics proved effective.

"Turner wanted to quit after the fifth round, saying his stomach was full of swallowed blood, but his handlers made him try one more round. After that round he was sure he wanted to quit, and no amount of urging could get him off his stool. Burley's leaping left hand, never missing, had mashed his nose and lips into sodden pulp. His own best punches had missed and he saw no reason for going on with the monotonous torture. No doubt he had swallowed a quantity of blood. He had also a quantity of pride and, in as much as there was no future in the evening's work for him, he let his wisdom dictate to courage and called it a night.

Burley was brilliant in his manoeuvres against his big, heavy-handed opponent. He came in quickly. It was slow torture for the Texas giant. When he discovered his best counter efforts couldn't come within a foot of his elusive target he decided there was no sense in submitting to further humiliation—and bloodshed. Turner might have been fairly effective against a big slow heavyweight. Against the wasp-like Burley, he was not much better than a heavy gymnasium bag."

Dick Callum, Minneapolis Daily Tribune

Branded a quitter by most of the crowd and some of the press the following day, Turner's worst fears had been realised. It had taken Charley Burley only six rounds of boxing to accomplish what Billy Conn couldn't do in ten.

In his column 'Lowdown on Sports' for the Minneapolis Star, Charles Johnson examined the Texan in a slightly more sympathetic light. He reasoned that the amount of damage Turner had sustained at the hands of Burley would have finished most other fighters, regardless of size. He cited the 'nasty, fast left hand' of Charley, along with the left hooks to the body and the long overhand right, as the weapons that brought about the conclusion to this 'curiosity'. Indeed, Johnson was adamant that the fans didn't like it - the gate of only $1,600 would support this - and that the Minneapolis commission should rethink its move over giving Charley special dispensation to compete in the heavier weight classes. The weights for the fight had been Turner 220 pounds, Charley Burley

150 pounds. A massive seventy pounds weight difference. Charley had proved that he could beat much heavier men and had sent out a message to Billy Conn.

Many years later, when he had retired from boxing and was a fight judge and real estate manager Turner was asked by legendary trainer Eddie Futch just how heavy he had been for the fight. Turner replied that he had been around 218 pounds, "and you know what? That little sucker knocked me cold. I woke up in the dressing room." Futch was one of Charley's biggest admirers and was instrumental in getting Charley elected to a number of halls of fame.

"Charley Burley is a legend in boxing, but the public doesn't know him because he never got the credit."

Eddie Futch

When he was in Pittsburgh with Larry Holmes for Holmes' world heavy-weight title defence against Renaldo Snipes in 1981, Futch told Larry all about the greatest fighter that the city had produced and suggested that they go and pay their respects. While they were visiting, the great trainer was telling his charge of the time Charley had beaten J.D. Turner in Minneapolis. When Futch was citing the differences in weight and reminding Holmes that he was around the same weight that Turner had been, Charley had to correct him as to just how light he was that day. Charley may have actually scaled closer to the welterweight limit for his fight with Turner, even though the Minneapolis commission had speci-fied a minimum weight for Charley of 160 pounds.

"No one saw me on the scales, they were embarrassed. I just wrote down a figure and ran out of the room."

Charley Burley

No matter how big Turner was it was obvious that he was not in the same class as Charley Burley. While he would go on to defeat the seven-feet, 255-pound giant Gilbert Stromquist for the heavyweight champion-ship of Texas a number of years later, big Jay had apparently witnessed enough violence in the ring. After the defeat by Charley, he headed for the comparative safety of the United States army and a one-year hiatus from the fight game.

Boxing broadcaster and historian Howard Branson tells a slightly different story on how the Burley and Turner fight came about. Branson claims to have seen Charley Burley in action several times and in his series of taped documentaries and recollections about the fight game he rates Charley Burley as the greatest fighter he ever saw. Branson's version of events leading up to the fight tell of how Burley was sparring in the ring when Turner, who was waiting his turn, made a racist remark. Charley confronted him over the slur and the two had to be separated by onlookers. This may or may not be true. What one has to remember is that Charley's family and friends recall Charley never challenged anyone to a fist fight and avoided such situations whenever possible. His usual reaction was to kid around, hug you, wrestle a little and then nearly break your neck in the process. Just to show you who was the boss. J.D. Turner however, may have been a little too big for those tactics to succeed.

With the win over the mammoth Texan, Tommy O'Loughlin wired Mike Jacobs in New York and informed him that Charley would box for free on the upcoming benefit show. He received no reply. On the basis of the victory over the much heavier J. D. Turner, Tommy O'Loughlin considered matching Charley with a Pittsburgh heavyweight by the name of Harry Bobo. Charley and the six-foot-four-inch, 210-pound Bobo were already familiar with each other, as they had trained together in Pittsburgh. Charley knew he could beat Bobo and a match between the two would have been a sell-out, especially if the fight fans in Pittsburgh had gained word of it.

Harry Bobo was a rated fighter and was in the top ten when Joe Louis was World Heavyweight Champion in the late 1930s. It is truly a measure of Charley Burley the fighter when you consider that most fight fans in Pittsburgh thought that Harry Bobo would provide Joe Louis with some interesting opposition, but the same fighter would probably not be able to beat Charley Burley. This collective opinion was most likely based on the fact that during the respective high points in their careers, which were not too many years apart, both men frequently sparred with each other. Bobby Lippi remembers the sessions well.

"This was the only time that they ever charged for people to come into the gym, when Harry Bobo and Charley Burley were training together. These guys were fighters, it was 'you take my head off and I'll take yours.' These were real training sessions, you understand. They used to charge a quarter per person and you saw the greatest, they were banging, they had those big gloves but it didn't make any difference."

Bobby Lippi

One enterprising fellow set up a hot dog stand outside the large window of the YMCA on Center Avenue and people would buy a hot dog and watch these sessions from the street. Charley learned a great deal from these encounters with Harry Bobo. He learned angles for punching against bigger men, he learned to be elusive, and above all he learned that he could take the punch of a genuine heavyweight contender. Whether or not these gym wars did anything for the confidence of Bobo it is difficult to tell. After all, here was a big man, a contender to the great Joe Louis, who was, more often than not, being given a lesson in boxing and fighting by a man who was little more than a welterweight.

The only obstacle to the match was the fact that Bobo had a high profile fight scheduled for the end of March against Lem Franklin. The management of the Pittsburgh heavyweight felt that a victory over Franklin would propel their man to bigger and better things within his own weight division and they wouldn't require a fight with the likes of Charley Burley. Tommy O'Loughlin was hoping for a Lem Franklin victory so that Harry Bobo's handlers would reconsider. However, it was not to be as Bobo stopped Franklin in the first round.

Unfortunately for Harry Bobo, the bigger and better fights did not occur. In a career lasting barely six years Bobo had a total of 43 professional fights, winning 34 of them. Among his victims were Lee Savold, Henry Cooper, Gus Dorazio and Lem Franklin. During the early 1940s former heavyweight champion of the world Jack Johnson was in Pittsburgh and he offered the promising Bobo some pointers down at the YMCA training sessions. Sadly for Harry Bobo, his dreams of a title fight faded, along with his boxing career and his sight, when he (reportedly) lost the sight in one eye due to an accident in the ring. Bobo was forced to retire from boxing in 1945.

The tactics employed by Tommy O'Loughlin in regards to getting Charley noticed by the East Coast fight fraternity appeared to be working. He was able to secure a bout for his fighter in New York City for April 20th. Many local fans were worried by reports in the Minneapolis press that the fight against Jay Turner may have been Charley's final appearance in the city. Tommy O'Loughlin decided that if he couldn't secure a fight against rated opposition in Minneapolis, then he would be forced to travel elsewhere.

Ruben Shank, another fighter making a lot of noise in the welter-weight division, was matched at the Armoury on April 10th as the head-liner versus Johnny Roszina. In an attempt to keep Charley busy and the local fight fans happy O'Loughlin matched him on the same card. For what was expected to be his final appearance in Minneapolis, Charley signed to fight the welterweight Cleo McNeil over eight rounds.

However, Charley stipulated certain conditions. He felt that, as he was somewhat more advanced in the fight game and could probably beat both Shank and Roszina on the same night, he should be the headliner. This did not appear to sit too well with Ruben Shank. This brash young fighter was convinced that he had the ability to beat Burley and made no secret of it. As far as he was concerned, he should be the headliner. Tommy O'Loughlin decided that the card would not suffer too much from having a double wind-up and decided to have both fights as main joint attractions.

The hard-punching and aggressive Akron-based McNeil informed all who would listen that he had the style to beat the fighter who many were by now calling the uncrowned welterweight champion of the world. McNeil tried to arouse the interest of the local fans via verbal banter in the press and was quoted as saying he thought he was too good for Charley adding, "I don't think Burley will like it in the stomach." McNeil was far from being a pushover for any fighter in his weight division and in his time had sprung a few surprises. He had dumped Dick Demeray out of a title fight with Henry Armstrong, dishing out a severe beating to a man who, at the time, was on a 17-bout unbeaten streak (and already held a decision over McNeil). He had also upset the 30-fight (29 knock-outs) winning streak of local favourite Charley Parham, forcing him to literally flee from the ring, an action that earned Parham a suspension from the NBA. On the occasion of his bout with Charley Burley though, McNeil must have felt like following Parham's example.

"Minneapolis fans always thought well of Cleo McNeil as an aver-age fighter, but last night Burley whipped him to within an inch of his life. He lasted five rounds, but could have been halted one round earlier by the referee. Remember it was a pretty good fighter Burley toyed with and stopped. In his easy victory Burley showed some stuff that only great fighters have. His right uppercut followed by a straight right in rapid-fire fashion, both punches carry terrific steam. You don't see second-raters getting away with that. He carries every punch in the book and finishing power in all of them. On the defensive side he is one of the finest boxers the welterweight division has ever had. But who can give him a fight? That was the question before McNeil came to town and it is still the question. It is doubtful that fans here will ever see him extended."

Minneapolis Press

In the other headliner, Shank beat Roszina and appeared to struggle doing so. A match between 'Cowboy' Shank and Charley Burley would never materialise, despite the amount of noise that Shank made in regards to his ability to whip Burley in the ring.

Charley Burley had such fantastic support in Minneapolis that even the local press felt inclined to help him out by way of an open letter to Mike Jacobs.

"Dear Mike, maybe you have started to hear something of a fighter we have out here named Charley Burley. Well, just between us, we know you have known about him for some time and have not been disposed to help him because some of the mob that doesn't want to see him on top has your ear. Let me tell you, he is a decent, family man, clean-living, hard-working, honest fighter and he deserves the chance it is in your power to give him.

If boxing is a sport then there is no sense in depriving a man of a chance just because he is so good he might make the most of it. Why shouldn't the best men go to the top? Why isn't that the best thing for your business? Burley is not fooling when he offers to give you his services for nothing in exchange for a chance to show you what he can do. All he asks is that you give him an opponent good enough so that he will get some credit for beating him. He wants to fight for nothing and he wants to fight no one but a top man. Isn't that fair?"

Dick Callum, Minneapolis Daily Star

From a neutral's point of view the proposal might well have been fair, but when was the fight game ever so? The reason Charley Burley wasn't good for business was because he could not be bought and therefore

133

there was no guarantee that money could be made on him.

The growing pressure from the media and the fans appeared to be having some effect and 1942 was beginning to look as though it might be Charley's year. Mike Jacobs in New York finally relented and decided to feature him at the Mecca of boxing, admittedly for a smaller venue showing, and had promised a bout at Madison Square Garden for May. Charley was given a chance to show his 'stuff' versus 'Showboat' Phil McQuillan at the St. Nick's arena. McQuillan, from Colorado, had fought a seven-round 'no contest' with Jack Chase several years before and by 1942 was considered something of a journeyman fighter. In an interview with Norm Meekison Eddie Futch recalled some details of McQuillan's career.

"He came to Detroit from Denver, he had heard about me and wanted me to work with him. I worked with him, he was a good fighter, but there was no one around to fight him at the time in Detroit. He was with me a couple of months and couldn't get any work, he was pretty clever and a good boxer and no one wanted to tangle with him in Detroit, so I suggested that he go to New York. He got work there and one day his manager asked him how he felt about Burley. He said he would fight him."

Eddie Futch

'Showboat' was a popular fighter and had fought in New York the previous year, losing to tough Chilean, Antonio Fernandez in a close bout. His second showing in the 'Big Apple' would last less than a round as Charley, eager to impress, forced him around the ring with a furious two-fisted attack that ceased only when 'Showboat' Phil was left flat-out following two swift uppercuts. The local fight fans were impressed, but the local managers bemoaned the fact that they had barely enough time to gauge Burley's true worth.

It could be argued that, in reality, the display put on by Charley shied them away from any thoughts of ever matching any of their fighters with him. While McQuillan was not truly world-class, he was considered fairly durable and a decent test for most. He never landed a single shot on Charley that night and the manner of his defeat was so conclusive that Phil McQuillan retired from boxing afterwards.

Charley had been brought to New York City so that the fistic fraternity could have first-hand experience of this fighting phenomenon. Although the viewing was brief it was enough for most and as far as local managers were concerned Charley became a gold-star member of the 'who needs him' club.

"Burley's good all right—too good. Frankly, he would have made himself more acceptable to name foes around here by merely winning a decision. Boxing is SUCH a funny business."

Lester Bromburg, World Telegram

It has been said by many, including Eddie Futch, that Charley's awesome display not only finished the career of Phil McQuillan, it also finished the career of Charley Burley as far as New York City was concerned.

Chapter Eight

The Cincinnati Cobra

During his trip to the city Charley stayed at the Theresa Hotel in Harlem, right across the street from the world-famous Apollo Theatre. The hotel was a favourite haunt of Robinson's as he kept several rooms and several women there during his time at the top as did heavyweight king Joe Louis. Kenny Halliday, a nephew of Charley's recalls a story about his uncle and Ray Robinson meeting at the hotel and how Robinson, not knowing who Burley was had trouble picking him out of a group of people. Kenny said that the reason for this was because Charley didn't look like a fighter. "He didn't have a mark on his face and he always dressed real nice." One thing that was always striking about Charley was the almost complete lack of facial scarring. Given the nature of his profession, the number of battles he contested and the company he kept in the ring, it is surprising that he wasn't more marked up.

While many of his contemporaries, such as Jack Chase, Holman Williams and Fritzie Zivic had their life's history permanently gouged into their faces – a short history of the painful life of a professional fighter written in Braille - Charley looked like he had never taken a punch in his life. He obviously didn't take as many as those that learned their craft the hard way. Charley believes that he may have had something approaching a sixth sense when it came to defence.

"I wasn't that big, but I could just know when a punch was coming and I stayed in shape, so I didn't have to worry about nothing."

Charley Burley

According to Kenny Halliday's story Charley and Sugar Ray shook hands and exchanged pleasantries. Kenny also recalls that when Charley found out that Robinson was fighting later that month in Minneapolis he knew he had to get on the same bill. Before that could happen though, he had to honour a contract for a fight against Joe Sutka in Chicago. There is a certain amount of incongruence to this story as Kenny remembers it as Charley had fought on the same bill as Robinson in Philadelphia the previous year. It is possible that they never met on that occasion or that the original meeting between the two described by Charley's nephew occurred at another time. He does, however, believe that it was at the Theresa Hotel.

Four days after his victory over McQuillan at the St. Nick's arena Charley knocked out Sutka in four rounds. The Chicago fighter had once lasted the course with Ezzard Charles and had twice extended Jimmy Bivins. It seemed a case of 'history repeating', as Charley's talents were never again showcased in Chicago.

"I fought and won one time each in Chicago and New York and never got back to either place."

Charley Burley

Back in Minneapolis Charley was matched on the Ray Robinson versus Dick Banner card at the Armoury. It must have been obvious to Charley that at the conclusion of the evening's proceedings comparisons would be made between himself and the Sugar Man. First in action, Charley was determined to impress. If anyone were to have asked his opponent, the unfortunate Sonny Wilson, about the performance of his conqueror that night then he probably wouldn't remember too much about it. The only time he made purposeful contact with Charley was when the two touched gloves prior to the ringing of the first bell. Wilson was knocked down three times in the first round, all for nine counts, and barely survived to hear the bell to end the opening session of a scheduled ten. At one minute and thirty-two seconds of the second round it was all over. A powerful right, flush on the side of the jaw, dropped Wilson as if he had been shot with a high-powered rifle. Face down, head and shoulders under the bottom rope, he remained out for almost as long as the fight itself had lasted. Ray Robinson, watching from ringside told his manager, "I'm too pretty to fight Charley Burley."

When it was Robinson's turn, he introduced Dick Banner to something resembling a leather-gloved conga, as he beat out a hard and heavy rhythm on the body and head of his opponent. Danced silly for the whole of the first round, the man from Savannah decided that the best way to get his own licks in was after the bell to end the session. Ray was not best pleased with the tactics employed by his dancing partner and once the second round got under way he crossed him right off his card. A crunching left hook dropped Banner for a short count and a following left-hook, right-hook combination left him flat out on the canvas.

On the night, Charley's performance would certainly compare favourably to that of Robinson's and would set the arguments raging about who would win if the two should meet in the ring. Curt Horrmann, the New York millionaire who controlled Ray's contract was apparently up for it as he congratulated Robinson in the dressing room after the fights.

"We found out what we wanted to know tonight, Ray. You are a better fighter than Burley, and he is a great one. Tommy O'Loughlin can have the fight for Minneapolis, but we will have to be paid for it. If Minneapolis can pay us the money we want, we will sign for it. I don't think a match between these two will draw so much in New York that it couldn't go somewhere else."

Curt Horrmann

Encouraged by Horrmann's comments, Tommy O'Loughlin went straight into negotiations for the fight. All he had to do was raise the finances to underwrite the event. From the reports in the following days' papers, it is apparent that most of the public, and the press in particular, were more impressed by Robinson's performance than that of Burley's.

"Now Mr. boxing fan, you have something to argue about. Which side will you take – the Charley Burley side or the Sugar Robinson side? No matter which side you choose you will find someone on the other side ready to give you a stout argument. The town is buzzing today as fans compare Robinson's two-round knockout of Dick Banner with Burley's two-round knockout of Sammy Wilson. It goes like this.

Robinson's faster than Burley.

Yes, but Burley's too experienced for Robinson.

Robinson carries a knockout in either hand.

Yes, but he hasn't any single punch as dangerous as Burley's right hand.

Robinson has the best left jab in the game today.

Yes, but Burley's too rugged for him.

Is that so? Well, Burley won't be so rugged when he has to make the welterweight limit. That will weaken him.

Robinson's left won't look so good against Burley's weaving style.

Say, listen, Robinson's left will look good against anything. It can out-point a trip-hammer.

Well, I'll take Burley.

O.K. I'll take Robinson."

Dick Callum, Minneapolis Daily Star

The local fans were desperate to see a Burley versus Robinson main event right there in Minneapolis. Tommy O'Loughlin and Charley Burley would have been happy to have the fight go ahead just about anywhere. While O'Loughlin did his utmost to secure it, Robinson's management had other plans. The up and coming 'Cowboy' Shank had also registered a KO in his win column on the same bill and he was proposed as a future opponent for Ray Robinson.

The real fireworks of the Burley and Robinson card came after the fights were over. In an uncharacteristic outburst Charley told the Morning Tribune that he was quitting the Twin City's and heading back to Pittsburgh. The reason he was quitting Minneapolis was that Tommy O'Loughlin and Bobby Eaton had paid him significantly less than Robinson for his nights work. However, Charley's sense of loyalty to the fans and reporters that had supported him since his move there prevented such an occurrence. He had good reason to be angry. Robinson was paid $1,000 for his two rounds of entertainment, while Charley was paid only $150.

Ranked fighters, Marty Servo and Sammy Angott were beaten by Ray in New York during May and July respectively and these victories cleared the path for a fight with Shank. In July of 1942, Ray knocked 'the cowboy' cold in under two rounds. Shank would probably have met a similar fate against Charley who was not sitting around idly waiting for either Shank or Robinson as he spent May and June doing battle with Ezzard Charles and Holman Williams.

Just three weeks after sharing the bill with Robinson, Charley was back in Pittsburgh for the first time in over a year. Local promoter Jake Mintz had a bout for him against Ken Overlin for May 25th. Overlin was coming off a ten-round points win over Paulie Mahonie in Buffalo and previous to that had contested two ten-round draws with Ezzard Charles and Wild Bill McDowell in Cincinnati and Newark respectively. Since losing the title over 15 rounds to Billy Soose in New York the previous year (1941), Overlin was on an 11-bout unbeaten streak

Charley was sure he could beat Overlin and set about his training determined to advance his career in spectacular fashion against another world-class opponent. However, the cold hand of fate waved in the direction of Charley Burley yet again as, with mere days to go before the anticipated encounter, Overlin pulled, or was pulled, out of the bout. With a large crowd expected and with thousands of tickets already sold, Mintz had to find another top-liner to go on with the Fritzie Zivic-Lew Jenkins fight. As luck would have it, for the promoter at least, Mintz had an interest in a young, up-and-coming middleweight who just happened to be available. 19 year-old Ezzard Charles of Cincinnati was brought in at the last minute to replace Overlin. The fight between young Charles and Charley Burley would be one of the most ferocious and hard-fought ring battles that any crowd at Forbes Field would be privileged to see.

Ezzard Mack Charles, who was born in Lawrenceville, Georgia, had turned professional in March 1940 after going a reported 42-0 as an amateur and winning the National AAU middleweight title the previous year. Up to this point in his career he had taken part in 28 professional contests, winning 25, (17 by knockout), had lost two and drawn one, a points loss and a draw with Ken Overlin and a points loss to the globe-trotting Evelio Mustelier, aka Kid Tunero. The Cuban born fighter was a veteran of 11 years and over 100 bouts. Prior to his win over young Ezzard Charles the Kid had lost back-to-back decisions to Holman Williams. Other opponents of the now 31-year-old Cuban were, Joe Sutka (L10), Antonio Fernandez, (two draws and a no decision), Jose Basora, (W10), Ken Overlin (W10) and honours even in two bouts with Marcel Thil.

140

The huge crowd at Forbes Field in Oakland awaited the main event with eager anticipation. Come the beginning of the main event, expectations rose and the highly charged atmosphere around the park began to seep into the consciousness of the crowd. They knew they were assured of a treat and they got what they expected.

For the full 10 rounds both men went at it, the bout swinging one way and then the other. In the fourth round Charley was caught with a solid shot whilst fighting inside and was forced onto the retreat. 'The Cincinnati Cobra's' ill-fated bout with Sam Baroudi was still some way off and Ezzard was punching with real venom and it was this power, in addition to his advantage in size, which enabled Charles to control the tempo of the fight. Displaying boxing and fighting prowess beyond his years, the young Cincinnati prodigy built up a marginal lead as the bout progressed.

Behind on points going into the final round Charley attempted to render the judges' score cards null and void by going for the knockout. As he pressed his younger foe he was caught with a crunching left hook, the power of which forced him to one knee, a following right hit him flush before he had a chance to rise. There was pandemonium as the crowd booed loudly and Charley's corner called for the Cincinnati fighter to be disqualified. However, Charley got up right away and indicated that he was in shape to continue. For what remained of the round and of the bout, Ezzard Charles retreated and boxed on the move, seemingly without throwing another meaningful punch.

As the bell signalled the end of the hard-fought bout, many of the 12,134 fans in attendance felt that Burley had done enough to win, although it had been close for much of the fight. Charley had been the favourite in the betting as it was considered that he had too much experience, power, and overall ability for the young upstart. It may have been that the weight disadvantage of 12 pound was too much for Charley on this occasion, as it was the hand of Ezzard Charles that was raised in victory once the scorecards were tallied.

Boxing politics may or may not have been a factor as Charles was a connected fighter on his way up; also the betting was where the real action and big money was. The people that controlled the fighters also controlled the betting and held sway with certain newspaper reporters in most major towns and city's. Without the benefit of television, fight fans often relied on the press reports to gauge the worth of an up-and-comer. A fighter could gain a reputation not just from his performances in the ring, but also from the reports that the press gave him. During

141

these times the press could make or break a fighter. Poor performances could be disguised or covered up by a glowing write-up, while reports on fighters such as Charley Burley often didn't make the national papers. This was just one method of promoting or even demoting a fighter.

> "It wasn't the over-exposure of TV that killed boxing, it was the pre-arranged fights that killed the game. Prior to TV you only knew what the fighter was doing in your home-town, you had to take the sportswriter's word about a fight that was fought in another city, which many times was not accurate. A lot of writers were paid off by the mob to tell a different story about the fight, I'm not talking about four- or six-round preliminary fights, I'm talking about world championship or top-contender fights."
>
> **Howard Branson**

With regard to Ezzard Charles' victory over Charley Burley, it could just be that the future heavyweight champion of the world was a little too big and powerful for Charley. But, when one considers the quality opponents Charley had beaten up to that point, and indeed the quality fighters he was yet to meet and defeat, it does not quite ring true that a 19 year-old fighter of comparatively limited experience could beat him in a straight fight. Ezzard Charles was, for many years, a largely underrated fighter.

Jake Mintz knew that he would have no trouble selling out another Ezzard Charles fight, even a return with Charley Burley, as this fight had grossed $31,686.50 and, to a promoter like Mintz, a match involving those kinds of numbers was too good an opportunity to pass up. Accordingly, Charles was signed to fight in the city again towards the end of the month, possibly against Georgie Abrams. That bout turned out to be a non-starter, so it was arranged that Charley Burley and Ezzard Charles would go at it once more. The second bout a little over four weeks later would break all records for the time at Hickey Park, both in terms of attendance and gate receipts.

Before the return, and while Ezzard Charles rested up, Charley would get in another fight with Holman Williams. Just three weeks after the first bout with Ezzard Charles, and only six days before the rematch, Charley Burley met Williams again, this time in Cincinnati. Since the last meeting between the two, Williams had lost two and won two, all on points, against 'Cocoa' Kid and Kid Tunero respectively.

The fight with Holman Williams went the full ten rounds and back in Pittsburgh for the return with Ezzard Charles, on Monday June 29th, Charley was beginning to show the signs of a busy schedule.

Proving to be the better man against Williams for a second time gave Charley the boost he needed for the return with Ezzard Charles and he was looking forward to gaining revenge for their previous meeting. According to Ray M. Todd in the September 1942 edition of Ring magazine the 4,200 customers, paid $6,843.30, beating the previous record of $6,000 set by Lou Brouillard and Anson Green in 1934. It seems that most of them were to go home slightly disappointed. As with most rematches, where the first meeting is a fight that is talked about for many years, the return was something of a letdown.

The fight fans in Pittsburgh had been relishing the return based upon what they had witnessed the first time around and the buzz that was created in the days following the initial, exciting encounter fuelled the demand for additional tickets.

On the night both men were a little slow to get going, but soon it was the Cincinnati fighter who started to dominate. At the start of the sixth round Charley made an attempt to regain some ground with a furious two-fisted attack and claimed that session convincingly. However, Ezzard, showing the skills and determination that would later make him a champion, came back effectively in the following round and swung the momentum of the fight back in his favour. Charley came back in the ninth round and continued the good work in the tenth and last round, by which time it was obvious that he needed a knockout to win. Ezzard was content to coast for the final three minutes and spent all of that session avoiding the attacks of the local fighter.

Pittsburgh Post Gazette sports writer, Al Abrams reported the following day that timidity had robbed the bout of any excitement. Al, a local man of Syrian descent, was raised in the same neighbourhood as Charley up on the Hill and according to Julia Burley he was one of Charley's biggest fans. He never missed the opportunity to write a glowing report when covering anything connected with Charley. On this occasion though, he was given very little of a positive nature to write about.

"While Charles' win over Burley last night was just as decisive as the one in their first meeting a month ago at Forbes Field, the battle was a far less spectacular affair, and at times bordered on the dull side. This was caused mostly by Burley's timidness, and utmost respect for the punching ability of his opponent. The Pittsburgh boy lost some of his timidity as the bout wore on, but still he couldn't do very much with a foe who kept on top of him most of the time.

Charles' repeat victory provided an old axiom of the prize ring, that a good big man can always whip a good little man. Ezzard, with height and reach in his favour, also had a pull of nine pounds at the weights, coming in at 160 to Burley's 151. He used all edges to good advantage, and although he lost the tenth round by a slight margin, was the stronger man of the two at the finish."

Al Abrams, Pittsburgh Post Gazette

The fans left Hickey Park that night knowing that young Ezzard Charles, who would go on to be the heavyweight champion of the world and one of the most grossly underrated champions of all-time, appeared to have the number on Charley Burley.

A post-fight interview with Charley Burley indicates that he, more than anyone else, realised his own limitations when it came to just how far out of his weight class he could safely venture.

"Burley was in better condition at a lower weight than for their first meeting, and he started out to make a boxing match of it, but Charles chugged away too steadily with both fists to counter blows and the fight soon resolved itself into pretty much the same sort of bout as their first one, and after it was over, Charley readily conceded he had met his master in the Cincinnati Negro.

'He's a good fighter,' he agreed, 'and he's too strong for me. He outweighed me a dozen pounds tonight. He's a full-fledged middleweight, while I still can make 147 pounds. Maybe I can lick most of the middleweights, but he's beaten me twice now. So I guess that's conclusive enough.'

Burley said Charles is not as hard a hitter as almost everybody seems to think. He hits well, he said, but not dangerously so. He hurt him only once last night."

Harry Keck, Pittsburgh Sun-Telegraph

After staging their own private little war the protagonists talked a while at a club downtown. Bobby Lippi recalls that Lou Shine, the owner of the

Ringside Bar on Centre Avenue, was in their company that night and he told him how they laughed and joked with each other, the hostilities of fighting for money temporarily forgotten.

Lou himself had been an old-time prizefighter and was more than familiar with the brutality inflicted upon the body during ring battles such as the one Pittsburgh had witnessed that night. For both fighters it had been a tough fight, more so for Charley Burley. He suffered greatly in search of victory and passed blood for several days after the fight. Julie remembers Charley's reliance on an old remedy after the Charles fight, "He'd be sore and hurtin', he'd be takin' Epsom salts baths."

Ezzard would go on to win his remaining six bouts of that year, scoring four knockouts, including one against Jose Basora, and posting two 10-round victories over Joey Maxim.

As his career progressed, Ezzard Charles would go on to beat the great Joe Louis and come within a nose of breaking Rocky Marciano's unbeaten streak and his reign as heavyweight champion of the world. Under the safety-conscious rules that govern the fight game today that would surely have been the case.

The second loss to Ezzard Charles was quite a setback for Charley in terms of world title aspirations. He was now approaching the end of his sixth year as a professional fighter and a world title fight seemed no closer now than it had back in 1936. The two encounters with the Cincinnati Cobra had been Charley's first fights in Pittsburgh for over a year and he would not fight in front of his home crowd again for another three years. He now needed to get himself back on top again and only a victory over a rated fighter would convince the fight crowd that Charley Burley was not yet ready to be written off. Also at this time Tommy O'Loughlin also sold half of his interest in Charley to New Orleans fight manager Sammy Goldman. This may have been a move designed to get Charley more bouts and therefore more exposure. It could also have been a sign that O'Loughlin was losing faith in his charge's abilities.

At the Victory Arena in New Orleans he battled old foe Holman Williams for the second time in as many months. The two fighters were now getting to know each other's style and after a couple of rounds of feinting for openings and defending counters from counters it may have looked to the 6,000 crowd present that the fight may go the distance. Charley had been putting steadily increasing pressure on the Detroit fighter and after round three, it was starting to tell. Williams was finding it more difficult to avoid his opponent's blows and he began to take shots that he would usually avoid. At the midway point of the bout, two of the officials had Williams ahead.

After eight rounds Williams had difficulty seeing Burley's punches as both eyes were swollen and closed, yet he still maintained a slight edge. Charley began to press the advantage he had in the ninth, as he forced Williams to spend more time on the ropes. Williams did his utmost to avoid what was developing into a sustained attack from Charley. Backing his opponent onto the ropes once more Charley landed a crushing left hook to the body and a following two solid smashes to the jaw and head knocked Williams through the ropes. It was at this point that the referee, Charley Daboney, halted the affair. This was the first time Williams had been stopped in over 65 fights, although Holman would have argued, along with some of the crowd, that the stoppage was a little premature. With close to six rounds left to complete, it was difficult to see how Williams could have lasted the course with his diminished vision.

After the fight, promoter Lou Messina bestowed the title of 'Colored' Middleweight champion upon the victor and talked about a return go with the number one rated middleweight, Ezzard Charles.

With proposed bouts in South America failing to materialise Charley returned to New Orleans just two months later to defend his 'title' and, more importantly, earn a pay-day, against Holman Williams. On that occasion the Detroit fighter fought out of his skin to regain the mythical championship.

Williams was content to jab and move while Charley attacked constantly, especially to the body. When Charley got close Williams clinched, grabbed and did whatever he could to avoid the ripping body shots being unloaded against him. The crowd was behind Holman all the way as he had become something of a favourite in the Crescent City. The decision in his favour after 15 rounds appeared to be met favourably by the crowd, whilst the reporters at ringside were split. Some thought Burley had made all of the running and if not for him it would have been a dull fight. Others felt that Holman Williams had put on another master class in the art of boxing.

"Holman Williams decisioned Charley Burley, reversing the recent Burley victory by scoring a well-earned 15-round decision. Burley was not at his best for this fight, but it is doubtful whether he would have taken Williams at his best on this night."

Ring Magazine, February 1943

Chapter Nine

The Black Murderers' Row

Nine months after the knockout win over 'Big Boy' Hogue, Charley was back on the West Coast, where he met Mexican slugger Cecilio Lozada in a scheduled ten-rounder. Charley started against Lozada in double-quick time, firing punches from all angles before dropping him with a sharp right hand punch behind the ear as the round ended. Charley repeated the dosage as the second got under way before finishing the job with a swift uppercut as the Mexican tried to retreat on shaky pins.

Charley was looking for another payday before the holiday season and was working out at the gym on a regular basis in order to stay in shape should he be called upon to fill a card or top a bill, but the rigours of the road were beginning to show.

> "He had so many fights in one year, you know, 17 fights and not a soft touch among them. The thing was, travelling coast-to-coast and he travelled by car. Nowadays they get on a plane for a couple of hours. I remember Charley telling me about fighting Ezzard Charles, and Charles outweighed him by some 20 pounds, then travelling down to New Orleans, then back to Pittsburgh and he'd drive in the car you know. He was remarkable."
>
> **Blackie Nelson**

Charley admitted to his friend that he was feeling totally exhausted, but realised it was due to a busy year. Despite this, he accepted a match with ranked light-heavyweight contender Lloyd Marshall in Los Angeles for December 13th after a proposed fight with slick Jack Chase fell through. Marshall was one of the best fighters on the West Coast at that time and in reality was probably one of the greatest fighters who ever laced on a glove. Many boxing fans and historians who are aware of Marshall's career are frustrated because it is very difficult to gauge his true worth due to his involvement with the shadier side of boxing in America.

Born in Madison County, Georgia in 1914, Marshall was raised on a farm by his hard-working mother who appeared to lead a nomadic existence, toiling in and around many of the southern states before finally settling in Cleveland. It was here that young Lloyd found boxing and proved to be an exceptional talent. In over 200 bouts he was defeated only 17 times, with two of those losses coming in the 1934 national championships semi-finals when he opposed Fred Apostoli and the 1935 final at middleweight when he lost to Dave Clark. As an amateur, Lloyd, like Charley, passed up a chance to compete in the 1936 Olympic selection tournament. Marshall's reasons were slightly more practical, as he had plans to turn professional and earn something to contribute to the upkeep of the family.

With the dollar motivating the Cleveland prospect, just as it would later in his career, he turned to the punch-for-pay ranks in that Olympic year with ex-fighter Johnny Papke as his manager. After winning 12 on the spin, Marshall began to get the impression that he was being avoided locally and at one point considered quitting the game. Around this time a ball player by the name of Frank Doljack, a former outfielder for the Detroit Tigers, came upon the Cleveland fighter and suggested that Lloyd might do better for himself on the West Coast, where Doljack himself just happened to be heading. Unfortunately for Marshall and his voluntary pilot, the fight game was not too hot in their final destination of Sacramento at the time and while the ball player practised with his new team, Marshall was reduced to living under the grandstand at the ballpark. When Doljack was selected to travel with the team on the road, he left Marshall in the capable hands of Jim Edwards who was a steward at the Hotel Clunie.

Lloyd had engaged in just the one bout at the time and due to illness, which Edwards nursed him through, he would not get another fight for six months. Times were hard, but once fully recovered Lloyd set about earning a crust for himself and the charitable Edwards, who now had the fighter living with him at his home. As the transplanted Clevelander progressed his skills drew interest from various corners of the fight game, most of whom where intent in stealing him away from his new manager. Interference from outsiders, mostly trying to poison Lloyd against Edwards, and the fact that Lloyd would not fight a black fighter, began to sour the relationship. Around this time Marshall took part in a fight that would have significant repercussions on the rest of his boxing career as, after gaining revenge over Johnny 'Bandit' Romero for an earlier defeat, he signed to fight Ken Overlin in San Francisco.

Overlin was a veteran of over 90 bouts, yet this vast amount of experience could not save him from the ten-round hammering he received at the hands of Marshall. Overlin, managed by the famous Chris Dundee, was also a connected fighter and, according to Blackie Nelson, some of his connections came calling the day after the Lloyd Marshall fight. They felt that he had not given his all and were suspicious of him conducting some 'business' of his own.

Overlin, who was by some accounts something of an unsavoury character himself, especially when it came to money, pointed out the damage to his eyes and ribs as evidence that Marshall was indeed the genuine article and more than capable of beating most middleweights out there.

"While boxing exhibitions with Ken Overlin in the South Pacific Ken told me Lloyd was the greatest fighter he ever fought."

Blackie Nelson

Overlin successfully convinced his visitors that there was very little that he could have done against Marshall. Thus, Ken Overlin's connections became Lloyd Marshall's connections and the 'Black Murderers' Row' member soon found himself caught up in all manner of 'business' fights. Overlin himself was the middleweight champion of the world from 1940, when he beat Ceferino Garcia over 15 rounds, to 1941 when he lost it the same way to Billy Soose. He lost only 16 of 152 bouts and was stopped just once, (by Freddie Steele in an NBA middleweight title fight in 1937).

After he retired from the ring in 1944 he ran a bar in Valejo, California where he supplemented his income by relieving drunken servicemen of cash and cheques by overcharging and short-changing them. Blackie Nelson worked with the former champion as a serviceman in the South Pacific. Often they would perform in exhibitions with each other and Fred Apostoli, another former champion. Blackie became quite friendly with Overlin and remembers that he liked to run games such as craps and other gambling activities, usually earning himself a decent amount of money. Blackie suggests that it was probably this greedy nature that got Overlin involved in business fights during his 13-year career.

For the bout with Charley Burley, Marshall was tabbed the underdog. In the fight itself he failed to perform like one as he looked to end it with just about every shot he threw.

"Marshall spun Burley abruptly to the deck at the tailend of the first round after Charley, leaping about him agilely, speared him with numerous punches. They were fighting in close when Lloyd shot a right to the head and Burley dropped like an elevator. He took a four count but was not seriously hurt.

Again in the fourth round, they were close when Marshall connected suddenly to the jaw, this time with a left hook. Burley fell to the canvas, bounding up at two. Lloyd threatened to whack Burley floorward in the second and in the third also. In the second he hurled a terrific right that clipped Burley on the jaw as he was going away, thus lessening the force of the blow.

Marshall plastered Burley up against the ropes in the third and blasted a right to the jaw that turned Charley's legs to rubber. He clutched Marshall, saved himself from falling and weathered the storm.

In between Marshall's mighty slams, Burley did plenty of scoring on a lighter and less impressive scale. Burley's heaviest cannonading appeared in the eighth, which saw him register with sharp chops to the chin."

Morton Moss, Los Angeles Examiner

The decision was a split one, with referee Bill Kirshner and Judge Charley Randolph going for Marshall 58-52 and 57-53 respectively and Judge whilst Judge Frankie Dolan voted for Burley 56-52. Joe Herman, the colourful trainer and gym owner from San Francisco, who worked Charley's corner from time to time, was down in Los Angeles for the Marshall versus Burley fight. He reported back the next day that Charley had been "fucked over" adding that Charley had made it look like an easy win. Charley had a different point of view:

"The roughest fight I had was Lloyd Marshall. He was a light-heavyweight. I lost a decision to him, and he's the only one who knocked me off my feet. A straight right hand in the first round."

Charley Burley

Charley Burley V Lloyd Marshall December 11 1942

"It was a tight, tough fight, but I caught Charley coming in and I kept the edge. I got the decision and I deserved it."

Lloyd Marshall

Charley, as usual, made no bones about his defeat to Marshall and, in all likelihood, it is possible that Charley felt that Marshall was the better man on the night, even if he did go into the bout with an injury to his thumb that made him practically one-handed. In fact it was reported some time later that the injury was so bad that Charley had it packed in ice to reduce the swelling immediately prior to being passed fit by the commission doctor. Some of the press reports tabbed Charley as "a washed up customer" and even "over the hill". It was figured by some that Marshall, with a win and a loss against Shorty Hogue, was not that special. Chappy Goldstein may have known that Marshall was the real deal when he refused a match for Charley against Lloyd in 1940. His reasoning at the time was that Charley was a welterweight and Marshall was a light-heavyweight. Whatever the reasoning then Charley Burley knew now that Marshall was special and history would back him up.

151

Another thing that Charley knew for sure after his fight with Marshall was that his hands were giving him trouble again and he had to pull out of a scheduled fight with (Alex) Watson Jones the following week in San Diego. Aaron 'Tiger' Wade stepped in as a late replacement and beat the unusually timid Jones on points.

Eighteen months after his victory over Burley Marshall beat Jake LaMotta in Cleveland over ten rounds. When he returned home, Lloyd told the West Coast fight fraternity that any one of the 'Black Murderers' Row' would have no problem beating the 'Bronx Bull' as it had been one of his easiest fights. Lloyd told Blackie Nelson that there were several fighters on the West Coast, most notably Charley Burley and Eddie Booker, who would defeat LaMotta easily.

It has been reported that Jake received one of the biggest beatings of his career the night he faced Marshall. His face was grotesquely swollen from the pounding it received from the fists of the California-based fighter. Despite beating nine out of the twelve world champions he faced, Lloyd Marshall never got anywhere near a world title fight.

"I remember Toby Irwin, an old-time referee, saying that he could always tell after the first round if Lloyd was out to win and that he once told him to 'get up, he wasn't pulling that off on him that night'."

Blackie Nelson

Blackie also remembered talking to Marshall in the gym when he arrived back home after the Freddie Mills fight in London. Marshall, it seems, arrived in England expecting to be given the lowdown on what was expected of him. It turned out that Marshall was there as an opponent for Freddie Mills that night, but somebody forgot to tell him. In his biography the promoter, Jack Solomons; a larger than life figure in British boxing for many years, recounted the circumstances surrounding the event.

"There was a lot of 'colour bar' talk going on in the sports columns about that time and, trying to be topical, I conceived the novelty of a Black v White card for my next show at Harringay. Mills v Marshall, I figured would be a sure-fire 'top' - attractive to the customers and calculated to advance my plan for Freddie's comeback. We duly collected the sad-faced Marshall: a Negro companion, welterweight Berry Wright; Johnny Rogers, their silver-haired old-timer manager and natty Matty Morton, one of the good-looking aces among American trainers and muscle-manipulators.

The sad-faced Marshall looked like uncle Tom after a session with Simon Legree, and his lazybones act in my gymnasium every day made the place as lively as an undertaker's office - especially as we were in the middle of an oppressive, too-weary-to-work heatwave. However, I quickly assessed the limpid Lloyd as a more-than-useful fighter. Despite the hangdog look and his apparent apathy, Mr. Marshall's moves in training convinced me that I had got hold of a real test for Freddie."

Jack Solomons

Marshall destroyed Mills that night and Solomons recalls, "That unhappy little episode cost me £9,000 in purse-money. I would have paid many times as much for it never to have happened." Indeed, the Black v White card resulted in a 5-1 victory for the black fighters and a huge setback for Mills. On the undercard Marshall's travelling companion, Berry Wright, won via a 2nd round knockout over Arthur Danahar. Randolph Turpin beat Mark Hart in six rounds, Ritchie 'Kid' Tanner won in eight over Dickie O'Sullivan, Jack Johnson knocked out Alby Hollister in two and Johnny Malloy did the same against Jackie Turpin.

Following the fight with Mills in London Lloyd returned to the USA where Ezzard Charles erased any doubts as to who may have been the better man by stopping him in the second round in Cincinnati. The Charles defeat was Lloyd's final bout of 1947 and the remaining four years of his career were hardly glorious. He fought only twice the following year (both wins), and fought six times in 1949, winning three and losing three. After that Lloyd may not have been as marketable as he had once been. Now fighting more frequently on the road he travelled to Germany, where he had five bouts - two wins, two defeats and a draw - before returning to the British Isles to oppose Don Cockell (losing on a disqualification in the seventh round), and Tommy Farr (won 10). While the Welsh heavyweight was considered a little too old to be fighting at 37 Lloyd Marshall was only a year younger, but it was the money kept him going His final three fights, in 1951, must have convinced Marshall that the promise of a payday couldn't justify the punishment, although he couldn't have suffered too much as he was stopped in less than a round by Don Cockell, five rounds by 'Bobo' Olson and one round by Harry 'Kid' Matthews. Lloyd had fought with the cuffs on several times and looking at his last couple of fights it is possible he did the same again just to earn a few more dollars.

Lloyd Marshall beat nine of the 12 world champions he had squared-off against including; Ken Overlin, Babe Risko, Teddy Yarosz, Lou Brouillard, Anton Christoforidis, and Jake LaMotta (middleweights), Joey Maxim and Freddie Mills (light-heavyweights), and Ezzard Charles (heavyweight champion). Speaking of Charles, in their 1943 fight Marshall knocked Charles to the canvas eight times in the eight rounds the fight lasted and Lloyd - justifiably proud of this accomplishment - felt that this feat had to be some kind of record. Despite such an impressive resume - or probably because of it - Lloyd Marshall never did get a shot at any title.

In an interview with Lester Bromberg for Boxing Scene in 1983, Lloyd attempted to explain the anomaly:

> "People were always asking after I beat those champs why I didn't win a championship. It's because I wouldn't have gotten fights with the champs if I tried to insist on it being a title fight. The younger fans, those who have only been around in the last several years, don't understand it. Well, in those old days a champ wouldn't get into the ring with you, especially in your hometown, with his title on the line. The manager'd say 'it's got to be over-the-weight, so we don't have to risk nothing. OK? If you win, maybe I'll fight you at the weight in a return.
>
> Now you know why I never became a champ. I never had a chance. I had a good manager, Johnny Rogers, who was as straight as they come and who took me for fights everywhere - London, Honolulu, Germany, you name it - and we got the dollar going, which was chicken-feed compared to today. I was a leading guy in the division, but I was black and if you knew the way things were in the 1930s and even the forties, you knew a black man couldn't get an honest break. It was nobodies fault really there were too many hangups of prejudice to get rid of in a hurry."

Lloyd Marshall

After his retirement from boxing Lloyd Marshall spent almost 30 years with the federal government working in industrial relations. He died in 1997, aged 83.

After the Marshall fight, and with the holiday season fast approaching, Charley had a chance to rest his hands, relax and spend time with his family in their new surroundings. Sunny California was definitely the place to be when recovering from a punishing schedule and Charley enjoyed every minute of it. Thanks to a busy year in the ring, Charley was able to provide a comfortable living for his wife Julia and their daughter Angeline.

Many years later, when reflecting upon his career, Charley said that he was able to earn enough so that it was the same as having a regular, steady job. The money he was able to make allowed them to live well enough and he was thankful for that fact. What was still eluding him however, was a title shot or even a big money fight with one of the highly rated white fighters. Like it or not, that was where the real cash was and in addition to his talents as a fighter, Charley had to contend with the acts of racism that also held him back, especially when on the road travelling to fights.

"He told me about going in the back door of restaurants to get himself something to eat and sometimes having to sleep in the car, they don't have nothing like that today."

Blackie Nelson

Settling on the West Coast, Charley may have been thankful that he had to do less travelling, as most fight locations were close enough that he could get home after a bout. The most attractive aspect of living in California was purely financial, as Charley was sure to make some money and keep himself busy in this part of the country. Some of the best fighters around at the time happened to reside in California – Jack Chase, Aaron 'Tiger' Wade, Archie Moore, Billy Smith, Bert Lytell, and the dangerous Eddie Booker to name a few. Not only were these guys among the best ring men on the West Coast, if not the world, they too were black. This would prove troublesome for them during their careers, as racism was as rife in sport as it was everywhere else. California also had a reputation for gambling and some of the biggest 'high-rollers' plied their trade there. With Tommy O'Loughlin setting up in The Manhattan Gym with his stable of

Charley Burley, Curley Martin and Chester Ellis it was hoped that he and his fighters could get something going on the West Coast.

One of the most under-rated and overlooked fighters of that era was the aforementioned Eddie Booker. Originally from Alto, Texas, Hilton Edward Booker campaigned at welterweight, middleweight and light heavyweight between 1935 and 1944. In over 80 fights, he had eight draws and only five defeats, all by decision. Half of his victories came via the short route, while he never once failed to go the distance, despite facing a veritable 'who's who' of world-rated fighters.

One of two boxing brothers (Earl Booker was a highly-rated light-weight campaigning at the same time), Eddie had an outstanding amateur career and carried that success over to the professional ranks under the tutelage of John Burdick. Eddie's pilot was often criticized by the boxing press for not putting the talented fighter in with a man before a thorough scouting report was completed and the opponent's worth assessed. If Burdick was guilty of anything it was of protecting his fighter by not allowing anyone else to dictate whom he should fight.

With a well-developed and muscular physique, Booker had the strength and ability to 'mix it up' when the chips were down and was happy to either fight or box – he genuinely loved to be in the ring. A slick-boxing, defensive stylist with decent power in both hands, particularly the left hook, Booker beat some of the better 'name' fighters of his time. Compared by some to heavyweight great Jack Johnson in regards to his ability to catch a punch and deliver a blow in the same motion with the same hand, Eddie was a methodical, conservative workman who fought as much with his mind as with his fists.

Based in San Francisco, Eddie made his daily dollars as a red-cap porter in a local hotel, where he sometimes had to suffer the indignation of a rich, white man's hatred towards a working-class African-American. 'Boy', was a term heard once too often as Mr. Booker was ordered to carry a bag or fetch a newspaper. Eddie's son, also Edward, is sickened still by the racial slurs his father had to endure in order to earn a living. The racism he suffered in his day-to-day work often spilled over into his career as a professional fighter and Eddie Booker's pleas for a title fight fell on the same deaf ears as the pleas of the rest of the Black Murderers' Row.

Unbeaten in his first 44 professional outings, Booker defeated Johnny Bassinelli, Remo Fernandez, Gail Harrington and the murderous-punching Jimmy Wakefield, before Fritzie Zivic dented his excellent record in New York in 1939. Required to boil down from middleweight to the welterweight limit, Eddie boxed well for the first half of the fight against the veteran Pittsburgher, but then ran out of gas and allowed his opponent to storm back in the final rounds and take the eight-round decision.

In his next bout, versus the experienced 'Cocoa' Kid, Booker was defeated for the second time, the only time he would suffer back-to-back defeats. In fact, he would only lose three more times in the remaining five years of his career. Eddie rebounded with a string of knockout victories before taking time out during 1940 due to badly damaged hands.

An 18-fight winning streak, during which time he won the California State Middleweight title in a ten-round match with rugged Shorty Hogue, established the talented Booker as a genuine middleweight title threat. An upset loss to Hogue in August 1941, which also cost him the state title, seemed to have removed Eddie from the contenders' list, but again he came back to post good wins over Johnny 'Bandit' Romero, Castillo Cruz and Shorty Hogue, (regaining the state title). He then went on to beat Izzy Janazzo, Bobby Birch and Lloyd Marshall amongst others.

By the time Charley Burley arrived on the West Coast, Booker was one of the top-rated fighters in the world. While a match between the two seemed like a natural there were plenty of other fairly high-profile fighters for Charley Burley to tangle with, even if none of them happened to be white. A proposed meeting between Booker and Burley for January 15th 1943 had to be cancelled by fledgling Oakland promoter Ray Carlen because Charley contracted the flu. Oakland Tribune Sports Editor, Lee Dunbar, felt there was more afoot than the flu as, just a couple of months later, Tommy O'Loughlin used the same excuse for Elmer Ray when it came to a fight with Harold Blackshear.

> "I spoke to Eddie about fighting Charley and he said he would if he had to but he wouldn't be too happy about it, because he thought that Charley was just about the best there was. Charley once told me that Eddie Booker would be the hardest fight he'd ever have."
>
> **Blackie Nelson**

Eddie Booker's series of fights with Archie Moore showcased his unquestionable skill, grit and honour. In a previous meeting, February 1941, the two engaged in a gruelling battle and Booker gave Archie's body such a beating that the Old Mongoose believes that's when his ulcer problem became critical. When Archie was rushed to hospital with his ulcer condition and was in need of a transfusion Eddie Booker was apparently the first in line to give a donation. Moore retired from the fight game after that battle only to return after a year off. The rest appeared to do him good as Archie won six bouts in a row, five by knockout, before tackling Booker again. Eddie had fought twenty times in the intervening year, winning 17 (6 knockouts), drawing two and losing one. An eighth round knockout of Shorty Hogue in August 1942 saw Eddie regain the state middleweight title he had lost to Jack Chase the year before. When Booker and Moore went at it again in December, Eddie's title was on the line.

The action was frenetic from the first bell and both fighters had their moments. Moore looked to end it early as he bounced Booker off the canvas twice in the first round. The defending champion was up both times without a count and hung on to survive 'till the bell.

In the second, third and fourth Eddie pounded away at Moore, but Archie hung in there, despite losing each of the three stanzas on all cards. The fifth round saw both men take a well-earned breather before Booker came out firing on all cylinders again after the bell went for the sixth. In that frame a solid right to the head, followed by "several jolting uppercuts to the head and solar plexus rocked Moore." Archie, probably realizing that the fight was slipping away from him, stormed out for the seventh forcing Booker to take a knee, again for a no-count, with a right to the body. The challenger then had the champion hanging on at the end of the round. Eddie tried to prevent the shift in momentum in the eighth session by hurting Moore with a left-hook to the head followed by a punishing body attack. Archie waved-off a solid low blow by Booker in the ninth, signalling to the referee that he was not hurt. The 'Ole' Mongoose' evened things up in the tenth and eleventh rounds by butting Booker in the face. Despite letting Eddie know that he too could fight dirty, Archie lost both rounds. Come the twelfth, and final round, it was looking like a successful defence for Booker as both fighters went toe-to-toe for the last three minutes. At the bell, judges Lt. Clayton Frye, Joe Stone and referee Benny Whitman came up with a draw decision.

Booker kept his title, but it may be that the fight with Moore cost him dearly. According to Eddie's daughter in law, who cared for him before he passed away in 1975, Eddie received the career-ending eye problem in the very same fight. His stepdaughter has vague memories of the incident.

"Because I was just a child then I don't recall a lot, only about his becoming blind and he became blind during a boxing match."

Loretta Bailey, Eddie Booker's stepdaughter

Exactly a month after the Moore bout Eddie lost his state title to Jack Chase in the first 15-round fight in California since 1914. Strangely, it was immediately after the bout with Chase that Booker entered the hospital. It is possible that it was in this fight that Eddie's eye problems emerged as his step-daughter remembers that the injury was a result of doctored gloves. Such an act would, in retrospect, seem unlikely of Moore, but more likely of Chase. Eddie Booker underwent eye surgery and remained in hospital for 24 days.

In February, 1943 Eddie's manager, Frank Schuler, told boxing writer Barney Kafka that his charge was under the care of an eye specialist and may never fight again. Eddie underwent further tests and was allowed to continue boxing as long as he agreed to be tested after each fight. Following a knockout victory over Harry 'Kid' Matthews in August of the same year the news from the commission doctor was not good. Eddie decided to get out of the game as soon as possible and even though he knew he was risking permanent blindness with each fight and every punch he took, he set about earning a nest egg for his family and his future.After a knockout win over Van McNutt, a 12-round points loss to Holman Williams and an inside-the-distance victory over heavyweight Paul Hartnek, Booker and Moore squared up for the third and last time in January 1944.

"Scoring five knockdowns, Eddie Booker polished-off Archie Moore in the eighth-round of a scheduled tenner at Hollywood last night, and Archie might have passed out a little earlier but for the fact that each of Eddie's flooring punches in the fifth, sixth and seventh occurred shortly before the bell and the gong saved him from fur-ther punishment.

But in the eighth, when Booker threw another of his deadly left-hooks to the chin, Moore hit the deck about the middle of the round and was so softened-up by the punching that he was a mark for another pot-shot when he got to his feet. Booker promptly tossed in another wallop and referee Johnny Indrisano didn't even bother to count this time. As Moore was sinking to the canvas he had

159

Booker's hand in the air, signifying a technical knockout.

Up to the time Booker uncovered his deck punch the fight was proceeding on an even-keel with not a great deal of action and the gallery-gods booing loud and strenuously at the lack of it. There was too much close-quarter stuff and no damage. Then came the fifth and Booker dropped Moore flat on his back. He barely climbed to his feet in time to beat the ten-count. The bell saved him, but after that it was just a question of time.

As two of Chase's foremost rivals for the state middleweight honours, Moore had slightly the better record, but Booker shot to the fore with his kayo last night."

The Press

After a ten-round points win over Frankie Nelson in Oakland- a bout for which Charley Burley was the original opponent, but was replaced at the last minute due to illness - Eddie gained revenge over Holman Williams, winning a decision over ten in San Francisco. Eddie Booker then walked away from the sport that had promised him so much, yet had ultimately let him down. One of the most talented fighters in any era and one of the few true gentlemen to grace the fight game, Eddie Booker was not only a victim of racism in sport, but also the seedier, slimy underbelly of boxing, the professional side of which, legendary writer Jimmy Cannon called, "The 'red-light district' of sports." Aside from occasionally helping out a number of professional fighters shortly after his retirement, Eddie concentrated on helping youngsters train for the Golden Gloves, while running his hardware store in San Francisco.

The talented Mr. Booker lived his remaining years blind in one eye and passed away in January 1975 after complications following a heart attack the previous April. Call it fate, or simple bad luck, Eddie Booker did not truly get out of life what he deserved and, years after his passing, it seems that the same spectres continue to haunt his family. According to Blackie Nelson Eddie's brother, Earl, lost his wife in a freak explosion at home, (along with his and Eddie's career mementos), while his mother passed away just three days before his induction to the California-based 'World Boxing Hall of Fame' in October 2000. Considering Rose Booker had lived to the grand old age of 103, this was a very cruel twist of fate indeed.

160

Eddie Booker, his California State Championship belt and manager Frank Schuler

After his brother's passing, Earl Booker reflected on Eddie's career with a justifiable amount of pride.

> "He was primarily a body puncher. He wasn't a sensational attraction, owing to his style. Many times people up in the gallery would boo him, because he used short, sharp punches they couldn't see from a distance.
>
> He was awfully good too at blocking punches thrown at him. Eddie usually wore his opponents down gradually and they'd just fold up from the pounding he dished out."

Earl Booker

If he were around and active today Eddie Booker would undoubtedly have become champion of the world. Just as Charley Burley, Holman Williams, Chase, Marshall, Lytell and the rest of the 'Black Murderers'

Row' would surely have been. While the honour of enshrinement into the Boxing Hall of Fame is the least these fighters deserve, in the case of Eddie Booker it is definitely a case of too little and too late.

As the big money fights and fighters were still eluding him, especially back East, Charley made the decision to remain on the West Coast. To supplement his pugilistic income he took on a 'regular' job and began working in a defence plant making aircraft for the war effort.

Charley had his sights set on the State Middleweight Championship, currently in the possession of Jack Chase, but first he would have to beat one of the other contenders for the title. A bout with Harvey Massey on the undercard or the Turkey Thompson - Bob Smith main event at the Oakland auditorium was arranged for February 3rd and Charley went to train at Harry Fines gym. Substantial crowds gathered to watch Charley Spar with Doug Ellison of Richmond, Virginia and the common consensus was that they had a future champion in their midst. The feelings were justified as Charley attempted to cement his position as one of the top middleweights in the country and a logical contender for the State crown.

"Charley Burley of Pittsburgh, Pa., worked on Harvey Massey with left hooks to the body and right crosses to the jaw to take every round and win a technical knockout decision over the Oakland fighter last night. Burley weighed 158, Massey 159.

Referee Jimmy Duffy wanted to stop the main event in the eighth, after Burley thumped Massey's face until it bled, but the game Oakland fighter pushed Duffy aside and continued taking it.

Despite the opinion of Dr. William Hatteroth, club physician, that Massey could continue, Duffy had his way after one minute of the ninth round and stopped the uneven contest when Burley had his opponent groggy from hard rights and lefts to the jaw."

The Press

Jack Chase, who had lost only once in 20 West Coast outings, indicated that he was happy to meet the transplanted Pittsburgher, but the title would not be at stake. Charley was still being billed out of Minneapolis and he would have to be a state resident for a minimum of six months in order to qualify for a state championship. Chase, an inch shorter than Charley at five feet eight inches, had lost only five of 55 fights since turning professional in 1936. The Texas-born fighter, who had been brought up without a father, was constantly in trouble as a youth. He spent a number of terms in the equivalent of juvenile hall as a teenager and also served several years in Colorado's Canon City prison after a robbery went wrong and he assaulted a guard with a lead pipe. Chase was a superb boxer with excellent ring skills and was considered something of a defensive wizard with blinding hand and foot speed. In his second year as a fighter he had lost on a fourth-round knockout to Ge Ge Gravante in Salt Lake City and despite meeting fighters such as Eddie Booker, Archie Moore, Bobby Birch and Ralph Chong he had not been stopped since. With almost half of his wins coming via the short route, Isaiah James Chase also had power to complement his skills. This was in evidence when opponent Roy Gillespie died after a beating at the hands of the Colorado resident in August 1941 when Chase was attempting to rebuild his life after a term in prison.

The non-title match between Chase and Burley on February 19th at the Hollywood Civic Auditorium was sold out as a crowd of 6,000 watched a classic display by a classy Charley Burley. Chase, weighing three pounds more than Charley at 155, could do little with the slick-boxing figure in front of him. A right-hand dropped Chase for a nine-count in the second as Charley, despite touching down for a no-count in the fourth, cruised to a relatively easy ten-round decision. The poor performance, and the fact that he was only credited with one of the ten rounds, was explained away by the reigning state champion as poor preparation in regards to conditioning for the contest. Charley had been the stronger of the two at the finish, so it might have been true that Chase had slackened off on his gym work before the fight. Also, the reigning state champion had only recently come through a tonsillectomy and had not been in the gym as much as he may have liked. Charley, however, was in top condition and remained in training for his next fight, just two weeks later.

The Burley family moved out of the hotel they had been staying in and relocated to an apartment complex before settling in a bungalow in San Diego. Charley had money for furniture and he and Julia went shopping at Beacons Furniture, an outlet that sold second-hand items that usually came out of the homes of the Hollywood movie stars. With their new home furnished the Burleys settled easily into the relaxed West Coast life-style and enjoyed the sun-drenched sights.

Charley stayed in shape and was ready to fight at short notice. It appears that Tommy O'Loughlin, who was promoting, but not managing Charley at this time, initially had far less trouble of putting good matches together in California, but there was hardly what might be called a 'soft touch' around and every opponent required careful consideration.

For what was his third fight in as many months, Charley was matched with the powerful Aaron Wade of San Francisco. Wade had been fighting since 1938 when he had won his only contest. His next bout, according to most sources, was in 1940 when he won five out of five, with three inside the distance victories. Two of his knockout victims that year were Bobby Pacho and 'Big Boy' Hogue. A pair of losses at the hands of Johnny Jackson led to a twelve-month hiatus from the sport for the 'Little Tiger' and when he returned to the ring, he won ten of ten with four knockouts. According to the Ring Record Book, by the time he met Charley Burley in March 1943 for the first of three meetings, Wade had lost only two of 20 fights. Other reports on the 'Little Tiger's' career, taken from the contemporary press, indicate that he had engaged in 100 fights with 58 knockouts to his credit. No wonder his manager Dell Van Liew was calling him a 'human stick of dynamite'. In the meeting between Burley and Wade however, only the reporting of explosions was in evidence.

Swelling to magnificent proportions a cheer in the local Auditorium and the torrent of sound burst through the doors and ruffled the surface of Lake Merrit. The vocal salute came immediately at the end of the third round of last nights fight between Charley Burley and Little Tiger Wade - a fight incidentally in which Burley ultimately won a 10-round decision - but it wasn't by any frenzied battling of the middleweights.

The gleeful uproar was the result of an eloquent, if ungrammatical, announcement by Eddie (Pesty) Ryan that US forces had knocked off some 22 Japanese warships and transports during the day.

Ryan's announcement was far and away the most exciting few moments of the Burley-Wade encounter which must go down on record as so much of a stinker the audience wasn't more than mildly irritated because Burley was given the nod. It was the consensus of most ringsiders, as well as the opinion of yours truly, that Wade was entitled to whatever doubtful honor was attached to receiving the verdict.

The suffering spectators, who paid $3195 for the show, would have been satisfied had Jimmy Duffy tossed both the Negro middleweights out of the ring. Burley didn't use his right more than four times during the evening and only once did he really level with the tender paw. In the sixth he hit Wade flush on the chin with his right and the Little Tiger's legs buckled.

Too much clinching, not enough fighting and a complete lack of spirit on the part of the participants made last nights bout one of the season's worst. Even if he had possessed two whole hands, Burley last night would probably have proved a pain in the neck. Obviously he was indulging in one of the 'bad nights' which assortedly haunt the Minneapolis middleweight.

Perhaps the finish caught referee Duffy's eye. Or maybe he felt sorry for Burley because of the sore maulie. Yes, and maybe if Tiger had shoved his arm under Duffy's nose while Jimmy was looking from one fighter to the other at the end of the tenth trying to make up his mind by the 'eenie, meenie, minee, moe' method he'd have been handed the duke."

Alan Ward, Oakland Tribune

In his next bout, several weeks later, Charley fought a return with veteran rival 'Cocoa' Kid in New Orleans. Despite scoring a knockdown in the second round and having the Kid swollen about the eyes, Charley had to be satisfied with a draw in a fight that most Crescent City reporters felt he had won by a "country mile." This result interrupted Charley's latest win streak at three.

A win and a draw against the talented Mr. Hardwick was nothing to be sniffed at. Holman Williams only managed to defeat him thrice in around a dozen matches and while he may have had a few miles on the clock at 30 years of age, 14 years as a pro and roughly 180 fights under his belt, the Kid still had plenty left. After his second bout with Charley Burley Cocoa Kid had enough to beat Holman Williams (again), Jack Chase, Joe Carter, Cecil Hudson and Gene Buffalo (who was himself a veteran by that point). Other top-flight opposition in his waning years included 'Oakland' Billy Smith, Archie Moore and Bert Lytell. Cocoa Kid called it a day in 1948 after losing to Bobby Mann in Trenton, New Jersey. He was often hired as a sparring partner and on one occasion was brought in to help Sugar Ray Robinson to prepare for a fight with Steve Belloise in 1949. Robinson learned that you couldn't afford to take liberties with a fighter of the Kid's calibre when an overhand right dropped him in one of their sessions.

Of the many talented black fighters that inhabited the same time and space as Charley Burley, Cocoa Kid is the only one to get a shot at a world title. Izzy Jannazzo won the vacant title in a 15 round decision over the Kid in October 1940. The new 'champion' defended the title once, winning a decision over Jimmy Leto the following year. With Fritzie Zivic winning the 'genuine' world title from Henry Armstrong just ten days previous, the Maryland version had little lustre and even less prestige. The fact that he got a shot at a 'title' didn't elevate Cocoa Kid's status, reputation or place in boxing history. It apparently did little of anything for this most talented of welterweights as he reportedly spent his later years ghosting around the seedy shadows of New York's Times Square begging for money to feed his drug habit.

Charley's next bout, against old foe Holman Williams back in Hollywood, can only be described as bizarre. With Charley ahead in the series three to two and with Williams out to avenge the only knockout defeat on his record up to that point, the two cagey professionals squared off for what promised to be a fascinating encounter at the Hollywood Stadium.

The press, labouring under the illusion that when these two talented fighters got together it was all-out war, promoted the fight as potentially one of the best in recent times in the Hollywood area. The sell-out crowd may have been expecting a battle royal as they sat patiently through the preliminary encounters of four four-round fights and a six-round semi-final. By the time Charley Burley and Holman Williams entered the ring for their scheduled ten-round headline fight, the crowd were undoubtedly looking forward to the promised fireworks. What they got however was the proverbial damp squib.

"Those two colored cuties, Charley Burley of Pittsburgh and Holman Williams of Detroit, met at the Hollywood Stadium and were tossed out of the ring by referee Abe Roth in the first minute of the last round."

Harry Winkler. Ring magazine, August 1943

What a large percentage of the fans and referee Abe Roth failed to appreciate was that both fighters possessed exceptional defensive skills and, having met five times already, were very familiar with each other's style. As the physical chess match progressed, the third man in the ring began to make things worse. Insisting that the fighters make more of it for the sake of the crowd, he caused both men, especially Charley, to throw and miss with more shots. With punches now being telegraphed out of eagerness to land, it was easier for Charley Burley and Holman Williams to avoid them. Charley missed much and clinched often, but he did force the action and hurt his opponent many times with powerful punches, while the Detroit fighter beat on Burley's body whenever the opportunity presented itself.

"In my opinion it was an injustice to both boxers, especially to Burley, to have the bout declared 'no contest' as late as the tenth round (although the referee's action met with the approval of most of the crowd), as it robbed the Pittsburgh Negro of his fourth victory over Williams."

Harry Winkler. Ring magazine, August 1943

The result meant that Charley was unbeaten in his last five bouts, although he now had one draw and a no contest amongst those. The boxing climate of the time meant that an investigation had to take place and both fighter's purses where withheld until a decision was reached.

The main problem for the commission came when a vote had to be taken on what action was appropriate. After all parties involved in the fight had been heard by the panel, commissioner Everett Sanders motioned that both fighters and the referee be cleared of any collusion, that they be paid and the referee's decision be upheld. A vote of two for and two against killed that off. Chairmen Julius Covey then motioned that the purses be withheld pending a physical examination of both fighters, that the referee's ruling stand and that the contest be re-fought for the original purse. Again a two and two vote quashed that suggestion. Commissioner Sanders felt that the fight was above board, as did chief inspector Willie Ritchie (who was out of town on the day of the hearing). When asked if he would consider the possibility of both fighters going at it again for the original purse, Hollywood Legion boss Charley McDonald said that he had watched the first five rounds of the fight and that both boys were "too smart for each other". He didn't feel he could sell it again and confessed to not wanting them back. In the end it was decided that physicals be taken by both fighters and a decision made on the back of that. It was discovered that Charley Burley had a bad hand (possibly from the earlier rounds), but otherwise there was nothing untoward to report. These facts were put to the commission and a ruling was made.

"Strange things go on in the state athletic commission. The 'body' met the other day on the question of the Charley Burley-Holman Williams fight, which was called no contest, and exonerated the two on any charges of a fixed fight, but there were only two commissioners present - Chairman Jules Covey and Member Everett Sanders. Missing were John Rustigan and Ed Pencevich. Next question being was it an official ruling? Or, where was the other half of the 'body'? Sounds like a whodunit."

Lisle Shoemaker, Nevada State Journal

Even though it was only June, Charley engaged in what was his last bout for the year when he took on Bobby Birch in San Diego. The reports on the fight lead one to believe that it was not the most exciting encounter on the card.

"Charley Burley, 156, Pittsburgh laced Bobby Birch, 154, New York to a fare-thee-well in a 10-round outdoor bout at Lane Field, San Diego. Birch appeared to have too much respect for Burley and boxed almost entirely on the defensive. When Bobby did take the offensive, his efforts were of the half-hearted variety. Burley spilled the New Yorker for a nine-count in the ninth."

Ring magazine, August 1943

The reason for Charley's inactivity after the Birch fight in June was that the state athletic commission handed down a suspension after he failed to make good on a contract to fight Eddie Cerda on a 9th July card promoted by Lynn Platner in San Diego. The fight with Birch, for the same promoter, drew a mere 300 paying customers - hardly the opportunity for a dig payday. Charley must have realised that his end of a similar take would not have been worth the effort as there has been no other reason offered for his 'failure to comply'. Cerda did fight on the promotion and won a ten-round decision over Charley's substitute, Terry Gibson. Due to the suspension, and a distinct lack of interest among the ranked middleweights to oppose him elsewhere, Charley made a decision to take work at a defence plant back in Pittsburgh.

It would be nine months before Charley was back in the ring, but by March of 1944 he was back to his old form as he knocked out Bobby Berger in San Diego. Just over three weeks later he was re-matched with Aaron 'Tiger' Wade for a ten-round contest. Since the first meeting twelve months previous, the well-muscled San Franciscan had won eight of nine fights with seven knockouts. The only man to last the course in a losing effort was the respected Archie Moore.

Also based in San Diego, Archie Moore had won and lost the California State middleweight title in two battles with Jack Chase and it was Chase who was the current title-holder. The only fighter to best Wade during this period was the champion, who won over ten rounds in San Francisco. Chase, who appeared to have something of the devil about him, was also responsible for shooting the 'Tiger' in December of 1943. Chase pleaded it was accidental and Wade was able to resume his ring career in February of 1944, when he scored a second-round knock-out of Alonzo Williams. Charley then positioned himself front and centre for a title fight with the state champion with a repeat ten-round victory over Aaron Wade at the Coliseum in San Diego.

The state middleweight title had something of a reputation and was labelled an 'ill-fitting crown'. It had been passed around for the previous 18 months and at various times had adorned the brow of Archie Moore, Eddie Booker and of course Jack Chase. Despite the fact that Chase had beaten Eddie Booker, Leon Zorrita, Archie Moore and Lloyd Marshall in fights for the Californian championship, Charley knew from his previous encounter with the reigning champion that he had the skills and punch to win the title.

After the first meeting between the two it was difficult for Tommy O'Loughlin to agree terms with the champion. Though confident in his own abilities, Chase wanted suitable financial reward for risking his belt and again concessions had to be made by Charley and his promoter. At last, after much hard work, a fight for the state championship had been made. So, 14 months after the initial meeting, the two met at the Hollywood Stadium on a warm Monday night in April. Charley Burley would get the chance to win a title that meant a little more than the 'Coloured' welterweight championship belt he still held and he meant to take full advantage of the opportunity. Both he and Jack Chase showed the Californian fight fans exactly what they were made of in a fight that more than lived up to the championship billing.

Despite a six-pound disadvantage in the weight, the challenger was determined to give his all for the belt and it wasn't too long before questions were being asked of him and his desire to succeed. In a fight that was described by one reporter as "fast and damaging" Charley floored Chase for a nine-count in the fourth and hurt him again just as the bell ended the round. Chase showed determination to match his undoubted skills, as he came back in the fifth and sixth rounds by clever use of jab-and-move tactics, refusing at any time during those six minutes to 'mix it up'. His confidence restored and his head cleared, the champion pressed the action in the seventh, managing to stagger Charley on two separate occasions, forcing him to clinch. Sensing a revival in his fortunes, Chase stepped up the pace again in the eighth round forcing Charley back towards the ropes where a blinding exchange of punches had the crowd roaring their appreciation. Another furious exchange resulted in Chase coming off second-best as he was caught with a couple of powerful shots that dipped his knees and cut him over the eye.

As the ninth stanza got under way it was obvious that Chase had not fully recovered from the bombs that Burley had detonated on his chin at the end of the previous round. Sensing his opponent's reluctance to meet in centre ring, Charley launched into a furious attack pummelling away at the groggy champion's jaw with a succession of murderous right-hand punches. The fusillade stopped only when Jack Chase pitched face-first to the canvas, where referee Abe Roth counted him out.

Stopped for only the second time in 75 fights, and for the first time in over 40 fights and close to eight years of competition, Jack Chase would undoubtedly request a rematch and a chance to regain his title from Burley, just as he had done so from Archie Moore.

"When Tommy O'Loughlin was here a few weeks ago with his heavy-weight Elmer Ray he was telling me about the trouble he was having trying to get a title fight for Charley Burley with Jack Chase, then holder of the State middleweight championship.

"If we ever get a crack at Chase's title, Burley will knock him out [for] sure," predicted O'Loughlin. He added that Burley was an extremely temperamental fighter. There are times when he acts as if he didn't care a rap whether he won or lost. But put him in front of an opponent whom he doesn't like and he's dynamite. "And Burley doesn't like Chase," said O'Loughlin. That's why I'm so certain he will cool Chase If they ever meet."

Alan Ward, Oakland Tribune

As the new California State Middleweight Champion, Charley Burley had plenty to be proud of. But, rather than let the fact inflate his head to the size of some of the egos parading around the Californian fight circuit, he went straight back to his 'day job' at the aircraft factory in San Diego.

In a lengthy conversation for Canadian boxing historian, Norm Meekison's Hall of Fame interviews, legendary boxing trainer, Eddie Futch told how Charley's next fight came about. Where Mr. Futch heard this version of events is unknown, but over the years it has been told so many times as to help add to the Burley legend.

"Hollywood Legion Stadium had a main event featuring Archie Moore and some opponent, I can't think of his name. The opponent failed to pass the physical at noon and the fight was due to go on at seven o'clock that night. So, they've got no main event because one of the fella's didn't pass. So, they got on the telephone and they called Burley, his wife answered and said that he was at work. She gave them the telephone number and they called there. They let them speak to Burley and they asked if Burley would come and box Archie and substitute for the guy that didn't pass the examination. Burley said yes. So, he finished up, went home, got his gear, got on a bus, rode 125 miles to Hollywood Legion Stadium, got there in time to be examined, get on his gear and go out there and give Archie Moore a lickin'."

Eddie Futch

Archie had an ego the size of the state and although he was highly regarded as a fighter, few of his opponents or contemporaries cared for his cocky attitude, although this would later change. In demeanour Archibald Lee Wright was the total opposite to Charley Burley, with total confidence in ability present in both, but utter boastfulness evident only in the gregarious Mr. Moore.

171

Arguably, Archie had much to be proud of. He had, like many other black fighters, come up from abject poverty and found a niche for himself in the world of the professional prizefighter. By 1944, Archie Moore was on the way back from an enforced retirement due to an ulcer operation. The ten-month hiatus in 1941 obviously served Archie well, as he returned to defeat previous conqueror Shorty Hogue. He had also beaten Jack Chase and had contested a second draw with Eddie Booker. The dangerous San Jose fighter had also knocked Archie out in eight rounds just four months prior to Charley Burley's meeting with Moore.

Jim Murray, co-founder of Sports Illustrated and writer for Time magazine and the Los Angeles Times, amongst others, drew a fascinating comparison between Archie and a mechanic after watching the Old Mongoose dismantle an opponent.

> "The early rounds of an Archie Moore fight always remind me of a guy opening the hood of an engine and exploring around inside for the weaker spots. Only, when he finds these, he doesn't repair them. He makes them worse. It's a trick a lot of mechanics have, but with Mr. Moore it's a high art form. A loose bolt here, a slick valve there, and by the time Arch has got through tinkering, the transmission falls out."

Jim Murray

While Archie was arguably the greatest ring mechanic ever, when he looked across the ring at Charley Burley that night at the Hollywood Legion Stadium, he may have seen a gunslinger looking back at him. As Archie remembers, Charley had, "the cold, grey eyes of a killer." Adding that Charley's stare could get "colder than an Eskimo's pad."

> "When you looked at Charley you knew you were in trouble. They [his eyes] had a bluey-grey colour. Very light."

Bobby Lippi

Julia Burley would tell you that Charley's eyes were hazel. A colour that seemingly has shades of blue, green and even brown. Whatever the shade, Charley's eyes, by all accounts had this look about them. A look that told you he meant business in the ring or out. A stare that fixed upon you and refused to budge until you could look no more. In his second book, 'Any Boy Can', Archie remembered Charley well, both in appearance and ability.

> "I remember how strange Burley looked - so youthful, so handsome - trying to look older by pencilling a thin moustache between his lip and his nose. His thin legs, however, reminded me of a stork.
>
> Fighting Charley Burley was almost inhuman, because he kept his punches coming at you like a riveting gun beats a tattoo on a rivet. He was a human machine gun the way he kept those punches spouting out, and nearly as dangerous."

Archie Moore

Once he had Archie Moore in his sights it was game over for the San Diego fighter. Down early in the first round from a smashing right-hand punch, Archie knew then that he was in for a rough night. The same punch dropped him for an eight-count in the third and Charley turned the trick again in the fourth, this time for a count of seven. Moore thought he had Charley cornered at one point and was looking to land with a deciding punch of his own.

A middleweight Moore had yet to develop his famous 'cross-arm' defence, although he would cover up crab-like from hooks and swings, and he could still be hit; especially with a straight right. Charley Burley was not only adept at delivering a text-book right-hand punch, he also had his own variation which arced in, over the opponent's guard and lead shoulder, landing flush on the side of the head. Even if the opponent had his chin tucked in behind his shoulder, the punch would connect up high around the ear, scrambling the senses of any fighter that could not get out of the way. Each time Charley hurt Moore and it looked as though he might go down again, he'd grab hold of Archie and hold him up.

> "This [the fourth round] was the last time that Moore was 'on the verge' until the last minute of the tenth round, in which he was punched around the ring and in a groggy condition at the final bell. Archie found Burley an elusive target rarely being able to tag Charley with a left jab, or finding a place to park a damaging left-hook.

173

The San Diego boxer was a sorry-looking warrior at the finish, his left eye being closed and the whole left side of his face badly swollen. Burley, scaling 155, was credited with nine of the rounds."

Ring Magazine, July 1944

Despite a six-pound advantage in the weight, Archie could do little with his adversary. The boxing lesson stayed with him for life and eighteen years later, in his syndicated newspaper column, Archie told the story of his meeting with Charley Burley.

"He was the best fighter I ever fought, and the best fighter I ever saw. I can remember him to this day. He was a grey-eyed, light-skinned Negro. And the way he walked and held his head and talked you knew he was something else.

I was getting along pretty well when they made the Burley match for me in '44. Looking back on it, I recall not being too impressed by Charley, of course. I knew he had to be a better-than-good fighter by the way he'd been scaring everybody to death on the coast. There had been stories about how he had chased heavyweights out of the gym, and stiffened sparring partners with the big training gloves. But you must take into consideration that I've never been burdened with false modesty.

The thing that sticks most in my mind about Burley was the way he defied gravity. He could lean way back on his heels and just make you miss. Well, you'd figure, this man's way off balance; he can't break an egg from that position. Then you'd get the surprise of your life. Charley Burley could knock you dead from that position, and he could do it with either hand.

He had me on the floor many times, but more than that he outboxed me. That's something I couldn't understand, because nobody had ever done that before. And no one, Incidentally, has done it since.

Afterwards my trainer told a writer that 'Charley Burley didn't just beat Archie Moore he beat him, beat him!' That remark hurts to this day. I never got another chance at Charley. Oh, I don't mean be was ducking me. He just got fed up with fighting for peanuts and he dropped out of sight."

Archie Moore

The respect, it appears, was mutual. Although Charley had a good deal less to say on the subject.

"He was a good puncher. We were both 'bobbers and weavers'. I beat him by just staying close."

Charley Burley

Charley's manager at the time, Travis Hatfield, a tall and rangy guy who always wore a Stetson hat, was a little concerned about the fight, especially as he had to be out of town on the night. He knew of Archie Moore's reputation, but he need not have been worried about Charley Burley.

"I heard this Travis guy saying he went to Mexico with a fighter on Saturday, came back Sunday, called Charley and asked him how his fight with Archie Moore went. Charley joked that Archie had knocked him out in the second round. He then bought a paper and read how Charley had scored three knockdowns and won a very easy decision over Moore."

Blackie Nelson

While the amiable Travis may have been Charley's manager of note, in reality it was his older and more experienced brother Carl who held the reigns.

"My brother handled him, then he gave him to me. So, I sold him twice for $5,000 each time and then got him back. I couldn't get him a fight."

Carl Hatfield

Babe McCoy had close ties to underworld figures and was associated with Mickey Cohen and others. It is fairly common knowledge that

McCoy had a hand in many 'pre-arranged' fights during his promotional career with his reach extending far beyond his Los Angeles base.

The story that Eddie Futch tells about the circumstances around the Archie Moore fight is obviously not true. After Charley relieved Jack Chase of the middleweight title, matchmaker Charley McDonald was keen to get the new champ in with Archie for a headliner on the 'Service Sports Fund inc.' benefit show at the Legion Stadium for April 28th. This ties in with Howard Branson's version of the build-up to the Moore-Burley fight. He recalls how Frank Matulla, head of the local teamsters union and a connected guy, had some action going on the fight and was concerned that Burley had not been seen in the gym for two weeks since signing to meet Archie. Branson also remembers how Matulla, in a conversation with Charley, expressed his concern at the lack of preparation saying that he would 'pray for him' in the fight with Moore. Burley's apparent response was that there was no need to pray for him and that Matulla should pray for Archie Moore. Charley's oft-times manager Carl Hatfield also supports the notion that the fight was indeed a scheduled event.

> "So, my friend in LA, Babe McCoy, who controlled the boxing game in LA, I brought him [Charley] to Babe. I cashed in $500 in war bonds and brought him to Babe. I told Babe I'd give him half interest because I couldn't get him a fight. He was the matchmaker for five arenas. Babe told all the fighters, 'You gotta fight Burley if you want to fight.'
>
> Burley put Archie in the hospital for three days."
>
> **Carl Hatfield**

The story told by Eddie Futch is the kind that grows up around the careers of old-time fighters as quickly as an entourage forms around a new champion. The facts are that the respected 'Knockout' magazine printed a front cover promoting the fight several days in advance. Charley Burley was Archie Moore's original opponent for the meeting at the Legion Stadium. Contemporary press reports also site Charley and Moore as a scheduled match.

> "Hollywood Legion Stadium has a pip coming up Friday - Charley Burley Vs Archie Moore. They'll meet at 162 pound, so Burley's

newly acquired state middleweight crown wont be at stake. Moore chilled Roman Starr in his last out, while Burley took away Jack Chase's 160 pound belt away in his most recent appearance hereabouts.

Babe McCoy would like to lure Jake LaMotta from the East for an Olympic special with Burley. It would do terrific business."

Al Wolf, Los Angeles Times

Knockouts of Al Gilbert in San Diego and Frankie Nelson in Hollywood prompted the Ring magazine to cite the year 1944 as one of Charley's best to date. The Nelson bout in particular was highlighted by some destructive punching by Charley who would have had Nelson out in the first had it not been for a judgement call by referee Reggie Gilmore as to whether or not Nelson had the required body parts off the canvas just as he lowered his arm for the fateful ten count. The decision by the referee to allow the bout to continue resulted in a one-sided contest, with Charley missing wildly at times during the ensuing six rounds of fighting as he attempted to finish off his tough rival. Nelson was down again for a nine count in the fifth as Charley continued to press for the stoppage. Nelson was sent back to the ropes by an overhand right to the jaw and Charley moved in for the finish in the seventh round. Hanging limply like a rag doll over the top strand, the brave Bostonian was rescued by Gilmore before Charley could add to the two knockdowns already scored. Matchmaker Charley McDonald attempted to sign Lloyd Marshall for the winner of the bout prior to the commencement of battle. The Sacramento-based fighter was interested, but only if the winner was Nelson.

Elmer 'Violent' Ray, a black heavyweight with a fearsome reputation, was being managed and promoted by Tommy O'Loughlin. Charley was back with the Minneapolis manager and promoter as Carl Hatfield had again sold his 'contract' for $5,000. Charley agreed to sparring sessions with the murderous punching heavyweight, but did little to further his cause during one of the subsequent sessions.

The 'Violent' tag did not get pinned upon Elmer because of his silky boxing skills, as he was one of the most destructive punchers in the heavyweight division. Unbeaten since Turkey Thompson stopped him in a round in Los Angeles in August of 1943, Ray had close to 20 knockouts in 30 fights. He was definitely the kind of guy you did not want to trade punches with unless you had to. As one of the sparring sessions progressed it became apparent that Ray wanted to give the spectators, who usually crowded the gym to watch Charley work, something to talk about. Elmer began to treat the spar as a contest and even though he knew that Charley was only weighing around 150-something pounds, he tried to score some points by attempting to separate Charley's head from his shoulders. With the slightest of head, body and shoulder movements Charley caused his sparring partner to miss repeatedly.

> "Charley was so smooth and had the best head movement of anybody I've ever seen. It was practically impossible to hit him solid. He seemed to anticipate every move that somebody was going to make. He was just like a cloud out there and he could punch like a fool. I know there's a few fighters that he let go the distance."

Blackie Nelson

When you consider that a lightweight couldn't catch him with a hard shot, it is little wonder that Charley never worried too much about heavyweights and their power. Obviously Charley didn't want to get hit clean by this particular heavyweight, but as a result of his defensive tactics he unintentionally began to make Ray look foolish as each time one of the heavyweight's shots missed, Charley was right there in front of him allowing him to try again. Elmer, sensing the reaction of the onlookers and feeling increasingly embarrassed, shoved Charley backwards, through the ropes and on to the ring apron. Charley, who was not wearing headgear (he rarely did for sparring sessions), got to his feet and dusted himself off before continuing. A definite buzz went around the jam-packed gym as a crowd gathered around the ring to observe what was going to happen next. Managers, trainers and fighters stopped what they were doing and stood silently awaiting the seemingly inevitable fireworks.

Most people that knew Charley also knew that he would not let anyone, regardless of size or reputation, make a fool of him. Ray, sensing that he had Charley rattled met him at ring centre and unloaded one of his patented bombs at Charley's jaw. Charley slipped the shot over his right shoulder while simultaneously delivering his own right to the point of Ray's chin. When he woke up several minutes later, Elmer Ray found that Charley was still in the ring waiting for him to make eye contact with him. When he did, Charley pointed his right glove at the 200-pound-plus heavyweight as if to say 'Don't mess with me.' His message received and understood Charley left the ring to hit the showers.

The whole gym started talking excitedly about what they had just seen. Essentially a heavy welterweight had just knocked a ranked heavyweight contender absolutely stone cold with one punch. This was a guy that would go on to beat Jersey Joe Walcott in a quest for a title shot of his own. Afterwards Elmer Ray admitted that Charley Burley hit harder than any heavyweight he had ever faced in the ring and, as far as he was aware, any other ranked heavyweight out there. Ray complained to Tommy O'Loughlin and intimated that it came down to a choice between him and Charley. Fights, and therefore paydays, were harder to come by for Burley, so again he found himself passed along.

In later years Charley and his family kept a dog, (actually they had a succession of canines over the years, all with the same name), Charley named him Elmer. Whether or not this is related to this particular incident or not, Julia Burley is unsure.

Charley's daughter, Angie, recalls a similar tale about her dad and Jersey Joe Walcott. The veteran heavyweight experienced the same fate when he too tried to make Charley look a fool in the gym. As can be appreciated, it is difficult to substantiate such stories, but contemporary newspaper pieces report that the Walcott camp employed Charley - along with Charley Banks and Johnny Wilson - when the heavyweight was in training for his June 1949 title fight against Ezzard Charles. Banks and Burley had both been in the ring with Charles, so it is easy to see the logic of Walcott's handlers. The same reports also indicate that Burley, for some reason, was 'released' after a short spell. What is known for sure however is that Charley Burley punched hard enough to knock out heavyweights and had demonstrated this ability on several occasions. When one considers that Charley always wore big sixteen-ounce gloves, yet was still able to chill big guys like Elmer Ray and Jersey Joe, it is little wonder that none of the higher-ranked fighters, and of course their managers, shied away. Historian Howard Branson, who recounted the Elmer Ray sparring incident, remembers that few were in a hurry to share a ring with the hard-punching fighter.

"He (Burley) would walk into a gymnasium and ranking fighters, particularly heavyweights would run to the showers so they wouldn't have to spar with him."

Howard Branson

179

Eight weeks after the Frankie Nelson fight Charley met previous opponent Gene Buffalo in San Francisco. Buffalo once ran around with the singer Ethel Waters and, according to Howard Branson, is supposed to have fleeced her for thousands of dollars. Despite numerous fights in very good company, Gene was not in the same class as Charley Burley, even if his new management George Moore and Henry Armstrong thought differently. Charley appeared to be the betting favourite, but Young Gene was 3-1 to go the distance with local press reports describing him as; "fast on his feet" and "capable of escaping danger." The same reporter (Will Connolly of the San Francisco Chronicle) also described Charley as "something of a hitter" and added that the local fans were "curious to see the man who knocked Chase on the seat of his blue silk pantaloons." adding that "any man who knocks him [Chase] out cold must be somebody indeed."

> "Burley had small opportunity to display his true worth against Gene Buffalo here. The Buffalo made Burley and himself look bad by his clown tactics, although most ringsiders agreed Burley throws a mighty punch with his right."

> **Will Connolly, San Francisco Chronicle**

A clubbing right-hand to Gene's jaw sent him reeling back to the ropes where Charley pinned him back with a sustained attack. The lack of resistance from Buffalo was enough to prompt referee Toby Irwin to rescue the Philadelphian in the fifth. Those curious to attend witnessed a demonstration of the power that had flattened Chase, but not everyone was impressed.

> "Burley missed dozens of haymakers in the Buffalo fiasco because his victim wouldn't stand still. The California middleweight champ strikes us as being a glorified street brawler. Every punch is a swing from the sidewalk. He doesn't punch straight. How he managed to tag the nifty Chase is beyond us. We'd hate to be in the way of one of Burley's whistlers, though. Even when he misses the breeze from his glove clears the ring of smoke."

> **Will Connolly, San Francisco Chronicle**

180

This latest stoppage boosted Charley to an impressive tally of five early finishes in seven starts and set up a return bout with Jack Chase for the State middleweight championship at the Civic Arena in San Francisco for September. With the title on the line and with Chase also rated with the top ten middleweights, Charley could not afford to slip up against the slick-boxing former champion.

Chase had been training harder than ever and was extremely fit. The local press maintained that he was looking like the fighter that beat both Eddie Booker and Archie Moore in previous title fights. Chase himself informed the press that he was feeling in top form as his training was winding down.

"If I lose this one it won't be because I'm not fit, but I still say I wasn't right when I lost to Burley recently."

Jack Chase

The state champion may have been telling the truth as he had a tonsillectomy to recover from and he was also flattened in sparring by turkey Thompson whilst preparing for the first fight with Charley.

Tommy O'Loughlin was causing a stir amongst the media as he felt that the fix might be in and that Chase couldn't lose. Prior to signing for the title fight with Charley Burley on the 11th September Chase had been signed for a fight with Lloyd Marshall on the 30th September. O'Loughlin suspected that such a big fight was pre-emptive given the fact that Chase first had to get past his man. Something he had not managed in two previous encounters. Charley Burley's biggest concern had to be the niggling hand injuries that were bothering him again after his recent run of knockout victories.

Eddie Muller, reporting from ringside, tells the story of an exciting fight that was to be the final meeting of these two great middleweights.

"Charley Burley retained his California middleweight boxing championship by defeating clever boxing Jack Chase in the main event at the Civic Auditorium last night. Burley won by a technical knockout in the twelfth round. Referee Frank Carter, judges Toby Irwin and Joe Gorman.

181

Round One

Both did plenty of left hand jabbing and blocking too, in a round which wound up fairly even. Chase kept away from Burley's right and only near the end of the session did Charley tag him with a right which landed high on the side of the head.

Round Two

Chase did a nice job with his educated left in this session. He brought blood from his foe's nose with straight jabs and kept Burley off balance most of the time. In the last minute Chase followed a stiff jab with a right cross which thudded against the champion's jaw.

Round Three

Burley found it difficult to nail Chase with any kind of solid blow. Jack, moving fast on his feet, got under Burley's leads or pulled away to counter punch neatly with his left. There was little infighting or clinching.

Round Four

Chase employed a two-fisted attack to take the fourth by a comfortable margin. Twice he steadied himself and scored with lefts and rights to Charley's face. Near the end of the round he deftly side-stepped as Burley, trying to land a right, sailed through the second and third strand of the ropes.

Round Five

Burley got an even break by getting in a number of jabs at the outset of the round and then burying a left hook wrist deep into Chase's midsection. The blow hurt Jack and the latter had to bring forth all his cunning to escape a terrific right which Burley missed by a whisker.

Round Six

Burley, the belter, found his range and levelled his heavy guns. He uncorked a left to Chase's jaw that staggered Jack near the outset of the round. He tried to level with right crosses but Chase got away. Again a left hook hurt Jack. A right also caught him squarely on the chin before the bell.

Round Seven

Chase went to boxing and had the better of a somewhat tame canto. Both appeared to be waiting for openings and, as a result, neither got in any clean blows.

Round Eight

By stepping swiftly about his foe, Chase gave the fans a thrill as he jabbed consistently with his left and at the same time made Burley miss with his well-loaded punches. However, towards the close of the round, Burley managed to get in a right but Chase took the blow without flinching.

Round Nine

After trailing going into the final minute, Burley whistled over a right and left hook, which caught Chase flush. Jack took a stiff right earlier but also retaliated with two short rights to Burley's jaw, which set the latter back on his heels.

Round Ten

Chase was too careful in this session. Burley landed what clean blows were scored. Burley received a slight cut under his left eye. A left into the body didn't do Chase much good.

Round Eleven

Burley came in with a rush to out-score Chase. Instead of Jack getting in the lefts it was Burley who did the most effective work with this weapon. Chase seemed content to keep out of range, as he backpedaled at a fairly fast pace.

Round Twelve

Burley unloaded everything he had and splattered Chase to the floor three times. He started off by digging a left hook to Jack's body. Then he chased him to the ropes and showered him with a volley of lefts and rights. Jack took them and then went through the ropes after receiving another barrage. He took a count of seven. Two rights to the jaw put Chase down for eight and when another right floored him referee Frankie Carter stopped it."

Referee Frankie Carter raised the bruised and aching hand of Charley Burley in victory, a hand that was yet again damaged during the champion's do-or-die assault upon his game challenger.

Jack Chase would continue to fight for another four years after this third loss to Charley Burley, taking part in close to 30 more fights. He would win the California State light-heavyweight title in a battle with Watson Jones at the end of 1944 and remained a top ranked fighter until Archie Moore knocked him out in nine rounds in 1947. Chase then abandoned his successful cleaning and landscaping business in California (which he once used to supplement his ring earnings) and moved to Portland, Oregon where he trained a number of fighters. He finally hung up the gloves in 1948 and made some efforts to give back to the community by carrying out a number of voluntary roles for those less fortunate.

Another opportunity for a payday materialised in 1949 when the former state champion played a corner man in the classic boxing movie 'The Setup' with Robert Ryan. The movie's climactic battle between 'Stoker' Thompson (played by Ryan), and Tiger Nelson is regarded as one of the better fight scenes in any boxing movie. The 'connected' Tiger Nelson was played by Hal Fieberling who used to be a main-event heavyweight on the West Coast. Hal's buddy, Archie Moore, remembered him as "a 200-pounder, big and strong, and a real good puncher." One day Hal worked out with Burley.

"I was never so humiliated in my life. That Burley was a freak. He knew Just what he wanted to make you do and he went ahead and made you do it. When I crawled out of that ring after that work-out

I went back to where the lockers where and I sat down and cried like a baby. To think that a little guy like that could make such a fool out of me."

Hal Fieberling

Here comes trouble

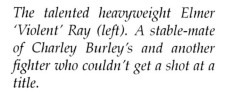

The talented heavyweight Elmer 'Violent' Ray (left). A stable-mate of Charley Burley's and another fighter who couldn't get a shot at a title.

Jack Chase (above) the only real killer on the Black Murderers' Row.

Aaron 'Little Tiger' Wade (left). Thrice a victim of Charley Burley in the ring and once a shooting victim of Jack Chase in a bar.

Chapter Ten

Back to the 'Burgh

With his recent successes, Charley was now firmly entrenched among the top five middleweights in the world. He was unbeaten in two years and 14 fights and had engaged in two winning bouts for the California state title. Unfortunately for him, and many others like him, all world titles remained frozen for the duration of the war. But, even if a title shot were available in the middleweight division or the welterweight class, a weight Charley could still make, it would have been of little use as his hands were again proving troublesome and as a result he would remain inactive for close to seven months.

By March 1945 and with his hands now apparently healed, Charley was signed to fight Joe Carter in San Francisco. Charley had started the year rated behind Jake LaMotta and Holman Williams for Tony Zale's middleweight title and was aware that he had to beat the dangerous New Yorker in order to stay in contention. Periods of inactivity due to injury and managerial conflicts had hampered Charley in the past and he couldn't afford any more setbacks.

The 24-year-old Carter, who was an orphan at nine, took up boxing for recreational purposes when he was studying to be an electrician at trade school. Though beginning his amateur career relatively late at 16, he amassed a record of 70 wins and 10 losses, winning a junior diamond belt tournament at welterweight. With over 50 fights in only two years of professional boxing, Carter had mixed in good class, beating Ruben Shank, Wild Bill McDowell, Van McNutt and 'Cocoa' Kid while losing on points to Lloyd Marshall and drawing with Holman Williams and Jose Basora. Carter's biggest win locally had been a ten-round victory over Aaron 'Tiger' Wade.

Carter's smooth-flowing, fast-punching style reminded some of an aggressive Jack Chase. With good boxing skills and fast, powerful combinations, he was difficult to hit and usually won his bouts by sheer volume of leather landed. Observers of the training sessions held at Newman's gym in town were very impressed with the amazing amount of work that Carter was getting through and many felt that he had the

187

speed, movement and fitness to trouble Charley Burley.

An extensive build-up for both fighters by the newspapers, and of course their managers, assured promoter Benny Ford of a sell-out crowd for the event at the Civic Auditorium. His only problem before fight-time was the insistence of Joe Carter's manager, George Winn, that judges be used for the fight. In New York judges were used for all major fights and with Burley and Carter both rated in the top five, George Winn insisted that this was indeed a major fight. Winn protested that his demands were not based upon recent results in the Bay Area where, it was contended by San Francisco News sports editor Bud Spencer, there hadn't been a major fight contested during the previous six months without the interference of mobsters. Spencer knew that Charley Burley was no dry tank artist and had been informed that Carter was also of sufficient moral standing so as to make an honest go of it.

With the undercard in place, Ford obtained the services of Joe Gorman as referee and Frankie Brown and Toby Irwin as judges for the main event. With close to $14,000 in tickets sold for the eagerly anticipated match-up and the box-office still open for business the day before the fight, a new wrinkle developed. The State Boxing Commissioner William P. Haughton threatened to stop the match based on evidence that Joe Carter was practically blind in his right eye. George Winn admitted that his charge did have deficient eyesight, but had been that way since he started out as an amateur. He argued that despite this slight handicap Carter had still been successful in 45 of 54 professional bouts. With ten percent of the night's profits going to the Charley Paddock Memorial Fund to supply much needed sports equipment for servicemen all over the world, Haughton was out-voted by his fellow commissioners and the match went ahead

"To those who enjoy the art of boxing, the Charley Burley-Joe Carter bout on Monday night was a real treat. Students of the ring say the pair showed them more stuff than they've had the good fortune of seeing in many years. Jerry Collins, an old pal of Johnny McCarthy went so far as to say that Burley is the greatest middle-weight he has seen since Stanley Ketchel. "He does everything for a purpose," explained Jerry, "even if he couldn't punch he'd still be a great fighter in my book."

Burley's lack of speed afoot doesn't handicap him. As a matter of fact his shuffle-in style proves deceptive because he can body feint without changing his stance.

His movements appear slow but the fellow seldom makes a mistake. When he turns slightly to one side for a right-hand delivery he can get his right foot in front of him in a split second. In this position he has the full weight of his power behind those punishing wallops."

Eddie Muller, San Francisco Examiner

Reporter Eddie Muller was obviously impressed by Charley's contribution to the evening's entertainment, but Joe Carter's skills were also acknowledged.

"You can't take any credit away from Carter, despite the fact that he lost the decision. He has plenty of ring class. Like Burley, he knows the value of feinting for openings.

However, he wasn't able to carry the fight continuously because Burley was murderous with his left hook to the body, used as a counter blow.

Burley doesn't have to hit you on the jaw or chin to hurt you. The punches which land high on the head, or even on the shoulders for that matter, shake you up from stem to stern.

The knockdown which Burley scored in the third round was the result of a short left hook to the face. He clouted Carter square on other occasions, but the New York gamester managed to remain upright. He escaped much punishment by skilfully bobbing under or ducking away from those terrific shots Burley threw."

Eddie Muller, San Francisco Examiner

With only the second, fourth and tenth rounds showing anything like an even match, Charley dominated the proceedings and dropped his fleet-footed opponent in the first and the third with those thunderous left hooks to the jaw. Content to let Carter box on the move for the first two minutes of practically every one of the ten rounds, Charley stalked his man until he stopped moving then let his most hurtful punches fly and came away with a unanimous decision over the highly-fancied speedster. Referee Joe Gorman gave the bout to Charley by a score of 58-52, while judges Frankie Brown and Toby Irwin had it for the winner by four and five points respectively.

The win proved that Charley's boxing skills had not suffered too much through his enforced lay-off and that his hands appeared to be holding up OK. However, one reporter at ringside noted that Charley had thrown exactly two left hooks to the head during the entire fight, landing and scoring knockdowns with both of them. The rest of his hooking attack was confined to the body and this was seen as a sign that not all was well with the injury-prone mitt.

> "I was overseas when Charley fought a kid called Joe Carter in San Francisco in 1945. They told me that Carter, who I believe then was undefeated, could really box and Charley made him look like an amateur – won going away. I asked Charley about it, but being the gentleman he only spoke well of Carter. I never once ever heard Charley talk bad of another fighter. He was a fine gentleman. He is still, in my humble opinion, the greatest. Along with being a perfect gentleman, no trash-talking smart-alex (sic"
>
> **Blackie Nelson**

For their efforts Charley Burley and Joe Carter each earned 25% of the $10,000 net amount made on the gate. With a ringside collection raising close to $1,500 the evening's cause did rather well. Pleased at the turnout and with Burley's performance, Benny Ford proposed a meeting between the transplanted Pittsburgher and Holman Williams for a slot he had available on March 26th. Charley was keen on another meeting with his old foe and agreed in principle to the match. Ford now needed to iron out the details between the fighters, but before he could get the fight signed, a dark cloud appeared on the horizon for Charley Burley.

After two years of living on the West Coast, Charley was drawn back to Pittsburgh by news of his mother's poor health. Charley's younger sister, Zella, travelled out to San Diego to visit Charley and Julia to give them the news. Charley, naturally, was very concerned for his mother and decided to move back to Pittsburgh immediately. On his arrival back in his home city he discovered that his mother was not as sick as the rest of the family would have them believe.

"They kept writing him saying 'mom's old, she's got a bad heart, you gotta come back.' We came back home because he was the only boy and they kept writing him sad stories."

Julia Burley

Julia thinks that because Charley had a regular job at the defence plant, was fighting on a fairly regular basis and was also California State champion, his sisters thought that he was making more than he could spend. They wanted to share in some of his supposed wealth and started playing on their mother's poor health to lure their successful brother back to the Smoky City. Charley was relieved to find his mother was not too ill after all, but neither he, nor Julia, was happy that they had been taken away from sunny California. Julia always thought that her family would make San Diego their permanent home.

"If it hadn't have been for Charley's sisters we would still be there. Charley's sister [Zella], came to visit me, she liked it so much she came back to Pittsburgh and moved to California and stayed there."

Julia Burley

Now that it looked as though they were going to be in Pittsburgh for the foreseeable future, Charley needed a place for he and his family to stay. Initially he, Julia and Angie would stay at his mother's place off Crawford Street, but this soon became a problem for Julia. Charley's mother was largely bed-ridden and was using a walking stick to get about the house and as a result was not as able to do the usual daily cleaning routine. While she did have daughters that maybe should have helped her out, one of them living right next-door, Julia remembers that her mother-in-law transferred much of the housekeeping chores to her:

"I left home. I said 'I'm leaving, I'm not taking it!' His sisters were there everyday with their babies and she had dogs, she had a bird, she had a chicken. I said 'I'm not taking it anymore.' I went up to Ms. McKnight's because I didn't want to go back home to my mother with Angie."

Julia Burley

191

Ms. McKnight's son Bobby had been a pal of Charley's for many years and had worked with Charley for his fights in Pittsburgh and both families knew each other very well. The McKnights had a boarding house on the Hill and Julia had no hesitation in going up there. Upon his return home that day, Charley found his wife and daughter gone and his mother in a foul mood. When he went up to see Julia and attempt to straighten things out, he was given an ultimatum, either to remain with Julia or to return to his mother's house and live there.

Julia asked young Bobby Lippi to go to Charley's mother's house and pick up her things, which she had already packed, and bring them to the boarding house. Bobby took a Jitney to collect the bags and suffered a tirade of foul-mouthed abuse from Charley's mother who swiped at him with her walking stick every time he went past. On returning to Ms. McKnight's he found that Charley was getting things straight with Julia and that he would have to go back to Ms. Burley's with the bags. Knowing Charley's mother's mood, Bobby decided to hedge his bets and play it safe so as to save more walking and carrying.

"He [Charley] gave me two more dollars for a Jitney – I went down to the corner and put them inside the numbers joint and I went back for them later."

Bobby Lippi

The housing situation may have been resolved for the moment, but the time may also have been right for Charley and his family to have a place of their own. Charley's mother's house, off Crawford Avenue was clean, but it belonged in another era.

"You had to go through the alley, through that funny little archway, into the courtyard. I thought 'oh my god', it was another world! That's why when I went into the house I was surprised. Nothing matched. There weren't two things the same. She had an old chair – other people's furniture. But, it was clean."

Bobby Lippi

"She didn't have no money though, that's why [nothing matched].
Boy it was clean! She scrubbed and she cleaned and she wanted you
to do the same. It was a good, brick house. There was the apartment building on one side, her daughter had the other house."

Julia Burley

Eventually Charley secured a house on Manilla Street, off Bedford
Avenue and only two blocks up from Crawford Street. Charley could still
be close to his ailing mother and Julia would only have to cook and clean
for her own family and not the entire Burley brood. Now that he and his
family were more settled, Charley was able to concentrate more fully on
his boxing career.

Four months after the victory over Joe Carter, Charley met old foe
Holman Williams for what was the seventh and final meeting between
the two. Charley was ahead in the series three to two, with the one no
contest. As a result of hand injuries and the move back to Pittsburgh,
Charley had contested only three bouts in 12 months prior to the Williams
fight in Buffalo and it showed. If you were going to fight Holman
Williams you had better be prepared or he would take advantage of any
weakness that you had. Williams, employing his usual defensive style,
gave Charley the first couple of rounds. He succeeded in keeping out of
the way of Charley's vaunted power-punches and was able to eke out a
close 12-round decision. The scoring, in rounds, was seen as 9-3, 7-5 and
8-4 with all three arbiters casting for Williams. That made the series even
at three wins each, with one no contest.

After his third victory over Charley, Holman Williams went on to beat
Bert Lytell in New Orleans and Archie Moore in Baltimore, both over the
ten-round distance. 1945 was to be a fairly successful year for Williams,
despite getting off to a bad start by losing to Cocoa Kid in New York. In
fourteen meetings Holman Williams managed only three wins against
the Hartford-based Cuban. In this, his 14th year as a professional fighter,
Williams won 13 of 16 fights, with losses to 'Cocoa' Kid and Archie
Moore and a draw with Bert Lytell. In the second fight of the year with
Moore, also in Baltimore, Williams was stopped for only the second time
in his career up to that point, going out in the eleventh round.

For what were the remaining three years of a fantastic career it was
largely a downhill ride for the talented Holman Williams. Although he
still had enough to beat Aaron 'Tiger' Wade, dynamite-punching Bob

193

Satterfield, Deacon Johnny Brown, Henry Hall and O'Neil Bell amongst others, he would lose 11 of his remaining 22 fights. The years began to catch up with him and his defensive style started to suffer due to a decline in his reflexes. He lost to Bert Lytell and Jose Basora twice, Jake LaMotta, Marcel Cerdan, Henry Brimm, Sam Baroudi, and Jean Walzak.

His career ended in June 1948 when he was beaten over ten rounds in Trinidad by Gentle Daniel. In a career spanning 17 years, Williams compiled a record of 144 wins, 34 by KO. He lost 28 times on points and was stopped only three times. It has been said that he engaged in over 300 professional fights, if so, many of these bouts have yet to be added to his record.

Several years after his retirement from active competition, Holman moved from Detroit to Akron, Ohio. He teamed up with Lee Thornton training local fighters and remained with Thornton when he opened the 'Club Wonder'. At the club Holman would also carry out maintenance duties and look after the place, often doubling as a watchman over the weekends. On Saturday July 15th 1967 he was on duty in the club when a terrible fire destroyed the building. Newspaper reports at the time indicated that the fire had been set deliberately. On the Monday prior to the suspected arson attack Arthur Snell, Summit County Assistant Prosecutor, was shot to death after an altercation with two men in the club. It was suspected that the fire was linked to the shooting.

Fire officials stated that Williams was probably asleep at the time, awoke to find the building ablaze, tried to escape, but was overcome by the smoke. His body was found near the bar. Holman Williams, one of the greatest and, it has to be said, one of the most historically neglected fighters of all time was dead at 52. In a 1988 interview with author Ronald K. Fried, Charley remembered his most frequent adversary with great affection and respect.

"Me and him, we had some times together! New Orleans I remember. I think I knocked him out once. He was a runner and a good boxer. It'd be hard to catch him. He was a great fighter, you can't take that away from him."

Charley Burley

Holman Williams
Possibly one of the most talented and graceful
fighters ever to enter a boxing ring.

It was around the time of his return to Pittsburgh, when Charley was "Top of the heap", as Bobby Lippi puts it, that the NAACP came calling for Charley in order to 'sign him up' to promote the cause. While Charley may have agreed with the driving principles of the National Association for the Advancement of Colored People, he did not want to be a member.

> "They wanted to do everything with Charley Burley. They wanted to enhance their image, to promote themselves."

Bobby Lippi

"Even that Black Panther thing, Eldridge Cleaver – is that him? He wanted Charley, but Charley didn't want to belong to nothing."

Julia Burley

Julia remembers that, due to Charley's refusal to join up with anything, she became a Ward Committee-woman and a representative of the Fifth Ward.

"I worked with Charlie Solomon, I worked with him and I went to jail with him (laughs). They were voting dead people. My own dead grandmother was voting! Charlie Solomon had a six-bedroom house with a hundred people living there. He had all those people registered at his own address."

Julia Burley

For his next fight, and his first in Pittsburgh since losing to Ezzard Charles three years previous, Charley was matched with 'Wild' Oscar Boyd of Buffalo, New York. The main event was Jimmy Bivins versus Curtis 'Hatchetman' Sheppard, which went on before Charley had a chance to show the 4,630 locals in attendance that he was still the best fighter to come out of the city. Bivins, maintaining his status as the number one civilian challenger for heavyweight title honours, beat Sheppard after ten hard-fought rounds.

When Charley was up he made very short work of the inexperienced Mr. Boyd, who, according to reporter Al Abrams, did not live up to his nickname.

"A club fighting Charley Burley was unveiled before the fans in the second 10-rounder on the program put on after the main bout. After driving his opponent, Wild Oscar Boyd, of Buffalo, bow-legged with a couple of stiff rights to the chin in the first round, Charley finished him off with a light right to the eye after 51 seconds of the second round."

Al Abrams, Pittsburgh Post Gazette

The same report indicated that the finish came so fast that few fans actually saw or knew what had happened. Murderous punching light-heavyweight Bob Satterfield and middleweight champion Tony Zale also stopped Boyd; none of them however, were able to turn the trick as quickly as Charley Burley.

Despite the recent move to Manilla Street, Charley was looking out for a bigger, and more robust dwelling for his family, this time the answer to the problem was not too far away as Paul Lippi, father of Bobby, lived right around the corner on Bedford Avenue. As he and his family were moving house he thought that Charley and Julia could move into their present address once they were gone. Paul told Charley he would square it with the owners of the building and that everything should be OK as they were Italians just like the Lippis.

Paul Lippi asked the landlady if it would be agreeable for the Burleys to take over the tenancy of the house, but he was refused. It was not the actual refusal that angered him, but the reason that was given. The landlady told Paul that she would not rent to Charley because he was black. Paul Lippi was a gorilla of a man, with huge hands and fingers like a bunch of bananas. An intimidating man at the best of times, he became enraged at this woman, who barely came up to the badge on his police officer's uniform, but then realized that he would do better to play her at her own game.

Paul Lippi had seen it all before. He had gone to work shining shoes at age twelve after his father died. He had worked in lumberyards and coalmines, had lied about his age to join the navy and had been involved in large-scale black-market operations before joining the police force. He wasn't going to let anyone get the better of him and he knew how to correct the situation that he faced.

> "So, my dad is 'OK, you don't want to rent to Charley? I'll send the building inspector up here and fix you'. Well, that one took care of that. My father, you know, he was rough, you know what I mean? He didn't take no shit. If you were right – that's all you had to be was right. But if you were wrong..."

Bobby Lippi

The tactics used by Paul Lippi had the desired effect and the owner of the building relented. Charley and Julia now had a bigger and better place to live and moved into the large house at 1712 Bedford Avenue. One day, while the Burleys were enjoying lunch in their home, Paul Lippi swept in. Without speech or ceremony he pushed his son Bobby towards the table.

"Here he is," he told Charley, before marching straight back out of the door. Charley motioned for Bobby to sit down but said nothing. "That's how my boxing career really started." Bobby remembers.

Young Bobby had no intentions of becoming a prizefighter, but his father would rather he pursued that career than the one he had lined up for himself. In his younger and more impetuous years, Bobby's greatest ambition had been to become a numbers writer as this was an activity that had been earning him good money since he was around 12 years old. That all started on the fourth of July in the summer of 1942 when Bobby became the victim of one of his own practical jokes, a date he remembers well for a good reason.

He had found a lump of tar, tore it into three strips, braided it and added a ribbon around the bottom so that it resembled a pigtail. The plan was to sneak up on one of his pals and stick it to the back of their head, only Bobby wasn't quick enough and it was he who ended up with a head full of tar. Of course, you cannot get tar out of hair without the hair coming with it. So, the only solution was to get his head shaved. Bobby remembers that his mother was not best pleased with his new look – whose mother would be? But, strangely, the new look started to earn Bobby some extra pocket money.

The local number joint was a few yards down from the corner of Manila and Bedford Avenue where Bobby and his friends hung out. People passing on their way to the joint started rubbing his head for luck, which was a source of great laughter for Bobby's pals until one day some guy gave him 50 cents as a reward for the luck he had brought. Bobby started hanging out at the top of the alley where the number joint was situated, just in case anyone else wanted to rub his head for luck and pay him for the privilege.

Eventually, he got to know most of the faces and names of the constant flow of people that went in there to place their wager and the guys that operated the place also befriended 'bald Bob'. When the joint was forced to move a couple of blocks down the street, he was paid 50 cents to direct the traffic.

Bobby then graduated to taking the slips and the stake money from the people that passed by on the street and running it down the alley to the number joint. He was paid for running and, if anyone got lucky, he was tipped occasionally. With an allowance of 16 cents per week it is easy to see how this easy money would have appealed to an impressionable teenager. Especially when the rest of the numbers guys were wearing the sharp suits and driving the biggest and best cars on the Hill.

Bobby's career as a fighter had been limited to a few amateur bouts. He had won a novice championship and was proud of himself and the reputation he had as a scrapper. One day Bobby took home a beautiful silk robe, the words 'Golden Gloves Champion' emblazoned across the back. His dad told him that he "ain't no champion" and took the robe from him. Bobby had been given the robe by local boxing star 'Booby' Pratt and was upset that this piece of memorabilia was taken from him. He never saw it again. Paul Lippi was growing tired of his son's street fighting and told Bobby that if he was going to continue fighting he should at least earn some money for it, that he should do it properly and that he should learn from the best. Hence the lunchtime visit to Charley Burley's house.

When he initially went to the gym to train with Charley, the first thing that Bobby noticed was the awful condition of Charley's boxing shoes. "He had the worst shoes. They looked like they had been worked down a coal mine." When Bobby made the mistake of putting brand new white laces in his own boots, Charley went to work on dirtying them up for him. While it may have been a case of 'look the part and feel the part' for Bobby Lippi, Charley Burley was of the opinion that 'less was more' and, as Bobby Lippi remembers of his mentor's Spartan attitude, "Anything that could spoil you was out".

Charley was now training at Pop O'Brien's, a local gym one block up from Wylie and Fullerton Avenues, just by Washington Park. The gym was part of the main bathhouse in the Hill district and it was frequented by the multitude of ethnic races that lived in relative harmony in the area. The bathhouse was the only real washing or bathing facility around, not including the community water pump near Washington and Bedford Avenues. The facilities at Washington Park were not available for the black population to use and even though the Homestead Greys Negro baseball team used the park itself extensively, they were also excluded from using the park's washing and bathing amenities.

Pop O'Brien had been a prizefighter back in the days of Jack Johnson and Stanley Ketchel and his gym had been in existence for a number of years. The gym, which took up the whole of the top floor in the bathhouse, had its own unique character, as do most well established boxing gyms. Jackie Wilson, the world featherweight champion, also trained there. Wilson, who was six years older than Charley Burley, used to spar with many of the fighters in the gym and he and Charley would often do their gym and road work together. In addition to the many fighters intent on whipping themselves into fighting shape up in the gym, anyone working out there had to contend with the rising heat from downstairs. The hot water and steam from the bathhouse would ensure that there was a hot, if moist, gym upstairs all year long. This was probably a most welcome luxury in the cold Pittsburgh winters, especially up on The Hill, but in the summer months a fighter would really have to have been dedicated to work through round after round of bag work, skipping, callisthenics and sparring.

In the gym (besides Charley) was Eddie Hines, who was an unbeaten bantamweight just starting out in the professional game. A fighter in the same mould as Sugar Ray Robinson, Hines had all of the moves and speed to spare, but no real power. Bobby Maloney, a rough and tumble welterweight who had a decent punch, was also part of the gym set-up. Maloney had a very spotty record and had been stopped five times in six losses from around 16 fights. Maloney lacked self-control and it was possibly Maloney's lack of discipline that resulted in him being knocked out so frequently. Never able to hold back or remain composed when the situation required, Maloney would go in all guns blazing, in a hit or be hit assault that sometimes worked and sometimes didn't. On one occasion when Charley was sparring with the free-swinging welterweight, things got a little out of hand and when Maloney became a little too fired up Charley had to knock him out. When Bobby Lippi was learning the game, Charley cut Bobby Maloney plenty of slack in his sparring sessions with the youngster.

> "I was cocky. I had won some two-bit championship, but I knew nothing. When I first went to the gym Charley would let Eddie Hines and them guys beat my brains in. I had to learn that you couldn't just go running in there and I had to learn that a right hand wasn't just to punch the other guy's head in. The right hand is kept high to stop the left hooks."
>
> **Bobby Lippi**

For hours on end Charley would make Bobby walk up and down the gym with his feet in a boxing stance. With his hands by his sides Bobby would have to slide his feet forward towards an imaginary opponent, while at the same time bending forwards and backwards from the waist. Thousands of repetitions of sliding into range, then laying-back from imaginary punches, before being allowed to throw a punch of any kind soon became frustrating. But Bobby was determined to stick at it.

200

Learning to use the jab to good effect was even less enjoyable.

> "The same with the left jab, my elbow was so sore! I had to SNAP
> that jab out, not drop it. If you dropped it BAM, an overhand right
> came at you. So you kept it up. It went out, it came back and when
> it came back, a hook came right off of it."

Bobby Lippi

Charley had Bobby think of his arms as being real loose, like long strands
of thick rubber cord. Each of his fists had to be a rock on the end of the
rubber cord.

> "When I finally got it, it was amazing. It was like having a pool ball
> in a sock. You understand? That's some weapon!"

Bobby Lippi

The repetition of punching, punching, always punching may have
left Bobby with a constantly sore elbow, but he also had a devastating
jab. Charley then moved him onto the next stage, which was sparring.
Another fighter who was in the gym at the time was a middleweight by
the name of Nate Smith. He was the type of fighter who looked great
in the gym, but in the ring was where he had his problems. Nate didn't
really like to get hit and Bobby Lippi, who was far lighter than Smith,
used to love their sparring sessions together. He would punch the middleweight all around the ring, as Nate would become very defensive
once he started to take shots.

When Nate was married, he and his bride had nowhere to live and
very little cash. His chosen profession was earning him very little money
due to his lack of ability and his wife was out of work at the time. Charley
figured he could help and he and Julia decided that the Smiths could live
with them at their big house. Nate brought shame to himself one day by
stealing a gun belonging to Charley and also his collection of coins. The
Smiths and the booty disappeared from the Burley home never to return.
Julia Burley remembers how with the coins in particular nowhere to be
found, Charley became concerned enough to seek the advice of Archie
Moore's mother, Lorena Reynolds, who was living in Pittsburgh at the
time. Charley originally thought that he had misplaced his collection
and was relieved to obtain what appeared to be relatively simple advice

on how to remember their whereabouts. He was advised that if he slept with dry-toasted bread under his pillow, the location of the lost items would be revealed in a dream. Being from the country and having a mother that still carried with her a lot of the 'old world' beliefs, Charley was also quite superstitious. He had a raccoon bone on a key chain that he carried around, which was looked upon as a good luck charm. Charley followed the instruction to the letter, but the next morning all he woke up to was a head and a bed full of crumbs. He had been the victim of a practical joke and in some small way Archie's mother had gained one back for her son.

Nate Smith would not be the only fighter to cause Charley personal problems as Eddie Hines went one better and was responsible for Charley Burley being prosecuted on dope pedalling charges in 1951. Eddie Hines liked to smoke and not the usual Lucky Strikes that Charley Burley was fond of, he liked to smoke other substances. One day, when he was struggling to score, he asked Charley to help him out. Through 'a friend of a friend' Charley bought some dope for Eddie and took it down to the gym. Things however, went a little 'pear-shaped' and as a result of the police findings Charley was taken downtown and placed in a cell. While there, a white 'gentleman' objected long and loud about being locked up with 'Niggers'. The complaints lasted about as long as it took Paul Lippi to arrive at work and discover what was going on. He knew Charley was innocent and that someone was just trying to score some points and maybe get their name in the papers by saying 'I arrested Charley Burley'. Paul Lippi confronted Eddie Hines over the dope incident and when Eddie confessed to being the guilty party, Paul returned to the station to assure Charley that he would certainly be allowed to go free. Paul also told Charley that he thought he should have a little fun with the racist in the next cell.

> "My dad, he'll gain on you in a minute, he picked this up, 'Oh, you don't like Niggers? Well, we got a nigger here in the next cell. I'll unlock your door and you go and kick this nigger's ass OK.' And he just bull-shitted this guy, unlocked his cell, then he unlocked Charley's cell. When this guy saw Charley he knew. You knew when you looked at Charley you're facing real serious trouble. The guy backs off and that was the end of that."

> **Bobby Lippi**

Charley was brought before the courts in September 1951 to answer charges of violating the state narcotics act. He admitted that he was just doing a friend a favour by obtaining and supplying illegal substances adding, "I guess it was the wrong kind of favour". He escaped with a caution, but Eddie Hines would end up paying for his mistakes in other ways. Bad habits finally caught up with the fighter and his boxing career took a nosedive after he became the travelling companion of a well-known singer. The usual tale of 'bright lights, big city' and a seemingly inexhaustible supply of drink and drugs led to Eddie becoming a hopeless alcoholic. He started on the good stuff, but eventually would settle for anything he could get hold of, as he became the epitome of a down-and-out wino bum. Eddie Hines, a talented and once promising fighter was dead before he was 40.

The incident involving Eddie Hines would not be Charley's final brush with the law when it came to narcotics as, in July of 1969, he wound up as a key figure in the (apparent) murder of a local drug dealer. While Charley had, at one time, tried to supplement his ring earnings with a job at the defence plant, a work colleague of his on the trucks had a similar plan. David Jordan was a huge man, way over six feet, and for this reason was known to all as 'Trees'. Mr. Jordan, who was around 15 years younger than Charley Burley, worked on the trucks as and when required, for example if someone called up sick he would step in. As the work was spotty at best, he had an idea that he was going to make himself some money and was going to follow in the footsteps of a local drug dealer by the name of Raymond Jackson. Trees figured he could use the spare cash, flash clothes, the fancy car and the 'big man' reputation that went with the territory, so he approached Raymond Jackson and bought himself a franchise. Now Trees had the goods, the customers and his own 'strong arm' in the form of Charley Burley, or so he is telling everyone. Charley knows nothing of this supposed arrangement, but before too long people believed it to be true, even though most people that knew Charley figured he would never go for anything like that. They were right. All Trees needed was a dealer to do the legwork and distribute the merchandise for him. Unfortunately for Trees his circle of friends did not include too many hustlers, pimps or dealers and he made the mistake of picking on the only guy he knew with such a pedigree; a local guy known, for some long-forgotten reason, as Malibu.

After his first big buy, Trees gave Malibu the dope on a 'sale or return' basis, which was his second mistake. Trees thought Malibu will be fine with it as his girlfriend at the time, a real sweetheart who had for many years tried to get Malibu to clean up his act, was keeping him on the straight and narrow, or so she thought. Malibu took the drugs and promptly went missing and his girlfriend started to panic. She called the police and told them that Malibu had been gone for over four days and that he must be dead and that Trees and Charley Burley must have killed him.

> "I said I was going to rough him [Malibu] up or something, or get Charley to do it."

> **David 'Trees' Jordan**

Malibu's girlfriend became even more anxious after she received annonymous letters telling here that Malibu was dead. She called the police and the story made the local papers.

> "The search for the missing Donald Flannigan, 31, whom Miss Yvonne Jackson, 142 Erin St. told police had been missing since a man called 'Trees' allegedly in company with a Charley Burley, 53, of the Lower Hill, fired several shots at him in a chase up Protectory St. on June 23, was still on this week.

> Capt. Theresa Rocco of the Missing Persons Bureau told the Courier that no trace of Flannigan nor any leads as to his whereabouts had been forwarded. She did confirm that letters which Miss Yvonne Jackson said she had received intimating that Flannigan had been killed and his body was lying in a vacant house somewhere in the Hill District had been inspected by police who were probing their origin.

> Sgt. John Stock of the Homocide Squad told the Courier that while his division was interested in the case, they only had a supplemental investigation going on 'until or if a body is found.'"

> **The Pittsburgh Courier**

The Pittsburgh Courier's editor, for some reasn, decided to run a story on the editorial page accusing the police department of sleeping on the job, because they had shown little interest in following up on the 'tip-off'.

Of course the police knew that the whole thing was bullshit and that Malibu would eventually turn up; even though Trees was not helping the situation by mouthing off how he was going to 'kill the son-of-a-bitch' for stealing his merchandise.

Charley paid a visit to the offices of the Courier and told them that he he had no connection with the case, did not carry a gun or had any dealings with narcotics. According to Bobby Lippi, who remembers the whole incident, the Courier continued to insist that Charley Burley and David Jordan be arrested and the whole thing given due attention, something that, as far as the police were concerned, was not going to happen. Charley had this reputation and respect amongst the Pittsburgh Police department that was second-to-none and Bobby Lippi and Julia Burley believe that if Charley Burley hadn't been Charley Burley then he would have wound up in jail for a spell. The police knew Malibu was a junkie, they knew Trees was just trying to cash in on his friendship with Charley and above all else, they knew Charley Burley. However, this didn't stop the police from picking Charley up one day when he was on his way home from work. They offered him a lift home and when he was in the car he was warned about hanging out with David Jordan and the trouble it might land him in. Trees himself knows that Charley was totally innocent and that it was just him and his mouth that started the whole thing off.

"Charley was a thoroughbred, he wasn't into stuff like that. He was a good old guy. I wouldn't want his good name tarnished with a story like that. It was something out of nothing."

David 'Trees' Jordan

Around a week later, Malibu arrived back in Pittsburgh. It appeared that he had this 'lady' up in Greensburg, where he would go and shack up now and again. His predicament over the drugs meant that this was one of those occasions, though Trees thinks that Malibu had his girlfriend go to the police deliberately while he laid low for a few days, so as to pre-empt any retaliatory strike by him. Whatever the real story, the situation now meant that Malibu was untouchable. Who was going to touch him now with the furore surrounding his short disappearance? He knew David Jordan could do nothing to him now that everything was out in the open, so he had no problem coming back to the city. The strange part of the tale is that Malibu died around three months later, strangely enough in an empty house. Malibu would leave the Ringside bar, go across the street and then shoot up the heroin. But he was a little too greedy and didn't want to share his gear. If no one was there with him when he went out, then there was always that chance that he might not make it back. Trees is of the opinion that Malibu's greed and the fact that he wouldn't share his score with anyone cost him his life.

> "He died a couple of months later in an abandoned house. He injected battery acid – a hot shot."

> **David 'Trees' Jordan**

Trees, who obviously hadn't learned his lesson from the first incident, again tried to turn it around to enhance his reputation, suggesting that he might have had something to do with Malibu's demise, a sort of, "You mess with Trees and this is what happens to you.", scenario. Charley was mad at Trees, wondering how and why he had got him into such a mess, but he remained friends with his work buddy.

Back in 1945, and a month after beating Oscar Boyd, Charley was matched with old foe Aaron Wade in Pittsburgh. Charley beat the bull-necked 'Little Tiger' in what turned out to be a relatively dull fight. Harry Keck of the Pittsburgh Sun-Telegraph suggested that the encounter "Should have been set to music". Not too many others at ringside were impressed either. Despite victories over the likes of Archie Moore, Oakland Billy Smith, Sam Baroudi and Bert Lytell, Tiger Wade never managed a result against Charley Burley in three meetings. Wade did however hang around long enough to accomplish something that all of the above could only dream of; a match with Ray Robinson. The problem was Wade, who started his career in 1935, had been inactive for two years and was a month off his 34th birthday when the opportunity arose. Sadly, the years told and he was stopped in three rounds. The fight with Robinson was his last ever and whilst he was occasionally mentioned in the local press, the Little Tiger quickly dropped out of sight and faded from public memory. He died in San Francisco in 1985.

Chapter Eleven

What's Your Price?

Charley had only been home in Pittsburgh for a few months and was getting back into the routine of hanging around his old haunts along Centre and Wylie Avenues. Dressed as sharp as could be and 'looking the part', as usual, he managed to attract the attention of a group of men who thought that they might be able to get themselves a reputation by challenging Charley Burley.

In what was essentially a mugging, Charley was set upon one evening at one of the busiest corners on the Hill, down at Roberts Street and Wylie. With him was his nephew Abby Williams, who could do very little about what was occurring as it was all over in a flurry of rushing feet, fast flailing arms and some rather destructive punching. Bobby Lippi was told the story by Abby, who knew of his uncle's reputation, but had now witnessed it first hand.

"Abby picked up a milk crate or something, but Charley didn't need no help. I mean, the guy could fight and he could hit."

Bobby Lippi

Before his sister Leona's son had a chance to do anything, Charley had knocked out three guys with about as many punches. Abby related the story to Bobby Lippi the following day, but Julia didn't get to find out about it for a long time because Charley told her very little about that kind of event, as he didn't want to worry her. Just like the time when he was mugged and lost his diamond ring. That time the guys got away with it, but Charley never told his wife what had happened. His attitude, as always, was 'Well, that's the way it is' and he knew that there was nothing he could do to change past events.

As a rule, Charley would not street-fight, because he knew that, being a professional fighter, it could hurt him. But sometimes things got a little out of hand and Charley had to do something about it.

"The guy pulled a knife on me and I didn't know. I'm doing that stupid thing, you know, I'm taking my coat off. And CLIP, Charley hit him and the guy got to (convulsing) and pissed all over himself and we ran, we ran. Another time a guy pulled a gun on Charley's niece. She was good-looking and attractive, but she was a player and she picked who she would allow to play with her, you know what I mean.

This guy, he didn't give a damn about her, he didn't give a damn about Charley Burley or anyone else. Well, Charley had enough, he goes over and this guy pulls out a gun, puts it right in Charley's face, and shoots. POOM! It was a blank gun. Charley damn near killed him. You don't scare Charley Burley, because from fear, that anger that's generated. Well, he tried to stuff the guy into the sewer and if he'd have got the lid off! The guy was a pussycat, but if you got him riled-up God ain't gonna do nothin'. He'll fight God!"

Bobby Lippi

At the end of the summer of 1945, the Dapper Dan charity organization made an offer of $17,000 to George Gainford for his fighter Sugar Ray Robinson to meet Charley in Pittsburgh. An offer which Robinson's manager accepted, but which Ray turned down. Although Gainford was listed as Robinson's manager in Pennsylvania the Sugar Man insisted that he was not authorized to make matches for him. Curiously, Robinson contradicted himself only nine months later when explaining his reported ducking of other ranked welterweights. In the trade paper 'Referee and Redhead' Robinson addressed fight fans in an open letter.

"Reports are being circulated that I am ducking Joe Curcio and Tommy Bell. Here's my side of the story: After several years campaigning I've earned recognition, but I had to make concessions to name fighters to get bouts. The Fritzie Zivic and Sammy Angott matches a few years back netted me very little, but a chance to exhibit my wares. If Curcio and Bell are earnest in their desire to make the match, let them meet the demands of my manager, George Gainford."

Ray 'Sugar' Robinson

Robinson at the time was possibly the hottest promotional property in the game and was sweeping all before him on his march towards a welterweight title fight, with Tommy Bell some 15 months down the line. The only blemish on Ray's record up to this point had been a defeat on points over ten rounds, at the hands of tough Bronx middleweight Jake LaMotta. A loss Robinson had avenged twice since. A match between Charley and Robinson would make for a great elimination match. As it transpired the charity was stalled for time and eventually Robinson withdrew. Later, Pittsburgh promoter Art Rooney offered Robinson $25,000 for a fight with Charley Burley at Forbes Field in Oakland, just outside of the city. The money was certainly tempting, but for the fight to go ahead there would have to be certain stipulations. Charley himself has recounted the events surrounding the possible matchup many times.

"Jake Mintz came to me one time and said I might be able to get a contract for three fights with Robinson, but he told me that part of the deal would be that I would have to go down in the first one. I questioned whether I would get a rematch after the first fight and didn't give him an answer."

Charley Burley

To purposely lose a fight was totally unthinkable to Charley, even though he was struggling to get a decent pay day, he refused to meet Ray under the conditions that Robinson's camp were insisting upon. Consequently, Art Rooney was unable to make the match, despite the large purse on offer. Bribes have always been a part of boxing and probably always will be. Many famous fighters have, at one time or another, received an offer to do business.

"I received several bribes. All fighters receive bribes. I will say even the biggest fighters that ever lived. I will say Joe Louis and Jack Dempsey, I will say some guy, some nut, would come to them, even with Dempsey."

Ike Williams

When testifying before the Kefauver Committee's investigation into boxing in 1960 Williams recalls how he was offered $3,000 to lose to

Chicago's Freddy Dawson in a title defence. The offer came from Blinky Palermo. On the night of the fight an acquaintance of Ike's told him that they were going to 'steal the fight' from him. The defending champion called a press conference in his dressing room and informed the media that if he lost the contest he would have an exclusive for them. The tactic appeared to work as Williams won over 15 rounds and he never had anything incriminating to tell the press. One story that Ike did mention to a reporter in later years was the incident involving Sugar Ray Robinson's tank job against light-heavyweight champion Joey Maxim in 1953. As for a Robinson versus Charley Burley fight, boxing's insiders knew that a bout between the two would be a real connoisseur's match and would be one that attracted plenty of attention.

The next bout up for Charley was against Dave Clark in Cincinnati. At this point in his career Clark was looking for a crack at the middleweight title, which was in the possession of Tony Zale, and was only interested in matches that would afford him some progress towards a title fight. Clark, who had been 1936 national amateur middleweight champion, had beaten former welterweight champion Izzy Janazzo by decision over ten rounds in Cincinnati less than three months previous. Charley also had a similar goal in mind and he approached the fight knowing that a victory over yet another ranked contender could only add weight to his often ignored plea for a championship bout.

The championship was 'on ice' at this time as Zale was occupied in the service of his country and would not re-enter the ring until the following year, January 7th., 1946, and would not defend his title until September of that year. In the meantime no one else would contest the middleweight championship and although the heavyweights had a 'duration' champion in the shape of Jimmy Bivins, the lighter divisions would manage without.

Charley arrived in Cincinnati on the weekend before the fight, which was to be held on Tuesday September 4th 1945. He travelled from Pittsburgh with his trainer Bobby McKnight and Bobby Lippi. The trio made their way to Ezzard Charles' hotel, the Coliseum, where they would be staying. Over the weekend, Charley managed to get in enough light roadwork to shake off his 'train legs'.

On the morning of the fight, the group made their way to the Cotton Club for breakfast. This is where the fun began. During breakfast Charley was introduced to the owner of the Cincinnati Reds baseball team, who was there for the photo-opportunity as well as being a boxing fan. Charley went along with it, although that sort of situation usually made him feel uncomfortable, as he was not happy being patronised. It was shortly after the photo shoot that Charley made the acquaintance of a number of Dave Clark 'supporters'. They had a proposal for Charley, although it is unclear what the benefits to Charley may have been, should he have accepted.

> "Some gangsters came by and were trying to talk to Charley, tried to push me off to the side and Charley wouldn't let them, 'cause I didn't know what was going on. And they wanted Charley to carry Dave Clark for the ten rounds. Charley said, 'No! If he can make it, but I'm gonna knock him out.'"

Bobby Lippi

According to Bobby Lippi, the reason they wanted Charley to carry Dave Clark for the ten-round duration was because they were negotiating with Ray Robinson to fight Clark, which nobody was aware of at the time. If Dave Clark was capable of going ten rounds with Charley Burley the betting odds switch and the suckers start coming in for Dave Clark when he opposed Robinson. If he looks good against Burley, he may have a chance versus Robinson. This would have given the interested parties a chance to make a killing on the betting odds.

Robinson had recently beaten Jimmy McDaniels via a second-round knockout and would face LaMotta for a fourth time just three weeks after the Burley-Clark bout. It had been suggested, in a Cincinnati newspaper article previewing Charley's fight with Dave Clark, that LaMotta had also been ducking Charley.

In response to carrying Clark, Charley said no because he was an honest prizefighter, he would not make deals, and he would not carry a fighter – especially when told he had to. He felt that if you're going to beat him, you're going to have to beat him straight up. He knew if he carried a guy they're going to steal the fight off him and he wasn't prepared to let that happen, you had to beat him fair and square. Besides, Charley was scheduled to fight world-ranked light-heavyweight 'Oakland' Billy Smith at the start of October in San Francisco, (Charley was still the official California State middleweight champion at this time). It would have been foolish to jeopardise such a lucrative match for the sake of a no-hope like Dave Clark.

Because the reply to their request was made with such finality and with a totally dead-pan expression Mr. Clark's supporters realised that they were not going to get what they wanted, but that was fine by them, because they had a contingency plan.

"The weigh-in is supposed to be at 11 o'clock in the morning, they changed the time to one o'clock in the afternoon. That's to mess up Charley's eating habits see, and then they started on me! What was I doing going into Ezzard Charles'? That was a black hotel. It caught up with us. And the Cotton Club! I was not allowed to sit out in the Cotton Club, I had to go back in the kitchen. I mean, this is ridiculous!"

Bobby Lippi

They even went as far as to cite the liquor laws in an attempt to keep him away from Charley during the party's time at the Cotton Club. All of this was designed to get Charley mad and it was beginning to have the desired effect.

That night at the Parkway arena, Charley arrived to discover that he didn't even have a dressing-room inside. The promoter asked one of his assistants to show Charley to his designated room and Bobby Lippi expected that they would be sharing with some of the other fighters on the card as was usual. To their surprise they discovered that Charley had been allocated the office of the parking lot attendant. That's where it was, actually out in the parking lot.

The office was small, cramped and very, very dusty. Charley had no place to hang his clothes and worst of all, no place to put his beautiful grey fedora hat that he always took such great pride in wearing. No matter where he put his hat it would get filthy with dust. He'd put it down somewhere, pick it back up and dust it off, put it down somewhere else and then repeat the process over and over several times before he ran out of places to try.

"This definitely got him mad but he just kept it in and Charley don't say too much when he's mad, it's just a slow burn."

Bobby Lippi

There was no room to warm up in the office, so the group made their way to the arena which involved a long walk from the parking lot to get into the main building and then from the usual dressing-room area to the ring. Once inside Charley found a place to warm up before he, Bobby McKnight and Bobby Lippi made their way to the ring where the announcer was going to introduce the young Mr. Lippi as Charley's protégé. Bobby McKnight was handed the gloves for the bout and was amazed to find that he had been given larger and softer 10oz gloves instead of the regulation size 6oz gloves. Charley just shrugged his shoulders and gave him a look as if to say 'what the hell' and extended his hand for it to be gloved up. Bobby McKnight tried to push some of the padding back away from the knuckle area so as to offer less protection to the features of Mr. Clark, who was arguably the innocent party in these shenanigans.

Bobby Lippi was introduced to the crowd and started to walk across to the centre of the ring but tripped on the canvas. This resulted in an uproar of laughter from the crowd. They had the canvas real loose and ruffled so as to make manoeuvring quite difficult for Charley. It would have been difficult to plant one's feet and obtain the necessary drive for a knockout punch. Now Bobby Lippi was mad and didn't really want to go over to the opposite corner and shake hands with Dave Clark when the ring announcer directed him to do so. Charley got madder still and after the bell to sound the beginning of the fight he went out and proceeded to take all of his anger out on his opponent.

As far as punches thrown goes, it was not a totally one-sided affair. Clark caught Charley with a number of jabs and right hand punches that appeared to have little effect. With Clark throwing leather, but moving towards the corner, Charley lay back from a jab and countered with a powerful right hand shot that landed flush on the side of Clark's jaw. He dropped face-first on to the canvas were he remained motionless until long after the ten count had been completed. The fight lasted 2:10 including the count and Charley never even worked up a sweat. A fair-sized proportion of the crowd voiced their displeasure, as they were very upset that the main event had lasted such a short time. This may have been due to the fact that some may not have seen the finishing punch.

Bobby Lippi recalls that many of the supporters had yet to find their seats and settle in for the big bout before it was all over. The people that had rushed to the restroom, or for a beer or hot-dog, missed the pay-off punch and the main event. Although his night's work was very impressive from a performance point of view, the victor had to listen to the jeers and whistles of the unappreciative crowd as he exited the ring.

Again, Charley's ability had affected his popularity and possible acceptance by the fight fans. Charley may have argued that he was not there to be flashy or crowd-pleasing, he was there to fight. If the opponent couldn't go with him, then that was hardly his fault. On returning to the hotel Bobby found that someone had taken a box of perfumed soap he had bought to take back to his mother in Pittsburgh. The whole trip and their treatment in Cincinnati had been a bad experience for the young Mr. Lippi, but par for the course for Charley Burley.

"That was a joke, what they did in Cincinnati. You know, between Charley and my dad, I learned what the rackets were about. I stayed independent. I could have had number joints, but I would have worked for someone else."

Bobby Lippi

Technically, Charley had earned decent money for his night's work, working out at around six dollars per second, as he was paid a little over $800 for disposing of the hapless Dave Clark. Charley's biggest pay day would come a little over a month later in San Francisco in the ten-rounder against 'Oakland' Billy Smith when he would receive $3,000. Before the Billy Smith fight however, Charley managed to get in another nominal pay day down in New Orleans where, just three weeks after the win over Dave Clark, he scored a fourth round technical knockout over 15-year veteran Walter 'Speedy' Duval.

From New Orleans, Charley travelled back to the West Coast for the first of his two meetings with 'Oakland' Billy Smith. Ten days after the Duval victory, Charley opposed the highly-rated light-heavyweight in San Francisco. Smith, who was managed by Jack Attel, had a distinct weight advantage over Charley the day of the fight.

"I know Charley wasn't as heavy as they billed him for the two Billy Smith fights. I recall the first one. After a workout we weighed on the gym scales, he weighed 154. Two days later I believe it was 167 he was supposed to have weighed. I know at times he was billed at a heavier weight. He once told me that himself and I certainly believe him, he was a good honest man."

Blackie Nelson

Billy Smith was a well-put-together light-heavyweight with a physique that looked to be chiselled out of rich coffee-coloured marble. With very little body fat on his tall frame, any advantage he had in weight was all muscle. Smith had a decent record up to this point in his career and had met some highly regarded and rated fighters. A win and a loss versus Jack Chase, a three-round no contest with 'Cocoa' Kid and two victories against Watson Jones and Kenny Watkins had the local fans and media very interested in the light-heavyweight prospect. Smith, originally from Omaha, Nebraska, had re-located to Berkerley, California with his parents as a 17 year-old and continued to live with them at 1614 Tyler Street when starting out in the professional fight game (though Berkerley Billy Smith doesn't quite have the same ring to it). Young Mr. Smith picked up pointers from Lee Savold, Johnny Paycheck and Al Hostak when he first entered a gym in Omaha and while living in Berkley Billy's idol was old Australian champion Tiger Jack Payne who lived nearby. In the US Army from January 1943 to April 1944 the up-and-coming Smith was described as "religious and patriotic" in his local newspaper. Boxing historian Howard Branson remembers the only thing that went against Smith was his demeanour. It appears that Billy Smith, initially, was the kind of fighter that Charley just didn't like, because he was very cocky and had no time for fans or the media. Smith would often tell fans to 'take a walk' if they bothered him for an autograph or just wanted to say hello. But, as Archie Moore knew only too well, Charley Burley had a way of dealing with cocky fighters. He punched it out of them.

At the opening bell of their fight at the Oakland Coliseum, Charley went about his task in his usual business-like fashion, as he slid towards Smith with his hands low, almost daring the Oakland man to throw a punch. When Smith did throw, Charley was in position to counter. After dropping Smith with a right-hand to the jaw, Charley realised that he could beat the light-heavyweight at any time he chose. Instead Charley would stiffen Smith with solid counters and piercing leads and then hold him up before he fell. According to some eye-witness reports the Oakland fighter appeared to be out on his feet at least four times during the ten-round fight, but Charley allowed him to stay in there just so that he could beat up on him. Smith also played a part in his own survival by holding whenever he had the chance and by pinning Charley against the ropes and holding on to the top strand with both hands to keep him there.

There had been some talk in the papers that some of Charley Burley's bouts, like so many others around that time, had not been 'on the level'.

"I know Charley carried old Billy Smith there."

Blackie Nelson

By the end of the fight Smith was so severely beaten that one side of his face was swollen up like a watermelon. Yet again the disadvantage in weight proved to be of little consequence as Charley handled Smith like a man with a small boy, even though Billy Smith was physically the much bigger fighter. Howard Branson believes that Smith's attitude changed considerably after that fight and he was no longer abrupt or uncooperative with the fans or reporters. According to the local press in the days following the fight, an attitude was the last of Smith's worries. Irate fight fans wrote to the papers saying that Smith should apologise to he fans for his poor showing and that he demonstrated little heart or appetite in the fight with Burley.

Charley's ability to mix it with the bigger men and still come out on top undoubtedly had negative repercussions on his career. Big Jack Godfrey, late owner of the Fifth Avenue gym and fight trainer in Pittsburgh, recalled an incident when a visiting West Coast fighter arrived in Pittsburgh to fight Charley.

"Burley was supposed to fight a guy from California once by the name of Tiger Harris. After the weigh-in everybody went up to the Crawford Grill like people did before most fights. That night Tiger Harris was there eating and people started coming in saying, 'Hey, where's that guy's gonna fight Burley?' And somebody would point him out. People would look over at him and shake their heads like he was in some kind of trouble. People kept on doing this and when the time came for the fight nobody could find him He'd already taken the train back to California."

Jack Godfrey

Charley's final appearance in the ring for 1945 was on Friday November 23rd when he was guest of honour at the Centre Avenue YMCA boxing show. The event was a fund raiser that had been organised in order to purchase a new boxing ring.

Ring magazine's final ratings for the year had Charley in 3rd spot, behind Holman Williams and Jake LaMotta, amongst the challengers for Tony Zale's middleweight title. Also in the ratings were Bert Lytell (13);

Cocoa Kid (14) and Tiger Wade (15). In the light-heavyweight division were Archie Moore and Lloyd Marshall at one and two respectively, while Nate Bolden was in at number eight behind Gus Lesnevich, the reigning 175-pound champion. At heavyweight Jimmy Bivins and Elmer Ray were both in the top five.

Sporting a pencil-thin moustache and possessing "the cold, grey eyes of a killer", the middleweight Charley Burley that Archie Moore remembers from the mid-1940s.

Chapter Twelve

Robinson Ducks

By 1946 Charley was finding it even harder to get bouts and was becoming something of an 'ugly duckling' amongst the middleweights. By March, he was back in Pittsburgh for a fight with Charley Dodson, his first sign of action in close to five months. Enthused at Burley's return, the crowds turned out at the Aragon Arena to cheer the local fighter on against his imported opponent. Appreciative of the record-breaking crowd, Charley turned on the style and gave a fine display of body punching. A flurry of blows to the mid-section dropped the visitor for a count of nine in the first round, then late in the second stanza, a left hook to the body dropped Dodson to the canvas again. As the count reached two the bell rang to save the New Yorker, who had to be carried to his corner by his seconds. The intervening minute however proved insufficient time for a recovery and referee Ernie Sesto award the TKO victory to Charley. Prior to the fight, promoter Jake Mintz told Charley that he might have a deal with Ray Robinson's management for a bout in Pittsburgh for May 10th at Forbes Field. Charley had heard it all before and probably wondered what the catch would be this time around. To him, the fight would be a reality when he and Sugar Ray were looking at each other from opposite corners of a ring.

Local man Morris 'Pippi' Slutsky - a Russian Jew - had recently acquired Charley's contract and, as his manager, was doing what he thought was his best to get Charley good bouts against rated opposition. According to some, the former Hill District butcher and businessman had one small failing, an all-consuming love of money. Always one to spot a good opportunity when it came knocking, 'Pippi' Slutsky figured he could make himself some money piloting Charley Burley.

Actually getting Charley's contract, however, would prove to be a lot more difficult than the butcher envisaged. Charley had been through several managers, sometimes out of choice, and the tangled morass of previous pilots was so complex that a lawyer had to be called in to resolve the situation. At the end of it all, Slutsky came away with Charley Burley's contract and $3,000 less in his pocket. This amount was probably small potatoes to Charley's new manager, as Slutsky did not confine his business interests to providing meat to the population of the Hill District. "They [Slutsky's] made a fortune out of all that black market stuff," remembers Julia Burley. Bobby Lippi used to do some work for Slutsky around that time and he could often be found unloading trucks down at one of the yards. Bobby remembers that he would usually work a few consecutive days when circumstances dictated Slutsky needed the extra hands. After many hours of hard physical work all he was paid was one dollar. Bobby wised up quickly and decided if Slutsky was going to cheat him, then he'd do the same right back.

> "I'm going to tell you about Pippi Slutsky, see. That no good son-of-a-... During the war, with the sugar stamps and the meat stamps and what-have-you, this guy would pay me a dollar, didn't take me long to wake up, you understand. He'd say 'Come on Bob let's go down the yard', you know. And I'd help unload the trucks and this son-of-a-bitch would give me a dollar. And then I found out where the sugar stamps and the meat stamps and that were and I'd grab handfuls of them. The guy was making big bucks and besides that, you know, they had the garage and through the garage was every hot part of a car you needed. When I find all of this out I'm saying to myself, 'you cheating, thieving son-of-a-bitch', he's going to rob me. Well, I got even, but I was so stupid I didn't even get the right price. I gave away a hundred dollars worth of sugar stamps for twenty cents."

Bobby Lippi

As Charley's manager, Slutsky was making a fair fist of getting him fights and had managed to get Charley a bout on the West Coast against 'Playful' Paulie Peters for April 4th. Although his training regime usually consisted of nothing more than a liquid diet, Peters was determined to give it a real go against Charley. 'Playful' Paulie was so determined he actually turned up at the Newman Gym in San Francisco for ten consecutive sessions and worked out diligently under the guidance of local trainer Joe Herman.

The fight, which was to take place at the Civic Arena in San Francisco, was slated for 10 rounds and would be the headliner to three other fights. Charley was favoured in the betting purely because of his experience and ability. Peters was as game as they come once he got started, though he was notoriously slow to get going, and he would not be shy about swapping leather with the uncrowned middleweight champion of the world. The main event looked as though it would provide some entertainment as both boys were considered good punchers and Peters was on a reasonable streak having beaten hard-punching Fitzie Fitzpatrick, Larry Carter and West Coast favourite, Chester Slider.

The paying spectators watched all of the preliminaries end in a hurry, with Willie Brown, Dee Edwards, and Babe Picazo all winning in three rounds apiece against Horace Thompson, Leo Green, and Billy Carlisle respectively. When Johnny O'Neill won in under a round against Oliver Mayfield the crowd may have thought that they were getting short-changed for the collective $14,100 that they had handed over for a Monday evening's entertainment. At the start of the main event, the crowd may also have wondered if the last bout of the night would be worth the ticket price. During the first round of his fight with Charley Burley, Paulie Peters may also have wondered. Although it is likely that he thought less about the crowd's value for money and more about what it was he would he have to do to improve on the total of four punches he had managed to connect with during the opening couple of minutes. With the left side of his body and face pounded to a distinctly bright-red hue, the claret streaming from his nose, he may also have wondered how to escape the trip-hammer rights and jarring jabs that came at him at every turn. As he fell onto his stool at the close of the first round, 'Playful' Paulie wondered no more, as he was through. He told his corner that he had difficulty breathing and thought that he may have some broken ribs. The crowd, who had witnessed barely eleven rounds of action booed loudly. There was no explanation offered up from the ring as to the reason for the bout's sudden conclusion, merely that it was a technical knockout for Burley. West Coast promoter Don Chargin was a 14-year-old spectator that night and he still winces at the memory of the right hands that Charley landed to the body of Peters.

After his latest victory, Charley appealed through the newspapers for opponents to come forward and challenge for his California State middleweight title. He received no offers. If there was no one at middleweight, then Charley was prepared, once more, to go to the higher divisions. Previous victim Billy Smith was now the State light-heavyweight champion and his manager Jack Attell accepted a non-title fight against Charley for April 24th.

"Billy Smith, whose fighting style is governed largely by his frame of mind at the moment, has a great deal to gain and much to lose in his bout Wednesday night with Charley Burley at the Auditorium. Smith himself is well aware of the fact. He was aware of the importance of Promoter Tommy Simpson's 10-round main event when he agreed without argument or delay to the Burley match.

Smith fully understands that if he is soundly thrashed, and most especially humiliated, by Burley he will have lost fistic face in Oakland to such a degree he no longer will be a local drawing card of consequence. Yes, and Billy knows that if he hands Burley a whipping he will have erased the blotch on his record and reputation applied by Burley in a San Francisco bout about three months ago.

Smith never entirely has lived down the unpleasant reputation he acquired when he surrendered hands down to Charley Burley in San Francisco, attempting virtually no return of Charlie's punches but going into a shell for the full route and taking a lacing in a manner which evoked mingled pity and amusement from the audience. However, Smith subsequently redeemed himself in part. He went the distance with Heavyweight Jimmy Bivins although he lost the decision. Then he scored an upset knockout over Lloyd Marshall in the Oakland ring. So, if a confident Billy Smith wins from his former conqueror in the bout coining up all will have been forgiven and the local lightheavy will have become one of the hottest drawing cards this city has known. Including Earl Turner and Max Baer.

The alacrity with which Smith accepted the Burley assignment is indicative of Billy's belief he can whip the California middleweight champion. At least, it implies that Smith has no fear of the hard-hitting Burley and is anxious for another crack at Charley. Jack Attell, Smith's manager, says that his light heavyweight for weeks after his loss in San Francisco begged for a chance to redeem himself.

The coming bout has created a wide interest and it looms as a near sell-out even with a boost in admission prices."

Alan Ward, Oakland Tribune

The day before the meeting of the two State champions Charley weighed 153 pounds in the gym and had been trained to a peak by the recently retired Eddie Booker and his veteran promoter, manager and trainer, Frank Schuler. Come fight time it is most likely that Charley was under the 160 he was listed as. Often there wouldn't be an official weigh-in before the contest and the ritual of weighing himself and his opponent would puzzle Charley. He was going ahead with the fight anyway, so what was the weigh-in all about? Of course, for accurate record-keeping purposes the recording of weights is a necessity. If they are going to be inaccurate however, then there is little point.

Smith had recently won by knockout over Lloyd Marshall, though there were some in the fight game who though that all was not Kosher with the Oakland boy's victory. As one report, from the day after the March 20 1946 bout, indicated:

"Two sources close to the Oakland fight game told me this morning that Lloyd Marshall took a dive to Billy Smith last night. They know that the Gazette is one paper which is free to say as much.

I was at ringside and I'll admit that it did look as if Marshall went down of his own volition in the ninth, rather than of the effects of Billy's right to the jaw.

I asked Smith about the matter this morning and he said that he was certain that it was a legitimate knockout, adding that the blow was hard enough to do the business. Marshall had won five of the previous eight rounds.

My sources claim, among other things, that a man close to the boxing racket bet $1,500 just before the fighters entered the ring that Smith would win by kayo. Marshall had been a favourite all week.

Understand, I am not accusing Smith of any charges. A coming world's champion if ever I saw one, he's too smart and honest to take part in any such shenanigans. Ditto for his manager Jack Attell. Neither do I intend to involve Ray Carlen, the promoter of last night's battle. The Oakland game could do with three more men like him.

With his victory, Smith retained his state light-heavyweight title. he was paid 27 1/2 percent of the $20,844.92 gate while Marshall received 22 percent."

Jim Scott, Berkerley Daily Gazette

It was also reported that Marshall, who at the time was resting due to broken knuckles, was gunning for a rematch. Smith, the state champion who was now rated at number five amongst the world's top light-heavy-weights, was out for revenge against Charley and vowed that he would be a different fighter to the one who showed up for the first meeting between the two. The Oakland light-heavyweight even went on record promising, "No more holding and running." Smith said he was going to meet his opponent head-on and fight. Talk, as we all know, is cheap, and while Smith talked a good fight, he was as ineffective in his second bout with Charley as he had been in the first.

Charley's best round was the sixth, when he frequently caught the hometown fighter with sledgehammer rights. Referee Toby Irwin deducted points from Smith in the seventh for hitting on the break and while Smith came back in the eighth, he was penalised again by Irwin for rabbit-punching. At the close, it was a victory for Burley by six rounds to three, with one even.

"Billy Smith was a real light-heavyweight, probably weighed 182 or more the night of the fight. I doubt Charley weighed more than 159. They fought twice, Charley won both easy. There was talk that Charley carried him for another payday, that was fairly common back then, I thought he did in the first fight."

Blackie Nelson

The second fight against Billy Smith in Oakland is the only fight of Charley Burley's entire career that was filmed. The old, grainy black and white footage shows Charley handling the much heavier Smith with ease. Blackie Nelson has always thought that Charley allowed Smith to finish the fight so as not to scare away potential future opponents, most notably Sugar Ray Robinson, whose management had actually agreed to a date for a fight with Charley in Pittsburgh.

Again the fans were not impressed with Smith's performance against Charley Burley. The Oakland fighter's lack of effort, coupled with the hike in prices left more than one fan enraged. One of them, R.L Mercer of Oakland, wrote to the Tribune.

"If you sportswriters do not burn Billy Smith's posterior for the miserable showing he made against Charley Burley you will be guilty of letting the sports fans down.

It will take many gallons of perfume, freely sprinkled throughout the Auditorium, before the stench will be cleared away.

The card was bad. The main event was worse. It will be many moons before the fans will pay increased prices to see Billy Smith go into another event such as this alleged fracas. For effort he gets zero. For Sportsmanship he gets less."

Reader's letter, Oakland Tribune

Still reigning as California light-heavyweight champion, Billy Smith continued to fight on with reasonable success and moved to the East Coast where he became known as 'Boardwalk' Billy Smith after his Atlantic City base. Regardless of the pre-fix used, Billy Smith was another of the highly-rated black fighters of the day that didn't get anywhere near a title shot despite a solid career. Several years down the line, in a bizarre fight with Archie Moore, Smith, who was on the wrong side of a pasting at the hands of 'Ageless' Archie, simply turned his back, climbed out of the ring and went home - an action that earned him a suspension from boxing and effectively finished him as a popular attraction. Once his boxing career had wound down, the Oakland fighter became a highway patrol cop in Nebraska.

After his second victory over Billy Smith, Charley returned to Pittsburgh to prepare for the long-awaited fight with Ray Robinson. Charley was confident that he could beat Ray and was looking forward to proving that he was the better man. He paid a visit to his manager, 'Pippi' Slutsky to sort out the finer points of the deal for the fight with Robinson and to collect the rest of his purse for the Billy Smith fight. When Charley met Slutsky he received a double whammy. His manager told him that Robinson had put up the price, he was now asking for a guaranteed $50,000 plus a percentage of the gate. Also, Charley's end of the purse for his last fight was not what he had figured. Robinson and his management knew that there was no way that the fight would generate anywhere near that kind of money.

Robinson was beginning to get himself something of a reputation for not going through with fights if financial arrangements were not one hundred percent with him. Often this was looked upon as an 'out' if Ray didn't fancy the job too much and is a tactic that has been used by many fighters, managers and promoters over the years.

"He raised the price, Sugar Ray, he raised the price from $25,000, then he shot it up to $50,000 plus a percentage of the gate, you know. Another time Charley could have fought Ray Robinson if he'd have made a deal. He loses the first fight. It was rotten, it was rotten."

Bobby Lippi

"Walter Winchell suggested that Robinson should fight Burley and Robinson replied, 'Walter, I thought you were my friend.'"

Eddie Futch

Three years later, in 1949, Robinson fought Earl Turner in Oakland, California. The purse was a mere $7,500 with some additional payments of $938.00 plus some under the table cash of $500.00 amounting to a grand total of $8,938.00. This alone is a good indication of the type of money Robinson was demanding, and getting, around this time. Turner was a decent professional, having beaten Cecil Hudson and Cocoa Kid, amongst many others. By the time he tangled with Robinson though, he may have been on the slide, having lost several of his more recent fights by knockout. However, the financial arrangements for Robinson illustrates that each opponent had their price, depending upon how difficult Robinson or his management envisaged that opponent to be. If you were Charley Burley, it seemed that no amount of money could get Robinson in the ring with you. This incident concerning Charley was not the first time, nor would it be the last, that Ray Robinson would welch on a deal or make such extraordinary demands as to make the proposed event a non-starter.

Blackie Nelson got to meet with Robinson in the gym during preparations for the Earl Turner bout and he found Ray to be a complete gentleman. The champ even took time out to fetch a picture from his car to sign for Blackie, who always remained a fan of Robinson, even though he knew the flashy welterweight and middleweight had denied his good friend Charley Burley a potential big money fight.

There have been many arguments down the years as to whether or not Robinson or his management ever had any intention of going ahead with a fight against Charley Burley. When questioned on the subject after Robinson's passing, Charley had some insight of his own.

> "Ray ducked me. George Gainford [Robinson's manager] admitted that much. But, I can't say I blame him. There wasn't no money in us fighting each other. All we would have done is knock each other off."

> **Charley Burley**

The big fight with Robinson would not go ahead after all and Charley was bitterly disappointed. His frustration at having Robinson duck him yet again soon turned to anger when he realised that Slutsky was trying to cheat him out of his money. The gate for the Smith fight had been just over $15,000 of which Charley was due 30 percent, around $4,500. One third of this was due to the manager; this would have left Charley with $3,000. Slutsky however wanted to divide the money so that he received his third, which was $1,500, and the expenses of $500 would be deducted from Charley's end. What Slutsky wasn't aware of was that Charley knew that his manager had already received an advance from the promoter of $500 towards expenses. The former butcher was prepared to take his percentage plus the $500 advance, which would be a total of $2,000, and let Charley pay the expenses from his $3,000. Charley would only receive $500 more than his manager for risking his health and career against a dangerous and highly-rated light-heavyweight contender.

Greed had got the better of Morris 'Pippi' Slutsky and Charley would never forgive him for not being straight with him over the additional $500 he had already received. Soon after the incident Charley attempted to wash his hands of Slutsky, but he was still owed some of his money for the Smith fight and Slutsky was holding back on the payment while still trying to make matches for Charley, so as to make yet more money.

Slutsky did not only cause problems for Charley, he also gave the promoters of the Burley-Smith card a headache they didn't need as the impact of the Hill Butcher's greed rippled out to the loyal fans in California and eventually the promoters themselves. Slutsky not only pushed matchmaker Jimmy Murray to lean on promoters Carlin and Simpson to increase the usual ticket prices to a $2.00 minimum and $6.00 for ringside, he also insisted on additional travelling expenses for Charley. As Charley had fought Paulie Peters across the bridge in San Francisco just two weeks previous the additional expenses were hard to justify. Especially as Slutsky had an advance on them and still wanted Charley to pay out of his end.

The result was a fracturing of the promotional and matchmaking team that had provided many great match-ups for the fight fans of northern California as Jimmy Murray applied for his own promoters licence. Charley Burley (and/or his management), had probably caused promoter Ray Carlen one too many headaches as he never fought in California again.

With the collapse of the Ray Robinson fight, Charley would have no competition for the month of May. By June he had announced to the press that he was buying out Slutsky's contract with him. As the money situation was being sorted out, Charley was matched with Charlie Banks in July. The fight would be Charley's first in close to three months and it turned out to be a fairly run-of-the-mill type of affair, often spoiled by Banks' clowning, inept display coupled with Charley's inability to punch with any real force. At the end of round one Charley nailed Banks with a right and almost reeled back as the pain shot up his arm like an electric shock. Sitting on his stool during the minute rest, Charley told his handlers that he thought that his hand might be broken.

"That's why he didn't knock him out, I mean after the first round it's a one-handed fight and Charley just beat on him and beat on him and beat on him. It was a tough fight; this guy was a light heavyweight not a middleweight. This guy was big, looked like he had been lifting weights. And Bobby McKnight says 'Charley broke his hand', I said 'Well stop it', but Charley wouldn't have it. There was no quit, just no quit in the guy, none whatsoever."

Bobby Lippi

227

As concerned as Bobby Lippi may have been for his mentor, he knew that Charley Burley was always aware of how much he could take. Not wishing to take the chance of his hand holding up for the ten-round duration, Charley was content to make the Detroit puncher miss with his wild, over-arm swings and then counter with his own left. As dangerous as Banks was supposed to be, with 12 wins in a row and eight knockouts coming into this fight, Charley made him look foolish. Using the right only sparingly, Charley dropped Banks in the fourth round on the way to a ten-round decision. The crowd of 4,103 had seen occasional glimpses of neat boxing from Burley, but overall they could not have been impressed by the wrestling style employed by the visiting fighter, a style that caused both men to slip to the canvas on several occasions. Fortunately, when Charley had his hand inspected after the fight it was not broken, although there was damage.

Charley was now becoming all too aware of the futility of his cause. Since 1942, when he had entered the ring 17 times, the frequency of fights was decreasing on an annual basis and he was averaging a mere six fights per year. The most money he had made for a contest, on paper at least, had been the $3,000 for the second Billy Smith fight and none of his subsequent opponents had been of sufficient standing to enable him to earn that kind of money since.

A fight with the highly-regarded Bert Lytell in August would not only be Charley's final fight of the year, it would be his last in Pittsburgh for close to two years. Bobby Lippi remebered that the build-up to the Lytell contest would also have some interesting moments. The night before the fight, a few of the guys were sitting around at Charley's house playing cards. Later in the evening, the phone rang and some guy was on the other end asking for Charley Burley. The guy claimed he was a reporter looking for an angle on the fight. Charley took the call and listened to the guy on the other end telling him that Julie Burley was a whore and Charley Burley was a washed-up fighter and so on. Charley tended not to respond to such obvious baiting and on this occasion he just hung up the telephone. They all went back to the game and continued playing late into the night. The phone continued to ring around every half-hour or so and Bobby Lippi was answering the calls just for the hell of it.

"I'm laughing my ass off. We were up late playing cards anyway. Charley didn't give a damn about Bert Lytell or anyone else."

Bobby Lippi

This incident echos Archie Moore's 'embarrassment' at losing to Charley in 1944. Archie claimed the loss hurt even more when he heard that Charley had been up all night playing poker and drinking whisky.

On the day of the fight at the Zivic arena, Charley and Bert Lytell shared a dressing room, which was quite common then and is not such a rarity even today. They exchanged some casual talk as they prepared for the fight, but not a word was mentioned about the phone calls the previous evening, something Lytell was likely oblivious to anyway. The mood in the dressing room beforehand would be far different from it after they had fought.

Bert Lytell, if that was his real name, was something of an enigma in boxing circles. Reportedly from Fresno, California, Lytell was a genuine middleweight contender and one of the toughest fighters around. There is some confusion over who he was and where he was from and there is a dearth of information on this talented southpaw. Some reports have his real name as Calvin Coolidge Lytell from Oakland, California, and others that he learned his boxing in the Navy, where he had over 30 bouts in places like Panama, Cuba and the South Pacific. Other sources stated that he learned to fight in the Army and that he took his name from the silent-era movie star. West Coast fighter Chester Slider, who ended the career of Henry Armstrong, and his manager Harry Fine, who both hailed from Fresno, told inquisitive reporters that they had never heard of him around that town. It has been reported that Lytell signed up for military service at the recruiting offices in Fresno and that is the reason it was referred to as his hometown. One particular story concerning his boxing career indicates that Lytell, after being honourably discharged from the navy, walked into Stillman's Gym and after observing a couple of guys go at it in sparring told Bernie Bernstein that he could beat either of them. After a quick look at Lytell, Bernstein passed him along to manager Sammy Aaronson, who must have been as equally impressed as he got Lytell his professional start against Artie Towne (Artie - aka Henry Johnson - had his debut several months earlier and was 8-0 with 4 knockouts). Fighting as 'Chocolate Kid', Lytell lost that encounter, but was soon making progress in the middleweight division.

Regardless of the confusion over his name and origins Bert Lytell was good enough to fight and beat many highly-rated middleweights and light-heavyweights during the late 1940s and early 50s. Lytell, who early in his career fought as 'Chocolate Kid', was often avoided by most of the top-ranked middles of the time and is another one of the good crop of fighters that Sugar Ray Robinson managed to avoid.

During his career, Lytell would have many opponents in common with Charley, including Holman Williams, 'Cocoa' Kid and Archie Moore. Lytell was considered very difficult to beat and probably would have beaten most of the middleweights and light-heavyweights ranked above him, (he was ranked from time to time in the top ten, with his maximum rank being around number five). Since none of the white fighters, with the exception of Jake LaMotta and the long-neglected Walter 'Popeye' Woods, were keen to fight him, Lytell fought almost all the top African-American boxers of that time. Fighters like Art Towne, Sam Baroudi, Major Jones and other long-forgotten black fighters who were too tough and too good for their own good when it came to the ring. Lytell's fight with Jake LaMotta in 1945 was very close, with LaMotta 'winning' a ten-round decision; there was no rematch. Popeye Woods fought and beat Lytell twice (1945 and 1946) and was a very stern test for any middleweight around. He had beaten Solly Kreiger, Harry Balsamo, Glen Lee, Ralph DeJohn, Jimmie Clark and Australian greats Fred Henneberry and Jack McNamee in their own back yard. An impressive resume by anyone's standards.

Lytell was expected to offer Charley Burley a good deal of competition, but Charley was looking to add to his run of nine wins with five knockouts and was prepared to give as good as he got. When the fight started Charley began rather slowly, quite content to open up an early lead by employing his usual style and the tactics a southpaw would normally use against an orthodox fighter. Charley counter-punched Lytell, drawing his shots and landing heavily, if not often, with his own punches. On a number of occasions, the Fresno fighter was forced to hold on after taking terrific shots to the body. By the fifth round, Lytell was cut under the right eye and the rest of his features were beginning to show the effects of the beating he was taking. As the bout progressed it was apparent that Lytell, on that night, was no match for Charley Burley. At the close, referee Buck McTiernan had it 7-3, while judges A.J. Williams and Red Robinson had it 6-4 and 9-1 respectively for Burley.

Jimmy Miller of the Sun Telegraph was not impressed with Charley's lacklustre performance, stating: "If Charley Burley expects to pick off a big bout here this summer he had better start showing a little more life in his fights. The Hill Negro middleweight, unquestionably one of the best boxers in the game, was too docile in beating Bert Lytell."

According to Bobby Lippi it is likely that Lytell would have disagreed with Miller. He remembers that after the fight, Lytell appeared to be in a world of his own. He showered, changed and packed up his kit and then sat in the changing room "like a little boy waiting to be picked up from school." Bobby Lippi also remembers it as being quite pitiful. "He had no idea where he was". No one knows how long this condition lasted once he left the arena, but Bert Lytell did recover sufficiently to gain revenge over Charley when they next met.

In September of 1946, reigning welterweight champion Marty Servo announced his retirement. In December of the same year Ray Robinson became welterweight champion of the world by beating Tommy Bell on points over 15 rounds in New York. Ray had made it to the top after six years and over 70 bouts, fighting under what he called his own terms. Robinson always maintained that he earned his title shot without the assistance of Mike Jacobs and the 20th Century Sporting Club and it was not until he returned as a middleweight after a short retirement that he became involved in the seedier side of the fight game. Charley Burley had been publicly sympathetic towards Robinson and the way he had been by-passed as a title challenger when previous champion, Cochrane, had agreed to fight Marty Servo for the title instead of the highly-rated New Yorker. He also expressed his wishes that Robinson would not apply the same restrictive practices once he became champion. While, in his own mind at least, Robinson might have laboured honestly towards world recognition, it has to be said that he openly avoided any fighter that might have given him trouble. Reflecting on their respective careers after Robinson's death, Charley still had nothing bad to say about the man who could have made all the difference in the world to his own career.

"You know, to me the most remarkable thing about Ray's career is that he didn't even get a shot at the welterweight title till he was 26 – or the middleweight title till he was 30! You think he was the greatest? What do you think he'd a' been if he'd gotten his chances when he deserved them? You wanna know the truth? If I coulda' got my shot, I wouldn't have risked it fighting someone like Ray."

Charley Burley

Ray, or his team, rarely liked to take any risks. Robinson's management also had as part of their stable a fighter by the name of Henry Johnson, or Artie Towne, or Sonny Tufts, or whatever name the New Yorker decided to fight under. Yet another highly skilled performer with decent power in both hands, Towne was another of a long line of fighters who were routinely avoided by many of the white welterweights and middleweights of the day. In boxing parlance the middleweight was used as a 'policeman' for Ray Robinson and was often matched with fighters that were prospective opponents for the Sugar Man. If they looked a little too difficult then Towne was sent in to test them and maybe even clear the way for the main man in the stable. Bert Lytell was one such fighter, as he was beaten by the policeman at the very beginning of his career and again near the end, when he was looking for a match with Robinson in 1950.

Towne laboured as a fighter for many years, plying his trade up and down the East Coast of the United States and knocking out opponents with monotonous regularity. Although he was active and fighting anyone who would get into the ring with him, Artie still found it tough to earn a living and he retired for a couple of years before mounting a comeback in 1956. Fight fans in Liverpool, England, still talk about him in glowing terms as he visited the United Kingdom as an 'opponent' near the tail-end of his career. The late Jimmy Faux, a Liverpool-based boxing trainer who for many years worked with a number of British champions, remembered Towne with admiration. "Artie Towne, he was a cracker. We had him training at the Maple Leaf. What a gentleman." Despite training at what was an amateur club during the month he spent in Liverpool, Towne was a consummate professional and he left a lasting impression on the local fighters and fight crowd. A promising local heavyweight by the name of Dave Rent - who, as a professional, would go on to be managed by Al Weil in New York - took the opportunity to spar with Mr. Towne and was somewhat baffled by the visiting fighter's ability to make him miss with just about everything he threw. When questioned about this apparently fine-tuned radar Artie Towne told the boxing club's star attraction that all he had to do to figure out what was coming was to watch the heavyweight's feet. In the two fights Towne contested at the Liverpool Stadium it seems that more 'foot watching' was going on as he knocked out both Willie Armstrong and former British champion Johnny Sullivan in under a round. With a career lasting from 1944 to 1958 Artie Towne contested over 100 ring battles, losing only a dozen or so and while he was always rated on the fringe, he never came near to a title shot of any kind. Artie Towne also met a very tragic end as he was stabbed to death by muggers in New York in the late 1960s.

With the end of the year approaching and after ridding himself of Pippi Slutsky, Charley went to New York in search of work and new representation. One day, after sparring at Stillman's Gym, he was introduced by Whitey Bimstein to Lew Burston who, during his time in Paris, had acted as manager for a number of European fighters. Burston had been watching Charley in action and was impressed, he asked Charley if he had representation and when Charley answered 'no', Burston told him that he might be able to get him a fight with French middleweight Marcel Cerdan. Burston had connections with Cerdan and his manager Lucien Roupp and knew that the European champion was looking for ranked opposition in the United States. Several months previously Cerdan had beaten Holman Williams on points over 10 rounds in Paris and was looking to build on the success.

When Cerdan arrived in the United States, Charley was contacted to come to the gym and train and spar so that Burston could see them both in action. According to some reports, Cerdan practically ran out of the gym and Burston was informed that a fight between Burley and the Frenchman would be a non-starter. According to Bobby Lippi, Burston already had Charley's name on a contract to fight Cerdan, but couldn't get the Frenchman's signature for the bout. Impressed with what he had seen and not a man to be discouraged easily, Burston took over the management of Charley Burley and along with a co-manager, the sports writer Jersey Jones, proceeded to promote the Pittsburgher as best they could.

For the time being Charley Burley had a management team that seemed prepared to go that extra mile in doing what it took to get their new charge noticed. Excellent promotional photographs, proclaiming Charley as the 'world's-best middleweight' were distributed among the top managers and promoters. While the claim for Charley may have appeared to be a rather bold statement, considering the numerous world-class fighters around during this period, it was not news to the American fight fraternity, most of whom knew Burley's worth.

In addition to the money spent on promotional activity, Burston was able to raise $60,000 in escrow from prominent businessmen in Pittsburgh and New York and offers went out to practically all of the ranked middleweights, including Tony Zale, Rocky Graziano, Marcel Cerdan, Jake LaMotta, Steve Belloise and Artie Levine. In an article written by his co-manager for the 'Ringsider' newspaper in November 1946, Charley's guide pondered over his career to date.

"Burley is one of the most amazing cases I've run across, but I sincerely believe Charley is the best middleweight in the world and I'm launching an ambitious campaign to force official recognition

233

of him as the number one contender and the logical contender to the Tony Zale-Rocky Graziano winner."

Lew Burston

Despite such heavy backing and large dollar signs, there were no takers. Ray Robinson, who had yet to earn over $20,000 for displaying his talents, could not be tempted into the ring with Charley even for the generous amount on offer. Even though the money Burston and Jones were promising was $10,000 more than Robinson and his management had demanded for a match in Pittsburgh.

Bert Lytell (left) defeats 'Oakland' Billy Smith in Oakland. The Fresno-based southpaw, another of the oft-avoided black fighters of the 1940s, would go on to repeat the victory six months later in Cincinnati.

Chapter Thirteen

The Garbage Man

Charley saw no further paid ring action for the rest of the year and his final record for 1946 stood at five fights and five wins, two of them by KO. It was also the last time he would be listed in the top ten of the Ring Magazine's annual ratings. At the time, he was at the number two spot behind Jake LaMotta for Tony Zale's middleweight title. Realistically, he could have been ranked in the next division up, as Ezzard Charles, Archie Moore, Jack Chase and Billy Smith were ranked two, three, four and five respectively and Charley's record was two defeats and six wins against these highly-regarded light-heavyweights. The fact that he was still scaling under 160 probably had something to do with him retaining middleweight status.

Another period of enforced inactivity, due in part to managerial disputes and six weeks of pleurisy, saw Charley slip in the ratings. In his next fight, February 1947, Charley would lose for only the second time in five years. If it had not been for his pride and for the need of a payday, he would not have taken the bout. As he sought to regain his higher world ranking, a return with Bert Lytell was arranged for February 17th in Baltimore, Maryland. The week before the match, Charley fell ill and was advised not to go through with the fight, as he was very weak from what was initially thought to be a cold. Julia begged him not to fight, telling him that he could always reschedule it, but Charley argued that they needed the money.

Charley had handled Bert Lytell with relative ease in their previous meeting, but could do very little with the strong and capable Fresno fighter in the return bout. With an argument for what was a dull first round, Charley soon slipped behind to the constantly bobbing and weaving Lytell. Charley also shaded the sixth round and, urged on by his corner, also took the ninth. Either Charley didn't have enough that night or Lytell had too much. Either way, the Fresno southpaw won an easy victory and thus gained revenge for the previous defeat in Pittsburgh.

The cold that Charley had turned out to be pneumonia and, on the orders of his neighbour, Dr. Goldblum, he was confined to his bed for over a week. Julie smiles as she remembers how he, "took a bottle of whiskey with him for company." The illness took so much out of Charley that it would be seven months before he would be back in the ring and also meant that he had only two bouts in a year with a very limited income. Arguably, Charley's stubbornness had cost him greatly. The defeat by Lytell made it easier for managers to avoid him, as they could now argue that he wasn't ranked high enough or that there would be no prestige for their fighters in beating him as he was on the slide. Even if the reverse to Lytell was his first loss in three years. It appeared that Charley's loss to Lytell was greeted by a smile of smug satisfaction by at least one west coast fight reporter.

> "Some considerable surprise was expressed that Bert Lytell, a boxer out of Fresno who has done most of his ring work in the East won an easy 10-round decision from Charley Burley in Baltimore. Knowing Burley and his mental processes I'm not surprised—nor would there be a feeling of amazement if Charley lost to Rough House Oliver, one of our better known four rounders.
>
> Burley essentially has been a splendid fighter—and notice use of the past tense—but he is a temperamental prima donna with a weakness for swapping managers and invariably winding up with one less capable than the predecessor.
>
> It was significant that the boys waltzed through the second half to the displeasure of a small crowd, after Lytell had punched Burley all over the ring. Very significant. Why didn't Lytell keep punching the second half, huh?
>
> Burley has wanted to box in Oakland but the promotion here wouldn't have the guy if he offered to appear on a 10 per cent basis. The promotion has enough headaches normally without adding another. And Burley is a headache to any promoter."
>
> **Alan Ward, Oakland Tribune**

Bert Lytell would take Charley's place in the top ten and go on to have a very successful year, beating 'Cocoa' Kid, Sam Baroudi, Holman Williams and also Major Jones. His only setback for the year would be a points defeat over ten rounds to Archie Moore. Despite this apparent success, the Fresno southpaw would also fall short of gaining a title shot. World middleweight champion Randy Turpin used him as a sparring partner when the British fighter was defending his crown against the man he took it from, Ray Robinson, in New York in September 1951.

With no money available while Charley was sick and out of action, the Burley family struggled financially. It was around this time that Charley was being courted by self-made millionaire Harry Roth. 'The Count', as Roth was known, was a Pittsburgh sportsman, but had made most of his reported million-dollar fortune as a con man, amongst other things.

Bobby Lippi fondly remembers the Count as the archetypal confidence trickster, the type that made a fortune on the passenger ships and in upper-class gambling joints. Anywhere that he could find rich old ladies, tricksters like the Count would be there, weaving elaborate sob stories and tales of misfortune along with scams and schemes all of which were guaranteed to make him richer and the victims poorer. Although he had the talent and personality for the con game, Roth was apparently one of the nicest people you would ever meet and was always a reliable friend. In many ways he was the opposite of Charley's previous manager, Morris Slutsky, who used to get upset with Julia for taking gifts or money from the Count, saying that he could look after them. In truth, Slutsky was probably jealous of the real friendship that Roth had with the Burleys.

It is possible that the tight-fisted butcher could not comprehend the sportsman's genuine generosity. Julia Burley always thought well of 'Pippi' Slutsky and would not have a bad word said about him, even so, he did not come across as the type of person that you could rely on.

> "Fuck Slutsky – I saw him turn down Charley for $20, I saw him turn down Charley for meat, she [Julia] thinks Pippi was a good guy – Pippi was a shit-head."

Bobby Lippi

Julia never knew any of this because Charley didn't like to tell her. But, if Morris Slutsky was unhelpful during Charley's time of need, then the Count was his opposite. As a 'sportsman' the Count was naturally attracted to the fight game and at one time had a financial interest in an unbeaten welterweight prospect named Mike Koballa, who became a rated fighter in the early 1950s. Charley helped out with the likeable young welterweight's preparation, often training with him and giving him pointers. At one point, a couple of years down the line, Charley took control over Koballa's training regime, but was never paid for his services.

With his growing interest in boxing, and local fighters in particular, the Count figured he could make money for himself and for Charley by acting as Charley's manager, as he had connections and money and was prepared to use them. For the moment though, Charley insisted that he was staying with Lew Burston and Jersey Jones in New York. This fact never prevented the Count from helping out when he could, as he had the greatest respect for Charley as a fighter and as a man.

It was also around this time that Abe J. Greene, president of the National Boxing Association, began to worry about the promotional monopoly that was evident in boxing, especially amongst the middleweights. Although it was apparent that not too many of the ranked middleweights wanted any part of Charley Burley, Greene attempted to prevent the title action becoming stagnant for a projected year and a half, by naming Charley as the man who might be able to prevent such an occurrence. The eighteen-month wrap-up was threatened because the current champion, Tony Zale, and rival Rocky Graziano were slated for a return bout at Madison Square Garden on March 21st 1947, (the bout did not take place until July of that year). Also the New York State Athletic Commission had installed Jake LaMotta as the challenger for the winner of the Zale-Graziano rematch. These two factors, along with Mike Jacobs' promotional ties to French middleweight Marcel Cerdan, who also had to be part of the proposed scenario, meant that any other contender would be left out in the cold. The problem for the NBA and for Abe J. Greene was that all of this was to take place under the banner of one promoter.

Marcel Cerdan's victory over Georgie Abrams, in December the previous year, had allowed him to gate-crash the party and he was now being lined up to meet the winner of the Zale-Graziano-LaMotta round-robin for the title. LaMotta's squawking about being frozen out of the title picture was silenced by the promise of a title fight with the winner of the Zale-Graziano rematch. The proposal from Greene was that the winner of a Burley-LaMotta bout would get to fight Cerdan in an eliminator. This would clear the way for a legitimate contender for the winner of the forthcoming Zale-Graziano bout. The logic behind this proposal was, primarily, to prevent the wrapping-up of the title for an extended period under the one promoter and to develop a challenger who was beyond dispute. This challenger would have earned the right to a title shot by beating the rest of the ranked contenders who were all clamouring for a chance at the champion.

As things transpired Graziano relieved Zale of his title by stopping him in the sixth round of their rematch (July 16th 1947), paving the way for a third and deciding match. Marcel Cerdan, still part of the picture as far as Uncle Mike Jacobs was concerned, remained in contention by beating Billy Walker and Anton Raadik during the latter half of the year. Raadik, an Estonian fighter, almost spoiled the party, dropping the Frenchman three times in the final round of their fight in Chicago.

Charley remained hopeful of securing a match with a high-ranked contender and he awaited news of the proposed match-up with LaMotta or any of the other white fighters that were involved in the championship chase. Jake LaMotta was obviously unwilling to risk his ranking against Charley, as he would not sign to fight him. This proved to be the unravelling of the NBA's otherwise sound idea. The winner of a Burley-LaMotta bout could have met Marcel Cerdan for the right to fight either Zale or Graziano, once they had finished playing 'pass the parcel' with the championship belt.

The self-managed LaMotta appeared to be quite content to bide his time until he got an offer he says he couldn't refuse, as he lost to Cecil Hudson and Blinky Palermo's fighter, Billy Fox during the same period. The 'loss' to Billy Fox cost LaMotta $1,000 in fines and a seven-month suspension for failing to report an injury, which was Jake's excuse at the time. According to his own testimony before the Kefauver Committee's investigation into boxing in 1960, the defeat also ensured that he received his title shot further down the line.

Palermo and his associates allegedly made close to $35,000 on the betting, as the Bronx Bull had been favourite going into the fight. Fox was a mob fighter, mostly built-up on a diet of fighters who were less able or who would consider taking some extra money for the tank job. Sometimes an opponent's co-operation had to be coerced in order to get the desired result.

One such reported incident involved Fox and 'Wild' Bill McDowell. In October 1944, Fox was going for 'win' number 28 and, coincidentally, knockout number 28. The fight took place in Philadelphia, as had most of Fox's previous battles, and McDowell of Dallas, Texas, was a 20-1 underdog in the betting. After taking the mob fighter's best shots and scoring three knockdowns of his own, McDowell looked to be on for one of his easiest nights in the ring.

In a conversation with historian Howard Branson some years later,

'Wild' Bill claimed Fox couldn't box, couldn't take a punch and was in no way a fighter. Before the third round got under way, McDowell was told that he would have to throw the fight if he wanted any hope of getting out of Philadelphia alive. So, he "took a powder" in the third and walked away with his health and a $300 added bonus to his purse for his night's 'work'.

Once he had recovered from the bout of pneumonia that had cost him dearly in the fight with Bert Lytell and had kept him out of the ring for six months, Charley was again looking to fight anyone that was willing to climb into the ring with him. Try as he might, Lew Burston just could not get anything going for Charley in any of the major cities.

Local Pittsburgh promoter and manager P.J. 'Bunny' Buntag had a middleweight from Donora, Pennsylvania by the name of Lee Sala, who was a genuine up-and-comer. Sala had a slew of clean-cut knockouts on his early record and was progressing nicely due to his manager's excellent matchmaking.

> "I could demand $10,000 to $12,000 a fight for Sala, he always sold out. If I thought it wasn't a sure thing, I wouldn't take the fight. I wouldn't reject it, but I would demand a high enough purse to make it unlikely."
>
> **'Bunny' Buntag**

The astute manager reflects on how this tactic could be employed when faced with the possibility of fighting Charley.

> "Any manager who had a good fighter wouldn't fight Burley. Charley was the greatest fighter who ever lived. Why would you take a fight with him for $1,200 to $1,500 – maybe get knocked out and lose everything? I don't think anyone could lick him and no one would fight him."
>
> **'Bunny' Buntag**

Buntag's insight offers some explanation as to how some of the bigger name or more well connected fighters might avoid a fighter like Charley Burley. Nate Liff, a local boxing camp owner, who had seen some of the city's better fighters come and go, reinforced this evaluation of Charley's situation, "Managers knew they could get better pay days without taking as great a risk."

Lew Burston must have been wondering what he had got himself involved with, as every door appeared to be closed. He was warned that he would do very well to make any kind of matches for Burley, let alone championship fights, as the word was out that Charley Burley did not or would not 'do business.' With just about every rated fighter connected, via their managers, to Palermo and Carbo it was a near impossibility to progress unless you were in on the action. Julia Burley thinks that it was his character that prevented her husband from scaling the heights of world boxing fame.

"Charley was so honest that if he went to the store and they gave him too much change he'd give it back, but not me – not me and when the gangsters came and wanted something I'd say 'yeah'. I told him to fight for the money, but he wouldn't go for the money. He was too honest."

Julia Burley

After close to 12 years as a professional fighter, the grim realisation of the situation must have begun to sink in as Charley decided after his last fight in Virginia that the fight game just wasn't earning him enough money to support his family. Soon there would be a new addition in the form of a son. So, at 29 years of age, Charley Burley, scourge of the middleweights and the most feared fighter in any division, went to work for the city of Pittsburgh as a garbage collector.

Life on the garbage truck was a hard one and not the easiest way of earning a living. During the 1940s, 50s and 60s the work was made even more demanding by the fact that the truck itself was essentially a large flat-back with a huge skip on it. The rubbish men had to go into the yard and bring the garbage out to the street where it was then carried up a ladder and dumped into the container on the back of the truck. "It was a strain to bring it out on your back and – it was rough then." Charley recalled. When the container was full it had to be taken to the rubbish dump where the reverse process was carried out. The men would get into the truck and shovel the garbage out. When they had emptied it out they went back on the streets to begin the process over again. As with everything else, Charley figured if he was going to do something, he was going to do it right and he worked hard each and every day, never cheating himself or his employer. His work-mates remember how dedicated Charley was:

> "He'd run on the job. The guys would get tired 'cause it was tough, but not Charley. He could do 50 push-ups after working all day. He worked like he was training for a fight."

> **David 'Trees' Jordan**

The garbage truck and the everyday mundane toil of a regular working man got to be a way of life for Charley. He seemed content to sacrifice his boxing career, a means of employment that had served him reasonably well for the past 12 years, but was recently beginning to let him down. Instead of punishing his body through training and fighting some of the toughest fighters in the world, he laboured like an ordinary Joe in order to provide for his loving, supportive wife and his children Angeline and Charles junior. Every working day he'd be up early and head off to the depot, lunch pail in hand. After a hard day's toil he and his work buddies would go for a beer down on Centre Avenue before heading home for a bath and dinner. Julia remembers how her hard-working husband slowly, but surely, became as much a part of the job as it became him.

> "He'd walk to work from here, all the way down to the strip and he worked on a dirty job. He'd kill me, I'd say 'why are you drinking?' And he'd say 'you're a rubbish man, you smell all that crap all day you have to drink, every rubbish man drinks.'"

> **Julia Burley**

Apart from a brief spell on the construction, when the Alcoa Building was erected down in the city in 1950-51, Charley was essentially a garbage hauler for the rest of his working life. Carrying the work ethic that had made him such a physically fit and strong fighter in the ring into his daily job, Charley was a foreman on the construction in no time. If wood shavings or rubble needed to be swept up, Charley would grab a broom and sweep. If anything needed doing he would do it, never relying on anyone else to do it first. This attitude impressed his superiors and he was quickly put in charge.

On the South Side of the city, which was Charley's regular route, things were no different when collecting garbage. He was a firm favourite with the residents, as he always left their yards clean and never left so much as a scrap of paper lying around. Bobby Lippi is forever in awe of Charley's dedication. Whether it was in the gym, the ring, or at his work, the fighter turned rubbish-man did his best to provide for his family.

"I don't give a damn how cold it was, how much rain or snow, and there'd be times we'd come in at two o'clock in the morning. Five o'clock he was gone. The preacher and all of them people on the South Side loved him, because when they left your yard the stuff they'd spill, they picked it up. They had respect, see this is the thing. If I'm writing a story about Burley and wanna teach somebody a lesson – being a garbage man could teach a lot of people a lesson, about pride, honour, RESPECT, being a big man, you understand. And working on the rubbish truck well, I don't wanna know about nothing else."

Bobby Lippi

In August 1947 Charley took a fight against the anonymous Larry Cartwright in Huntington, West Virginia. A knockdown in the sixth round paved the way for the finishing right-hook in the following stanza. This seventh-round stoppage victory in late summer was Charley's final ring appearance for the year and earned him little more than pocket money. Although he was getting regular work on the garbage, Charley was still a registered fighter and at the end of the year (1947), the NBA declared that, according to their own ratings, Charley Burley was still a ranked contender.

"It's nice; it's really nice that they still think so much of me, but gee, I wish somebody would give me a chance to prove it in the ring. The only bouts I can get are against that wolf at the door. That guy is always willing to fight me and I've had a tough time outpointing him In the last year.

I don't know how I'd have managed if I hadn't hooked on as a helper on a city garbage truck last June and that's only on a part-time 'basis."

Charley Burley

Charley would have been grateful for the opportunity to justify the position. Yet, as the twelfth year of his career got under way, he still wasn't seeing enough action. The dire situation was perfectly reflected in Charley's decision to answer a call from Carl Hatfield and return to San Diego. Despite the manager's promises, bouts were still hard to come by and, totally frustrated at the lack of interest being shown from all sides, Charley decided he wanted to return to Pittsburgh.

Hatfield did manage to get him a 15-round main-event in Phoenix, Arizona, but the fight turned out to be a six-rounder and the payday was a paltry $150. Hardly a purse worthy of a championship contender and even then the opponent was not to keen to tangle with him, despite having a weight advantage of close to forty pounds. For his part, Charley just wanted to fight, get paid and go home and the desperation was beginning to show.

"Then his opponent said 'I aint gonna' fight Burley for no six rounds. Burley said 'Look kid, I just need enough money to go home to Pittsburgh. I won't knock you out until the fourth round.' The opponent said 'Christ, if you can call the round, I don't want to fight you.'"

Carl Hatfield

After being convinced that the fight, and the opposition, was of sufficient calibre to warrant a purse of $150 and that said pay day was enough to get him back to Pittsburgh, Charley stepped into the ring against one Battling Blackjack. Despite the time off from work and the time away from competitive fighting, Charley started in determined mood.

"Jesus Christ, Burley hit him and the guy didn't know where he was at. So he comes back to the corner and says 'Look, I gotta knock this guy out. He's butting me and might cut my eye.' As I climbed out of the ring, Burley flattened him. He was stretched out."

Carl Hatfield

Battling Blackjack, or Lonnie Craft as he was born, was a big guy. He had weighed 190 pounds for a 1939 loss to Johnny Risko and was big enough to challenge Clarence Henry and Zora Folley. Folley knocked him out in 1954 and five years later Battling Blackjack took the final count as he was executed in Arizona for the murder of his estranged wife.

It would be over a year before Charley would step into the ring again for the purposes of earning money, by which time he had seen out his commitment to Burston and Jones and had signed with a local man by the name of George Armstrong. The problem with Armstrong was he had no real connections in the sport and, as a result, earned himself zero dollars in purse percentages during the six months that he was Charley's manager.

With no fights and plenty of gym time Charley began helping other fighters learn their trade. Eddie Hines, Bobby Malone and Nate 'Available' Smith, who were all in the gym during the time that Charley was working with Bobby Lippi, were also on hand when Charley was recruited to assist with the further development of California heavy-weight, Rusty Payne. Fighting out of San Diego Rusty Payne had built-up a decent record against good opposition defeating 'Big Boy' Hogue, Kenny Watkins, Paul Hartnek and J.D. Turner amongst others, but with five losses and a draw from his previous 12 bouts, the young fighter's career looked to have stalled. Remembering Charley, and the encourage-ment he offered when he lived in San Diego, Payne and his management, the Hatfields, got in touch with him back in Pittsburgh.

During the time that Charley was working with Rusty Payne he ran up a streak of five consecutive knockouts, with 'Mean' Erv Sarlin and mur-derous-punching Curtis 'Hatchetman' Sheppard amongst the victims. Unfortunately, Bobby Lippi recalls, Rusty had a problem - besides the homosexual advances of his manager (Hollywood actor) Cesar Romero - he didn't like to train too hard. It also appeared that his recent suc-cess had gone to his head and somehow stopped his ears from working correctly. Rusty Payne just wouldn't listen to Charley. Most of the city's other fighters would be doing laps around the oval at Schenley Park, but Charley always preferred to work harder. He would run along the bridle path and that was all dips and turns. Going down the dips it would be easy to just coast. Not Charley, he ran down the slopes and would sprint up the next. Rusty Payne just didn't like to work as hard as his mentor and Charley couldn't work with someone who wouldn't listen. So that was the end of Rusty Payne's time in the gym with Charley Burley. Payne lost on points over ten rounds to Johnny Flynn in Pittsburgh in his last fight for 1948. He later went on to beat 'Hatchetman' Sheppard again over ten rounds and lost to Jimmy Bivins, also over the same distance. Without Charley Burley helping him, the muscular, black heavyweight went on to lose five of his next eight fights. While Charley may have been reluctant to waste his time with someone not willing to do what was necessary in the gym, he remained friendly with Rusty for many years afterwards.

At the outset of 1949 Bobby Lippi managed to get himself in a whole mess of trouble and ended up doing two and a half years in prison, largely as a result of being in possession of stolen goods. He and a bunch of guys had stolen a safe belonging to the owner of the McGraw Wool Company in the Fox Chapel area. Originally they had tried to get it into Charley and Julia's house on Bedford Avenue to crack it open. The house had a large cellar and Bobby figured that there they would remain undisturbed and unhurried, but Charley wasn't having anything to do with it and he sent Bobby and his friends away.

Always the first to admit that he did some crazy stuff as a young man, Bobby remembers how stupid they had been opening the safe in a nearby parking lot, late at night. With thousands of dollars worth of what they thought to be useless stocks and bonds in the safe, the boys thought that they had wasted their time until they found a cache of money and jewellery. The gang had a reported $3,500 in cash, so small fortune in negotiable stocks and bonds went down the river, literally, as the safe was dumped from the 5th Street bridge. Later attempts to recover the safe and certificates from the river were unsuccessful and Bobby figured that they were probably halfway to Mississippi by the time the divers started looking for them.

The gang set about enjoying the cash and the jewellery, some of which was spread amongst their friends. Julia Burley remembers Bobby giving her some of the booty.

"Oh! He gave me beautiful jewellery, sapphire earrings with diamonds. I thought it was junk jewellery; I put it on the dresser. Here's a knock on the door, detectives come."

Julia Burley

Julia recalls that the detectives asked her if she knew Robert Lippi and whether he had given her anything in the way of jewels. She thought that it was just costume jewellery because the stones looked too big to be genuine. To her everlasting surprise she discovered they were real and had to return them. Bobby maintains that if it hadn't been for one of the gang's associates getting shot by the police in a separate incident and spilling the beans, Julia would still have the earrings today. Even if that particular escapade had not gone pear-shaped, Bobby would probably have still done some time as he was always looking for a fast buck. The strange thing about the McGraw heist is that Bobby's dad, Paul Lippi (a force veteran at the time), spent close to two days with little sleep cracking the case; only to find his 18 year-old son was the ring-leader.

Although Bobby's original plan for a career as a numbers guy never came to fruition, he feels that boxing, and Charley Burley in particular, kept him out of serious trouble for a couple of years at least and led to his development and the man he grew up to be.

"Anything that would spoil you was out of the question. It wasn't allowed in the picture. Forget it! And it worked! Because, I tell you, the trouble that I got into, whew! I'm gonna tell you; Charley taught me how to fight. I'm very serious, very serious. If I hadn't have been the lightweight champion of the world, they'd have had to make room for me to fight, because I really had it together. Because Charley really taught me well, you understand? Some of these things you don't see anymore. I mean, double right-hands! I could hit you with a double right-hand. It was double-up, double-up! Double right-hands, double left-hook."

Bobby Lippi

Bobby also recalls how Charley's work ethic rubbed off on him and made him a mentally tougher person, because Charley led by example.

"With the half-a-brick in each hand when you were doing the road-work, that last hundred yards, I mean, you'd come flying in, with your legs high, you're drivin', man. Big Jack [Godfrey] and them guys said 'he's gonna burn him out.' Burn me out! He didn't burn nothin' out, because he did it. You're right alongside him. He don't

247

ask you to do nothin' that he can't do."

Bobby Lippi

By March of 1949 the whole boxing scene had changed yet again, arguably for the worse, as the International Boxing Club came into being. The new organisation, which was composed of former heavyweight champion Joe Louis and James D. Norris, (executive vice-president and secretary of the Chicago Stadium), was supposedly brought into existence to arrange bouts of national importance only. These matches were deemed to be heavyweight elimination fights for the championship, which would be promoted in Chicago, Detroit or New York City. The Stadium owners, coincidentally, also had a controlling interest in Detroit Olympia, and stock in Madison Square Garden. Their first promotion was a proposed bout between Ezzard Charles and Jersey Joe Walcott in June to determine the new heavyweight king. Due to his failing health Mike Jacobs, head of the 20th Century Sporting Club in New York, which had held exclusive rights to Louis' services ever since he won the title from James J. Braddock in Comiskey Park on June 22, 1937, would have nothing to do with the new set-up.

Initially there seemed to be no problem with a new organisation taking over where Mike Jacobs, and Tex Rickard before him, had left off, (the corruption that existed within the IBC would only later become apparent). While Norris may have been quoted as saying, "We got tired of having Jacobs tie up all the fighters for New York.", essentially he and his partners, Arthur Wirtz (who was also his partner in other business enterprises), and Joe Louis (who was only a figurehead), subsequently followed suit and tied up all the fighters for not only New York, but also Chicago and Detroit. Eventually St. Louis was added to their collection of promotional locations.

Mike Jacobs may well have been in poor health, but he wasn't about to step aside and let Norris, or anyone else for that matter, take control of the sport that had made him so fabulously rich and famous. While the IBC may have had ideas about promoting Ezzard Charles versus Jersey Joe Walcott for the vacant title, Jacobs fired a return shot across their bow just to keep them in check. A press release announcing the 20th Century Sporting Club's exclusive rights to Ezzard Charles for yet another year, with Jake Mintz named as one of three partners in the Charles contract, seemed to put Chicago in check for sole promotional rights for the fight. With New York or Chicago appearing to be the only candidates, promotional interests in Cincinnati put their case to the NBA, claiming there should be open bidding for the right to stage the Charles-Walcott bout. In an attempt to placate all concerned parties, the IBC added Pittsburgh, Cleveland and Philadelphia to the list of possible venues. The tentacles of the boxing 'octopus', as the IBC would come to be known, were slowly coiling around the whole boxing scene. The effects would be far-reaching but, as with everything else in life, this latest monopoly would not last forever. While it did last, it made very rich men out of a select few, whilst also lining the pockets of many other managers, promoters and fighters.

In Pittsburgh Harry Roth, 'The Count', was now back on the scene and he took over as Charley's manager, convinced that he could get him top-line fights against rated opposition. After a one-year absence from the ring and from the world rankings, Charley was signed to fight the respected Charlie 'Doc' Williams in New Orleans. Williams was a light-heavyweight out of New York and was rated as the number five challenger to champion Freddie Mills of England. Williams had achieved his recently bestowed, lofty status by virtue of his wins against Henry Hall, Bert Lytell, Buddy Farrell, J.C. Wilkins and two sterling efforts against Archie Moore. Credited with an excellent left jab the 'Doc's' fight against Charley Burley was seen as the classic boxer versus puncher, though Burley still had tremendous boxing skills to complement his undoubted power.

Promoter Abe Katz had relied upon his matchmaker Louis Messina to put together the card for the afternoon's show and when the matchmaking was complete, the show was advertised as being a 'Negro' fight card. With a three-round exhibition, one four-rounder, a five-round fight and a couple of six-round wind-ups to complement the headliner, the promoter banked on the lure of 'Doc' Williams versus Charley Burley to tempt the crowds indoors for the 3p.m. start.

Charley struggled somewhat with the heavier Williams, although he managed to hurt the light-heavyweight with body shots in the seventh and eighth rounds. After what Ring magazine called a "gamely contested, but losing, effort" against the New Yorker, Charley's manager made promises to the reporters in attendance that his fighter would be kept busy and would be matched with light-heavyweights or heavyweights if need be. He also made it known, although it must have been obvious by the choice of the highly-rated Williams as an opponent, that Charley Burley would not be fighting soft touches on the way to a title challenge. Roth may have had the money and may even have had the connections to sign up for bigger names, but he was not part of the new system that was developing under Norris and the IBC.

Bobby Lippi recalls that besides losing to 'Doc' Williams, Charley had to swallow what essentially amounted to a mugging. After the fight, Charley and Bobby McKnight went to the promoter to get paid. When they asked for the money, which was supposed to be a percentage of the gate plus expenses, all they were given was $150. Charley demanded more and as the argument grew more heated someone called the cops. Charley was advised to leave without causing any trouble, which he did. The trip to New Orleans was cut short by a day, as Charley and Bobby McKnight left soon after the fight. Charley once pointed out to Tommy O'Loughlin that he never had any luck in New Orleans. This last visit was apparently proof of that statement.

The light-heavyweight division at that time was a division of turmoil. Nine months earlier, in a shock result, Freddie Mills of England had relieved Gus Lesnevich of his championship belt. With the crown now sitting atop a British head, the 'American' light-heavyweight title again came into prominence. Middleweight Tommy Yarosz had gone up a division after dropping a ten-rounder to Jake LaMotta in December 1948 and his manager, Ray Arcel, went to the IBC to ask for its assistance in gaining an elimination bout with Gus Lesnevich for the aforementioned version of the title. However, Jack Kearns entered into negotiations for the same fight for his charge, Joey Maxim, and consequently put Maxim front and centre for a legitimate world title fight with Mills after the Italian light-heavyweight scored a 15-round decision over Lesnevich in May.

In June of 1949, Charles and Walcott fought at Comiskey Park in Chicago, with Charles winning the vacant heavyweight championship of the world via a 15-round decision. Although the fight reportedly drew 26,000 fans to the venue and grossed a quarter of a million dollars, the two principals settled for $53,000 apiece, including broadcast rights. Less than two months later, in what was his first defence of the title, Ezzard Charles received only $15,000 for beating Gus Lesnevich, who had recently failed against Maxim to win a light-heavyweight title. It was becoming increasingly apparent that, even during these early days of the IBC, you had to be 'in' to have any kind of hope of a title, or big-money fight. Things would become much worse with the development of television as the American nation's number one means of entertainment.

Although it would be close to three years before Archie Moore would be granted a world title chance against Joey Maxim, he too had been involved in the occasional business fight during his tough climb to the top. Blackie Nelson remembers being in a bar in San Diego one hot and sunny afternoon in 1948. Just as he was about to order his first drink, two guys in suits, overcoats and hats walked in as if they owned the place and one of them shouted for two drinks while his friend went to the telephone. When the business on the phone was finished, the one guy comes back and says to his friend sitting at the bar, "Moore is going to make it look good for the first." With that, they thanked the barman and headed out, leaving behind ten dollars for two drinks they hadn't even touched. Blackie passed comment to the barman on the heat and their surplus garments and asked who they were. The man behind the bar told Blackie that he didn't want to know and that if had any sense he would avoid them at all costs.

When Blackie told him what he had heard of their conversation, the barman advised him to get some money on Leonard Morrow, Archie Moore's opposition that night in Oakland. Blackie went to the fight, placed a bet on Morrow and came up trumps, as Moore was knocked out in the first round just as predicted.

There were unanswered questions concerning the bout and it would be many years before the Old Mongoose fought again in his adopted state; though he did reverse the result over a year later in Toledo, knocking-out Morrow in the tenth round. This is not to say that Moore was wrong to participate in such deals, he and plenty of other fighters had to do business just to earn money to eat and in some cases to further their career. But, despite doing the deals and playing his own games, it still took Archie Moore close to 15 years of fighting to obtain a title shot. Bearing this in mind, it is easy to see how a fighter like Archie Moore could have all the respect in the world for Charley Burley.

"Archie Moore loved Charley, he knew the deals, he knew the rottenness of the game, you understand. Archie played his little games too, but he came out on top, but Charley was different."

Bobby Lippi

Another 'alleged' fix involving Archie Moore occurred in 1944, but didn't really receive any attention until Archie was preparing for his world heavyweight championship bout with Rocky Marciano. According to Los Angeles Times writer, Braven Dyer, the California state boxing inspector at the time of Moore's knockout loss to Eddie Booker - former champion Willie Ritchie - thought that there was something not quite right about the contest. Dyer wrote to Eddie Booker to get his version of events and the long-retired middleweight shared his thoughts in a reply dated July, 1955.

> "The information which you have presented in your letter comes as a complete surprise. This is the first knowledge that has come to me that Willie Ritchie had wanted Archie Moore and Myself suspended following my knockout victory over Archie in 1944.
>
> But after having fought two very tough draws with Archie Moore previous to the 1944 meeting, I knew what a tough fight Moore puts up, so consequently I was in no hurry to meet Moore for a third time, and I so informed my manager, Frank Schuler. But at this time fighting was my business so the match was made. Later, after the fight, I learned that Archie had not desired to fight me either, but no one approached me prior to the fight with any kind of deal covering the fight.
>
> As for the fight, I had discovered Moore's weakness in our second fight, and I capitalized on that knowledge, but the bitter and desperate fight Archie put up in that third fight was as tough as the other two and how anyone can even intimate that Moore was not trying is beyond me. I personally believe there must have been a misunderstanding on someone's part...
>
> ...In view of the fact that I have nothing to hide regarding the Moore fight or any other fight in which I participated you may quote any or all of this statement."

> Yours in Sports
>
> **Eddie Booker**

According to former lightweight champion Ike Williams, another all-time great who apparently 'did business' when he had to was Sugar Ray Robinson. In his Hall of Fame interview with Norm Meekison Williams told how Robinson went into the tank against Joey Maxim when challenging for the world's light-heavyweight championship in 1952.

"About four or five years later [after the Robinson - Maxim fight], I used to read The New York Journal American every day, that's a fine paper. Bill Corum, who's a very fair writer, he wrote out about what a great fighter Ray Robinson was – and gentlemen, quote me please – he said, 'Ray Robinson, the greatest fighter that I've seen in 35 years of watching fights, took a dive against Joey Maxim. Maybe his friends will tell him to sue me, but he won't.' That's what he said.

I heard that Ray Robinson double-crossed the Negroes in Harlem in New York and they told him to get out of New York or 'we're gonna kill you.' So, you see, Ray wound up living in California."

Ike Williams

The double-cross theory comes out due to the fact that, according to Ike Williams, Maxim had also been instructed to throw the fight so that Robinson would win a third title. After the fight Robinson retired from boxing, only to return just over two years later. It was five years before he fought in New York again (January 1957), when, coincidentally, he lost his middleweight title to Gene Fullmer. The next time he defended his title in New York (September 1957), he also lost, this time to Carmen Basilio. It is possible that certain sections of the population got some of their money back on those nights. How true this tale is, it is difficult to tell. Ike Williams was a huge fan of Ray Robinson, calling him the greatest fighter who ever lived, and had nothing to gain by telling the story.

With his pride and self-respect dictating terms, Charley was not about to go into the tank for anyone. Not that Harry Roth was suggesting that he do so. A couple of months after the defeat to 'Doc' Williams, Charley signed up for a fight in Pittsburgh where he would meet Willie Wright of Youngstown, Ohio. In the Pittsburgh Sun-Telegraph, a local sports writer, promoting the upcoming fight, wondered if things might have been different for Charley.

"There's a fellow who should have been champion, but kept hopping from one manager to another and going in and out of retirement. It's too late now for him to achieve any high goal but he still should be able to beat many of the young fellows who do not have his ring savvy. Certainly the fans will be pulling for him."

Harry Keck, Pittsburgh Sun-Telegraph

While he may have been partly responsible for his own situation, it must have galled Charley to be fighting in an eight-round, under-card bout. If it did trouble him in any way he certainly didn't show it and he didn't let anything affect his performance. Two knockdowns in the second and fifth rounds paved the way for an easy victory for Charley in a semi-final bout to Charlie Affif and Jackie Burke. Bobby Lippi and Julia Burley remember 'Chink' Affif fondly. They recall that he was a good guy that got caught up with the racketeers. These parasites were apparently responsible for Affif leaving the fight game with very little to show for his career as Young Zivic.

Essentially, Charley was picking up pocket money during his recent comeback. The doors to the middleweight and light-heavyweight titles were not only closed to him, but, with the formation of the IBC, they were also securely bolted. Bobby Lippi is of the opinion that by 1948 it was all over for Charley.

Back on the garbage truck, Charley laboured away, waiting to hear any news of a fight. Harry Roth was having about as much success as previous managers in getting Charley any kind of action at all. Seven months after the Willie Wright contest Charley disposed of Chuck Higgins in double-quick time. Roy McHugh, reporting for the Pittsburgh Press, gave his view of the fight.

"Coming from Charley Burley, the words sounded familiar. "I'll fight anyone," he said last night after a quick and artistic knockout of Chuck Higgins.

Burley was merely repeating himself. For 13 years he has steadily proclaimed his availability. But tricky phantom punchers of Burley's stripe never make popular opponents, and the willingness was entirely on his side.

In a manner of speaking, Burley was too good for his own good. Still is, probably, even at 32. A feint, a left uppercut, a right chop and another left uppercut, this one just under the ribs, polished off Higgins. It happened at 1.17 of the first round.

254

Higgins is no setup. The muscular Elwood City middleweight had won 33 of his 34 fights up to last night. But this was a Charley Burley who made it easy to recall that he had been in the same ring as Fritzie Zivic, Billy Soose, Jimmy Bivins and Ezzard Charles.

It was Burley's first fight in seven months and only his fifth since 1946. However, he still had the name to attract an unusually heavy Aragon turnout, 1,100. With a $2,100 gross, Joe Brusco and Bill Drummer paid off on $1,600."

Roy McHugh, Pittsburgh Post Gazette

Barely a month later at the same venue, a somewhat smaller crowd of just over 700 braved the appalling weather to see Charley dispose of Detroit's Buddy Hodnet in six extremely one-sided rounds. A cold appeared to hamper Charley's efforts slightly and it took him a little longer than usual to get into his stride against a largely ineffective fighter, who seemed content to use his hands for purely defensive purposes. The slow start from Charley amused Hodnet somewhat and he sealed his own fate by laughing in Charley's face at the start of the sixth round. After that insult the assault upon his person was so savage that Hodnet attempted to turn away, but was hit on the side of the body with the punch that ended the fight. Although no one knew it at the time, this would be the final ring appearance of Charley Burley before his hometown fans.

Yet again the cold that Charley had turned to something much worse, as he developed pleurisy. The illness meant he had to pass up the opportunity to travel to the West Indies for a series of bouts featuring fellow Americans Bert Lytell, Jerome Richardson, Richie Dallas and Louis Ramos. Lytell, who had defeated Gentle Daniel and Easy Boy Francis, and Holman Williams, who had lost to Daniel during previous forays to the Islands, had given the West Indian populace a taste for American fighters. Promoter George Beckles had been hopeful of staging a successful tour in Trinidad, but his plans fell through and neither Charley Burley nor Bert Lytell travelled to southern shores that year.

While Charley was yet again faced with another delay to his boxing career, shameful bad luck that was becoming such a regular occurrence it appeared to be a part of his kit bag, Ray Robinson marched on. By defeating Robert Villemain in Philadelphia in June, Robinson became Pennsylvania 'World' middleweight champion. In reality, Charley could have no argument with being left out in the cold by his home state's commission, as he had not been active enough to gain a sufficiently high ranking in order to contest the vacant title. Besides, Villemain had the right credentials, having defeated reigning middleweight champion Jake LaMotta in a non-title fight just six months previously, while the ever-popular Robinson was now four from five versus the Bronx Bull and had been the victor in their last three meetings. Yet another possible and probably more influential reason for this match-up is that the chairman of the Pennsylvania state boxing commission was Leo Raines, friend of Blinky Palermo. Robinson and LaMotta were definitely connected. Villemain possibly so, while Charley Burley was not.

Although he didn't manage to travel to the West Indies, Charley did get to fight in South America once he was recovered from his illness as he made the journey to Peru to fight South American light-heavyweight champion Pilar Bastidas. According to Prof. Wilfred Stephenson, local correspondent for Ring magazine, it was the first time that an American fighter had been brought in to fight for money on a professional show in Peru in twenty years. The writer also indicated that local promoter Max Aguirre had Charley, Cocoa Kid and the respected Artie Towne signed up for fights. The fight, outdoors during the winter season, drew a decent sized crowd.

Some reports indicate that Charley didn't have it too easy with the big Uruguayan. Although one local scribe felt that, at the final bell, Bastidas looked miserable". The report of the 'action' from the following day's newspaper, 'Ultimas Noticias', highlighted the fact that Charley did not impress with his display, which consisted of 'calculated and minimal movements'. While the American visitor was admired for his 'fast fists' and his 'technical ability', he was labelled as being rather dull. This was a tag that was often hung upon Charley and it would appear that, to an extent, this might have been true. Charley did not take chances in the ring if he didn't have to. Doing just enough was often enough as long as the win was gained. He had contested close to 100 recorded professional fights (or over 100 if earlier reports on his career are to be believed) and a look at his record will show that he fought some of the better fighters of his day. Some were truly dangerous men, deadly punchers and genuine 'Hall of Fame' material. It appeared that the man who could do things in the ring that no other fighter, before or since, could do was just not exciting or crowd-pleasing enough and the sport of boxing, when stripped right down to its fundamentals, is all about entertainment.

"Although the North American made a hit at his training quarters, even putting some of his sparring partners into difficulties at times, he was not up to expectations when in action in the ring.

Burley came out of the fray without a scratch, but did not seem to have done his best: his slowness showed fatigue or lack of training. The fight was a ten-rounder. This correspondent interviewed him after the fight and he complained of aching pains all over his body owing to the dampness of the climate here, and it was obvious that he had a temperature."

Prof. Wilfred Stephenson, Ring magazine

Another local newspaper - El Comercio - wrote that the fight did not satisfy the fans as both fighters did very little. The reporter went on to say that "... the North American did show that he was a man that knows all the secrets of the ring and holds a very powerful right hand." Although he was not eligible to claim the title that Bastidas held, Charley considered his performance to be worthy of such an honour, as he told the press after the bout, "I suppose I can call myself some kind of champion now." The climate became such an issue with Charley that he didn't take part in the additional two fights that had been agreed upon. The experience had probably not been what he was expecting, but he had earned another payday, had another win, was still practically unmarked and in full possession of his faculties. Blackie Nelson feels that it was Charley's great skill that kept him in such fantastic condition despite a 14-year professional career.

"I thought [he was] the greatest I ever saw. Great reflexes, body movement, fast hands, slick as grease. Seemed to anticipate every move the other fighter was going to make. He could really slide and ride with a punch. Probably why he was never stopped or cut up. He was very deceptive on his feet. He wouldn't jump around like too many people, especially today. He was kinda like Louis, he wouldn't jump around either, but he was always on top. He'd keep the opponent from running and hiding. Both were very good at that. Charley was always a hard worker, always in shape. He didn't drink too much or crowd around. Smoked a little, but not bad, you know. "

Blackie Nelson

Back home to Pittsburgh and his humdrum job on the garbage truck, Charley Burley once again contemplated retirement. The trip to Peru had been long and lonely and he was tired of the luck that had dogged his fight career.

In May 1951 Charley was offered a series of bouts in Germany. Harry Roth felt that a trip to Europe might help re-establish Charley's career as he was getting no action whatsoever in the United States. The previous year Lloyd Marshall had embarked on a similar tour, fighting in Germany, England and Wales with varying degrees of success. During his tour of the European continent, Marshall, who was now approaching the end of his career, engaged in eight contests winning three and gaining a draw in another. According to one boxing insider, he also managed to leave behind a pregnant girlfriend who later gave birth to a son. Lloyd's alleged offspring grew up in Sweden and his own son (Marshall's grandchild) competed with some success for an amateur club in Western Europe.

Thousands of cross-country miles, dozens of seedy hotels, many nights curled up in the back of his car, hundreds of hard-fought rounds and close to 15 years since his last trip across the Atlantic, Charley sailed for Europe. Any excitement generated by the prospect of visiting another part of the European continent must have rapidly evaporated as, for reasons that are not totally clear or have been forgotten by the passing of years, not one of the arranged matches materialised. Again travels to foreign climes had failed to deliver on promises and Charley returned home on the SS Washington.

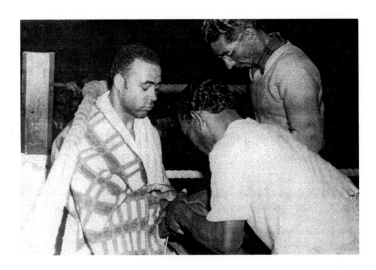

With the assistance of Peruvian boxing stalwarts Roberto Carrillo and Guillermo Penaloza (glasses) Charley gets ready for South American Light-heavyweight champion Pilar Bastidas. Whilst awaiting the first bell (below) Charley attempts to keep warm. The cold, damp climate put him off any more fights in Lima.

Chapter Fourteen

The End of the Line
The Begining of the Legend

A story that Bobby Lippi recalls about Charley during the period around the end of his career involves some confusing and contentious points. Julia Burley recalled an incident when Charley fought and the Ku Klux Klan were there. She remembers that incident as occurring in Oklahoma or somewhere similar. She also believes that the incident involving the Klan happened around 1948. As for a latter adventure, Bobby Lippi is unsure of the location - Oklahoma or Texas - but remembers some of the details.

"He went on the road taking on anybody that felt they could beat him. These are not in the record books. These were not considered professional fights.

They were setting up the Tank Towns. They went for about six weeks. He was guaranteed $250 a week, plus a percentage. [Julia Burley, at this point in the tale, still didn't remember]. He was like a 'Masked Marvel'. Nobody knew that this was Charley Burley; it was a set-up. It had to be '51 when he went. It was after Peru. They cheated him out of his money when he came back from Peru. [Bobby recalls how 'Pippi' Slutsky was again on the scene]. Charley went away [to fight] and they tried to kill him, hang him, in one of these 'Wild West' towns after he beat the guy, knocked him out. [Julia remembers the incident at this point, but thinks it was Oklahoma. She also recalls that Charley brought home a wrestler after the trip who stayed with them for a while. She also remembers that Charley was cheated out of some money again].

They had this black and white thing going on with the betting. All the money is on the white side, but they don't know that their guy is going to lose. They'd set it up, knock out the guy, collect the money and go on to the next own. They went to one town where

260

they stormed the ring. They had to go under the ring to get away. Charley got out and said 'To hell with this' and they came back."

Bobby Lippi

Julia remembers when Charley was away during that time and also remembers the story about the crowd storming the ring. What she wasn't aware of was the detail of what Charley was really doing on the road.

"I remember something about that, it was a barnstorming trip, but I thought he was boxing in professional fights."

Julia Burley

Bobby Lippi feels that it couldn't have been easy for Charley to have to earn money in such a manner. But, as he said to Julia Burley, "He was embarrassed, but he had to put food on the table." The fact that there was no television and that there was only the one film of Charley kicking around, it is not difficult to see why such an enterprise would work in distant locations. Charley had been a practical non-entity, fame-wise, during his peak years and it could be a fairly safe bet that no one out in the sticks would recognise him. His name may have been well-known, his reputation possibly more so, but his face could have been any one of thousands of black fighters trying to earn a dollar at that time. Apparently, Rocky Marciano got away with using his brother as an opponent at the outset of his own boxing career and even more recently professional fighters have used one name in one town and another name somewhere else.

Contemporary newspaper reports indicate that in October 1949 Charley teamed up with one Ralph Hayes, a boxing promoter and manager in Council Bluffs, Iowa. It seems that the idea was to engage Charley in a barnstorming trip of the smaller towns in the area. On October 18th Charley stopped Jack Burns who, despite a forty-pound weight advantage, was fortunate to last until the fourth of a scheduled eight-round 'exhibition'. Charley, scaling 158 pounds, dropped his opponent in the second round for a seven count, in the third for an eight count and again in the final round for a count of two before securing the knockout with a body attack. That contest took place on a wrestling bill and is the likely reason it was listed as an exhibition. It may also be where Julia Burley got the memory of Charley returning to Pittsburgh with a wrestler in-tow. Three days later Charley beat Jack Brennan of Kansas City in three rounds, and then fought heavyweight George Hayes on the same night. The former Iowa Golden Gloves champion accepted a challenge issued to anyone who felt they could go a round with Burley. He failed.

Julia remembers that Charley, on most occasions, would come home after being on the road with money and that particular jaunt was, as she recalls, no different. Once again, Charley returned to his job with the city and thought little about fighting again until, in August 1951, an opportunity for a fight against the highly-ranked light-heavyweight Harry 'Kid' Matthews came along. Charley, along with Rusty Payne and Archie Moore, was proposed as an opponent for Matthews for a Labour Day card in Washington. Charley spoke to Bobby Lippi about going back to the gym on a regular basis and maybe getting this and a few more paydays. By that time, Pop O'Brien's gym at the bathhouse was no longer there and the ring at the Irene Kaufman Settlement was gone. With the city's redevelopment of the Hill District a large number of the older places were being torn down and there appeared to be few, if any, suitable locations.

"What was a gym didn't even have a shower! They had an oil drum cut like this [a quarter of it cut away] that you stepped into on two two-by-fours with a hole in and a hose coming from the wall. After about a week of that, that was it, no more come back. Charley never talked about it again. And I'm glad, 'cause I would have got killed."

Bobby Lippi

Bobby knew then that it was over, because when Charley was in training he didn't drink and he cut out the Lucky Strikes cigarettes and his occasional cigar. If they went to a bar, Charley would abstain from alcohol and would drink only orange juice. However, on this occasion they went just down the street from the gym into a joint called the Blue Note (at the intersection of Wylie and Fullerton), where Charley ordered two beers and he never went back into a gym with the intention of boxing again.

The boxing career of Charley Burley was over and after his retirement he was largely forgotten about by the fight game. His steady job was enabling him to keep a roof over the heads of his family in addition to food on the table and Charley Burley seemed happy to forget fighting.

The heavy and dirty work of the rubbish truck would affect him in later years, but, for the time being, he worked hard throughout the week and relaxed at weekends by hanging around on Centre Avenue and its surrounding streets. He and Bobby would spend their time in bars, shooting pool (another game he excelled at) and generally having a good time. Bobby would take his wife up to Charley and Julie's house early in the day and then head off down the street.

Charley always liked to look his best when not in his work clothes and his 'rubbish man's hat'. His 'Friday night regalia' consisting of a one hundred-dollar Stetson, cashmere coat and yam-coloured Florsheim shoes made him stand out from the crowd. Always sharply dressed and sometimes better-looking due to cosmetic assistance they paraded on street corners and watched the world go by. Charley was also not above dabbing his shiny nose with a powder puff and the makeup routine was a ritual that Bobby Lippi took to emulating.

> "Hey, monkey see – monkey do. I had this greasy forehead, you know us greasy Dagos right? And if Charley Burley can use a powder puff…"
>
> **Bobby Lippi**

Bobby laughs at the memory now, but he and Charley were serious about their appearance when out on the street. Charley wouldn't go out without a crease in his pants, the sharp suit, a shirt and tie and the hat – "all brushed up". Bobby remembers that Charley didn't stop wearing a suit until 1953-54. He walked that walk – and, according to Bobby Lippi, never, ever started trouble, "It was always some other fool." Charley had a way of dealing with the smart guys or the guys that thought they could take him on. He'd get to kidding around, grab any smart ass around the neck and get to hugging them and destroying their balance. He let them know – 'hey, I'm Charley Burley', because there was no doubt over who he was. He was Charley Burley. One local fighter made the mistake of calling Charley a 'has-been' and word got back to him. Instead of challenging 'Sugar' Ray Jackson, Charley just fooled around with him, almost breaking his neck in the process.

Bobby Lippi felt that the song 'Standing on the Corner' (watching all the girls go by) could have been written by, or for, he and Charley because that's what they used to do. Charley was not one for conversation and usually only mentioned things once, but he sometimes had some humorous insights into what was going on down the street and with life in general. Standing on the corner or hanging around down the street, Bobby Lippi fondly remembers the hours and days spent with his mentor and friend.

> "He was a good guy. The kids would come around and he would always have, you know, quarters or something to pass out to the kids. All the whores and prostitutes and everyone down there, they all loved Charley, but they knew Charley had a wife at home and there was no games with Charley."

> **Bobby Lippi**

> "My Daddy was a gentleman."

> **Angie Burley**

Charley's reputation and the respect that the people in Pittsburgh, and in particular the Hill, had for him is reflected in countless stories that his family and friends tell. Charley was not above using this respect to his own advantage if a friend was in trouble or in need of a favour. Although he was unhappy with his work buddy 'Trees' for putting him in the middle of the Malibu drug incident by naming him as his strong-arm, Charley would, on occasion, do a little of that kind of stuff. One incident that occurred in 1970 involved a good friend of Charley's by the name of Al.

Down at the pool hall, Al was well known as the numbers guy and he always had a good-sized bankroll on his person. Because he was known and respected, Al became a little complacent about his money and where he kept it. One day he took some stake money from a punter and added it to the already large roll in his back pocket. However, Al neglected to tuck the roll all the way in. A guy in the bar, an African-American who needs to remain nameless for reasons that will become apparent, saw the money and its keeper's negligence. He went over to Al to start making small talk and, when the opportunity presented itself, popped the roll out of his pocket. A regular at the bar, an old railroad guy that used to sit in the corner wearing his regulation pinstripe cover-alls, saw everything that went down. The robber left the bar immediately and the railroad worker told Al what happened. The guy that stole the money was a drug dealer with a large and nasty reputation and the physical presence to match. Al had a problem, how to get the money back without getting killed. To him there's only one answer, Charley Burley. Al called Charley, who then called Bobby Lippi to drive him over to this guy's place. Not wishing to inflame the situation by turning up at the man's front door with a white guy in tow, Charley called another friend by the name of Blackie and the three met on the street where the drug dealer lived. Charley asked Bobby to wait in the car and he and Blackie knocked on the door to confront the guy over the money. The guy answered, talked to Charley for a short while, and then quite meekly handed over the money. It was only $300, not a vast amount to a numbers guy like Al, but it was the principle, as Al had a reputation to uphold. The man that stole the money has today cleaned up his act and can occasionally be seen on television preaching the word of the Lord.

Just as things were during his boxing career, Charley didn't always get what he wanted or what was due to him. After years of playing the same number, Charley finally appeared to have some luck as, in early 1960 his number, 536, finally came up. Unfortunately, he was refused the payout that he felt he was due and this put him in a rather tricky situation. The guy that Charley played his usual numbers with on that occasion was a former ball-player by the name of Joe Atkins. At odds of 750-1 Charley's numbers 'hit' and he expected a windfall of $1,012.50; instead he received only $300. Bobby Lippi was amazed at Charley's initial reaction, as it was a little out of character for him to become violent, "Charley thought about going down there and doing a number on him," he remembers. Charley however, had the good sense to listen to Julia and instead chose the legal route. Which made her very happy, as she was all too aware of what Charley was capable of. "Charley would have killed him, he would have killed him." Julia says now.

Atkins was arrested and, on the back of previous convictions in 1956 for operating a lottery and in 1959 for receiving stolen goods, was found guilty by a jury in less than ten minutes. Judge Anne Alpern turned the case over to the Probation Office, who carried out an investigation of Atkins prior to sentencing. Although the former ball-player was punished for the illegal operation of a lottery, Charley never received all of the prize money he was due.

Whatever Charley and Bobby got up to after work, come dinner time Charley always insisted that he and his seemingly constant companion go home to eat. No matter how much money he had on him, he would always argue "nobody cooks like my Julie" and he would head off home after first picking up a pint of his wife's favourite 'North Pole' ice cream. He and Bobby could be right down the other end of the street nearer to home and Charley would insist on walking back along to the store for the treat, before returning home for dinner. The ice cream got to be a daily ritual and Julia complained that she would get fat; to which Charley would reply "I like fat." Though he obviously loved his wife, and Julia loved him, there were times when the jealousy born out of real love got to rear its ugly head.

"Burley always had something going against him. He was good-looking, light-skinned and the white girls loved him. One of them still lives just around the corner here. She used to follow him around everywhere. He didn't want nothing to do with her, but word got around and that hurt him."

Jack Godfrey

The lady that Jack referred to used to frequent one of Charley's regular haunts down off Roberts Street.

"That blonde down on Protectory [Street], I mean she was a good-looking blonde. But what was going on down there was the poker table, because Charley loved poker."

Bobby Lippi

Bobby also remembers Julia's reaction to the rumours that were flying around about Charley and the woman at the gambling joint, and he is adamant about Charley's fidelity. He finds the whole thing quite absurd, though he still jokes good-naturedly about it. Julie remembers the incident and is open about how she felt at the time.

"Sure, I got jealous. Everyone gets jealous, it's only human nature!"

Julia Burley

When not down on the street or playing cards or shooting pool, they would all go fishing together up at Akerman's lake and spend a quiet day on the banks with a picnic. With lines dangling in the water, Bobby would often fall asleep. The women would talk, but Charley often just fished and watched the water, hopeful of a catch. One day, while taking part in one of the many fishing contests, Charley had a bite and by the size of the struggle he was having it was a pretty big fish. Usually, anyone next to you who saw you trying to land a catch would pull in their own fishing rods out of courtesy. On that occasion however, the guy next to Charley and Bobby refused to move, so Charley pulled out a knife and headed towards him. If Charley had any intentions of stabbing the guy, then the belligerent fisherman would have been dead on the spot, as he just stood there frozen with fear. Charley simply reached across and cut his line. It was not the action itself that left Bobby Lippi open-mouthed in disbelief; it was the fact that Charley Burley carried a knife. Charley landed the fish and the prize-money that had accumulated in the 'pot', winning just over $26.

On one fishing trip the pair ran into some trouble of the nastiest kind, when they were asked to move away from the lake by the owner, though this wasn't at their usual haunt, due to complaints from the residents across the other side of the water. They felt that blacks hanging around would 'lower the tone' so to speak and they didn't want them around their property. The owner was embarrassed and even apologetic, but Charley just got his stuff together and moved on. Needless to say, neither he nor Bobby ever went back there and Charley was quite philosophical about the whole thing, saying that it was " – their loss, they won't get to know me – Charley Burley." This was always his attitude and you have to admire Charley's acceptance of things he could not change. That is not to say that Charley never had a temper, he could be rather wicked, though never really violent. Julia remembers that Charley could swear with the best of them when upset; though, by all accounts, he was still some way behind his mother.

In the winter of 1951, Charley's mother passed away. Angeline Burley was in her mid-seventies, and although she was largely bed-ridden for her last few years, she was still a force to be reckoned with. It is probably just a strange coincidence that the termination of his boxing career occurred around the same time as his mother's death, as Charley basically 'gave up the ghost' after the barnstorming trip and the ill-fated tour of Europe. It appeared that he had definitely had enough.

"That was it. I couldn't take it anymore. It was hopeless. I came home and said 'What's the use?'"

Charley Burley

So, what of a career and a life after boxing? Today, many fighters with the personality of an Archie Moore or a Ray Robinson would wind up doing colour commentary for television. As it was, Moore and Robinson ploughed time, money and energy into American youth. For those that had earned the money and the titles, the worry that a lack of money brings was not a problem. Many of the popular white champions had earned enough to live a life of relative luxury and ease, even if some boxers are notorious spendthrifts. Willie Pep had it and lost it all, but at least he didn't end up shining shoes like Beau Jack or labouring in a warehouse, as did Ike Williams.

With the very rare and notable exception, it seemed that even the black fighters that 'made it' had trouble keeping it together financially, once the punch-for-pay days were over. Many fighters who have hit the heights and been long in the public eye have a very difficult time adjusting to the changes that retirement brings, not only from a financial perspective, but also from a recognition point of view. Many found it hard to cope once the spotlight faded and the fans stopped screaming. Charley Burley had no such problems. While well-known and respected he had eased his way out of the fight game over a period of about four years and had supplemented his pugilistic income with a regular pay-cheque from the city. He had little trouble settling into a 'normal' way of life and before the mid-1950s his family had grown to include another son in the form of David. As the Hill District vanished under the guise of urban renewal, Charley and his family moved to the Oakland area of the city, near to Forbes Field where they settled in a duplex at the top end of Robinson Street. Charley secured a position as the superintendent from the building's owners, a job he was able to perform in conjunction with his work for the city. In exchange for his services, Charley, Julia and their three children lived downstairs in one block, while he also kept an eye on the other buildings in the complex.

As the 1950s were reaching their conclusion Angie Burley was lured away by the bright lights and the jazz scene of New York where she married a musician named Doug Watkins. This double bass virtuoso recorded with Art Blakey and the original Jazz Messengers, amongst others, in addition to recording and releasing solo material. Sadly, Doug was killed in a car crash in 1962. This was the first of a string of tragedies that would plague the Burley family. Eventually, Angie would return home to Pittsburgh and her loving family.

The following year (1963), Charley paid a visit to Pittsburgh Post-Gazette sports writer Al Abrams. Abrams, who hadn't seen Charley in 15 years, thought he still looked in good enough shape to "whip a lot of the bums masquerading as fighters today."

Happy within himself and with his general 'lot' in life, Charley would often receive visits from old friends such as Archie Moore. Their fight in 1944 may have been all blood and thunder, but their friendship was based on mutual respect and admiration. In a letter to Charley, Archie Moore reflected these sentiments.

"Hi Champ, It was sure nice of you, Julie, Angie and David to welcome me and my family into your nice friendly home. Charlie you can count your blessings, what a fine family you have. I remain your friend."

Archie Moore, April 22nd 1973

Charley faded from the eye and the minds of the boxing public and for over 20 years Charley passed his days in relative obscurity. An article entitled 'Yesterdays', written by Joe Kaplan for the March 14, 1977 edition of Sports Illustrated, appeared to re-ignite the public's interest in Charley Burley. Kaplan mused at how one of the greatest fighters of his day had wound up hauling trash for the city of Pittsburgh. Charley confided that it was a money issue. "I was offered, but wouldn't take no dives. I wouldn't do it. I never took no Money and that's God's truth." Julia agreed saying that was Charley's mistake. "You could have had plenty of money. Now we don't have none."

Suddenly, to some small extent, Charley was back in the public eye as things started to happen. The new-found recognition may have been a nice reminder of his glory years, but it did little for Charley in the real world. A seemingly trivial accident at work, where an old rubbish can fell on his leg, left him incapacitated for a lot longer than expected. Twelve stitches were required to close the wound, but it became infected and refused to heal, resulting in surgery and two weeks' rest at the city's

Montefiore Hospital, the same hospital that had worked on Charley's hands in the late 1930s. Cuts and gashes aside, and Charley received plenty in his time, mostly due to the fact that he didn't even wear gloves to protect his hands at work, the labour involved in carrying the people of Pittsburgh's trash around for over 20 years began to take its toll. Charley developed arthritis in his back and the physical work became even more demanding.

While it may have been a case of 'too little too late' for the recognition now being heaped upon him, Charley enjoyed the attention to a certain degree; though he thought that people may be better off writing about the younger guys presently plying their trade in the hardest profession of them all. At the begining of the 1980s Charley found himself somewhat in demand as he was nominated for a number of awards. The Rochester Boxing Association, in their 5th annual awards ceremony, presented Charley with the 'Courage' award because of "his record as a great fighter in the ring and his exemplary conduct out of it." The April 1983 edition of Ring Magazine named Charley as an inductee to their Hall-of-Fame along with Bob Foster and Carlos Monzon.

Things started to happen again for Charley on the boxing front. The Hall of Fame recognition drew attention from other quarters and he was approached by James Washington Junior of the W.P.S. Fight Factory in California. Washington, a professional fighter in San Diego in the mid 1940s was looking to get into boxing promotion and, remembering Charley, felt that he was ideally suited to the training of his fighters. Washington told one reporter, who wondered who Burley was, "Charley Burley is the Vince Lombardi of boxing".

The unlikely location for these initial promotions was to be the U.S. territory of Guam. Washington, along with his corporate counsel Albert Atallah and local promoter Dave Quituga, had been developing the programme for a number of months and had approached the promoters of World Boxing Council junior lightweight title holder, Hector 'Macho' Camacho as a possible headliner for their first promotion.

After losing his youngest son David to health problems in 1985, Charley appeared to have little zest for life. He stopped going fishing, a pastime he truly loved, and he stopped going down the street. It would be a rare occasion that he would go out in any kind of a social manner and even when his old buddy Archie Moore would come to visit, he would just stay at home and talk.

The World Boxing Hall of Fame in California made Charley one of their inductees at a ceremony in 1987. Julia remembers that Charley really didn't want to go on the all-expenses-paid trip to the West Coast. She thought that he was being anti-social, though she also suspects that it may also have had something to do with Charley's dislike of being fussed over or patronised. They left for California on the Friday, went to the function on the Saturday, come Sunday Charley wanted to return home. Other inductees that year were Joe Brown, Jimmy Carter, Young Corbett III, Jackie Fields, Fidel LaBarba, Danny 'Little Red' Lopez, 'Philadelphia' Jack O'Brien, Willie Ritchie, Jack Sharkey, Dick Tiger and old nemesis Fritzie Zivic, who had sadly passed away three years earlier aged 71. Although Zivic was no longer around to help relive the days of their youth, Charley delighted in meeting contemporaries Ike Williams and former triple title-holder Henry Armstrong. Hurricane Hank was not enjoying the best of health at the time and Julie Burley's snap-shots of the occasion show the man once dubbed 'Mr. Perpetual Motion' getting around in a wheel-chair.

Charley made a number of trips back to the West Coast during this period and on one occasion he took the opportunity to meet up with his old nemesis, Sugar Ray Robinson. Charley looked forward to meeting Ray again, though Bobby Lippi remembers that he hardly had hand-shakes and hugs on his mind.

"When he went to California he wanted to beat the shit out of Sugar Ray, he wanted to beat Ray's ass on the spot. Cause he was mad at Sugar, because Sugar worked too many rotten deals. Sugar was in up to his neck with the racketeers and Charley was going to show him - not that he just screwed Charley Burley, but other people. Charley was the most deserving of them all. He should've been the champ.

Bobby Lippi

Bobby said that Charley told him that he felt sorry for Ray when he did meet up with him in California as Robinson was showing early signs of dementia and his nervous system was eroded to such an extent that he was constantly shaking. If there was evidence of any real ill-feeling between Charley and Sugar Ray it didn't show publicly. When Charley was honoured for his upcoming World Boxing Hall of Fame induction at a banquet in the Aurora Club in April 1986, he was the recipient of a telegram from the former welter and middleweight king.

271

"Congratulations on your night. Millie and I are thinking of you and always wish you the best. Finally."

Sugar Ray Robinson

Charley, Julia and Angie had moved out of the duplex on Robinson Street and were now living in the next street along, while Charles Junior, an electrician by trade and a Vietnam veteran lived across town. Julia Burley remembers how Charley's experiences of WWII and the impact it had on his career were reflected in the life of their eldest son. Charley had moved himself and his family to Minneapolis to further his boxing career the weekend the Japanese bombed Pearl Harbour. On a similar note the eldest of the Burley boys decided he was going to leave school as soon as possible, thereby foregoing college. He left high school at the end of the week and lo-and-behold, the USA joined the Vietnam War and he was drafted.

Bobby Lippi recalls that when Muhammad Ali changed his name and refused to be drafted, Charley, probably thinking about the perils his son was facing on foreign shores, would not call him Ali. Instead he insisted on referring to him as Cassius Clay. Bobby adds that Charley came to respect the self-proclaimed 'greatest' because of what he stood for and eventually referred to him as Muhammad Ali. The heavyweight champion obviously had respect for Charley Burley though as, according to Charley's nephew Kenny Halliday, he sent him tickets for his fight against Charlie Powell in Pittsburgh in 1963. Kenny remembers, because he went to the fight with the same tickets as Charley didn't want to go.

As the 1980s drew to a close, visits from family, friends and fans did little to lift Charley's spirits and his health was now beginning to falter. Charley may have felt that he had done his share of travelling and socialising, as he became more content at home and insisted that his Julie go out and enjoy herself at the bingo and occasional gambling trips to Atlantic City.

At the onset of the 1990s Charley was becomming increasingly frail and was begining to show signs of Alzheimer's disease. With her husband relying on a wheel-chair to get around, Julie had to spend what little money they had on home improvements in order to make Charley as comfortable as possible. The bedroom was moved downstairs and an additional bathroom was constructed on the side of the living-room. 1992 brought further recognition and induction into Canastota's International

Boxing Hall-of-Fame, but Charley was too ill to travel and he was increasingly confined indoors.

On sunnier days Charley would occasionally sit out on the porch and watch the world go by. Maybe he would think about the childhood he had, running barefoot and innocent in the mining slums of Pennsylvania or of growing up in the smoky city that was the Pittsburgh of old. Maybe he pondered on the time he spent developing into a fighter capable of competing with some of the world's best. Swapping punches just down the hill at Forbes Field where part of Pittsburgh University now stands. Whatever he mulled over, he had a rich and varied life to reflect upon. The only thing that was missing was his name on the roll of honour of boxing's elite world champions. As Charley himself once said in an interview shortly after Ray Robinson passed away, "God said 'which one of you wants to be Sugar Ray?' I guess I didn't raise my hand fast enough."

Many have wondered at the fact that Charley Burley never seemed to be bitter about not getting what he deserved out of the fight game. Big Jack Godfrey was always of the opinion that Charley was bitter until the end, while David 'Trees' Jordan recalls an occasion where Charley knocked out some guy who called him not so much a 'has been', but a 'never was'. The young man that looked up to Charley and wanted to be just like him felt that Charley was made of much better stuff.

"I think lesser people, with less force of character would have allowed that kind of thing to eat at them until they destroyed themselves and ended up a bum on the street, all because of this raw deal they got and be consumed by their bitterness."

August Wilson

Charley's closest and dearest friend knows that his mentor didn't carry such baggage around with him.

"Bitter? No. There's a better word that I can't think of. You know when you would have liked something to happen, but it didn't. I wouldn't say regret, because that was not Charley.

He knew! He knew how good he was and no one else needed to

tell him. He knew he would've been the champ, all he wanted was the shot, you know."

Bobby Lippi

Charley Burley died on October 16th 1992, the day of his great-grandson's first birthday. He was 75. As was typical of Charley's life and luck, as far as fame and boxing were concerned, the newspapers were on strike that week and there was nothing in the local press and consequently nothing in the boxing magazines about his passing. His old friend and sparring partner, Blackie Nelson, wrote in disgust to the trade press, including Boxing Illustrated and the Ring Magazine and they belatedly ran a short piece on the career of Charley Burley.

There was precious little written about Charley after his retirement and right on up until his death and even then there was little more than a nod of recognition. What has been written has been in the way of reflection on a boxing career that never took him where his talents deserved. Musings on how he wasn't flashy or crowd-pleasing enough in style, though he had substance in abundance, or how his moving from one manager to another somehow hampered him and his aspirations, are repeated over and over.

If, like Ray Robinson, Joe Louis or Henry Armstrong, Charley had availed himself of the services of a good, black manager, he may have obtained a better deal for himself. But, as all of his managers were white, it could be argued that, with the possible exception of Phil Goldstein and Tommy O'Loughlin, they might not have had the best interests of a mixed-race African-American at heart. As a result Charley came away from 14 years in the fight game with very little tangible reward. Money, as always, was the God and a sad fact of life in sport's 'red-light district' was that a very large percentage of fighters were just commodities. Racism reared its ugly head with monotonous regularity and it took a strong will to fight back, not only physically, but also conscientiously. Bought, sold and traded as little more than meat, many fighters paid the ultimate price in the hardest of all sports. For African-Americans, Italians, Jews and many other working classes, boxing may well have been a 'way out', but there was a hefty price to pay. One of Charley Burley's more redeeming traits may have been his sense of who he was and what it was like to be black in a sport that was a reflection of the society that spawned it.

In his book 'The 100 Greatest Fighters of all Time', boxing historian, writer, journalist and wit, Bert Sugar, summed it up well when he said of Burley, "Fame has been called a crazy old lady who hoards swatches of fabric and throws away plates of food. In Charley Burley's case, it threw away one of the greatest unrealised talents in the history of boxing."

The real truth behind Charley Burley's failure to win a world title may be a combination of many factors. Racism undoubtedly played its part, but the fact is that Charley, regardless of the colour of his skin, was a simple and honest man. The money and the opportunity were there for him when he was at the top of his game, he just couldn't have lived with himself had he taken the cash and gone into the tank.

"It wasn't my style. I think it paid off to a certain extent. You have a better feeling about yourself."

Charley Burley

In his eulogy to Charley, playwright August Wilson considered how the life of a tree cannot be fully appreciated until it is cut down and its rings counted. He made the same comparison to the life of Charley Burley. Only now, upon reflection, can we gain a true insight into not only the type of fighter he was, but also the type of man. It could be argued that he should have co-operated more with the powers that be, maybe then more people would know as much about him as they do of his contemporaries, LaMotta and Robinson, Zale and Graziano. Then again, he wouldn't have been who he was – Charley Burley.

"Charley should have had it all and it had nothing to do with his colour. He was honest – he was a very honest man."

Bobby Lippi

Charley Burley along with colleagues (above left) whilst working for the West Coast Fight Factory and (above right) in California visiting Junior Washington et al.

With boxing historian Jerry Fitch in Rochester, 1982 (photographed by Tony Liccione Snr.)

The author with Charley and Julia Burley at their Pittsburgh home in September, 1992 and with Bobby Lippi (below) at the Burley home in October 1997

*Height: 5'- 8"
Neck: 16"
Reach: 75"
Chest: 37" Chest, exp: 39 1/2"
Bicep: 12 1/2" Forearm: 11 1/2" Wrist: 7 1/2"
Waist: 30"
Thigh: 18" Calf: 14 1/2" Ankle: 9"
Weight: 142 - 162lb

*(also listed at 5'- 9")

Charles Duane Burley

BORN : September 6 1917; Bessemer, PA.
DIED : October 16 1992; Pittsburgh, PA.

MANAGERS
(1936-1940) Phil Goldstein; (1941) Luke Carney;
(1942-1945) Tommy O'Loughlin, Travis Hatfield - Carl Hatfield;
(1945-46) Morris Slutsky; (1946-48); Charley Rose, Lew Burston & Jersey Jones;
(1948-49) George Armstrong, Carl Hatfield; (1949-50) Harry Roth.

Amateur Record
49 total fights: Won 43 (KO 13): Lost 6

Golden Gloves Junior Lightweight Champion 1934
Golden Gloves Welterweight champion 1936
National AAU Welterweight runner-up 1936

(Bouts list - Incomplete)

1935
May   Leo Sweeney (Pittsburgh Boys Club) - LP
Oct 27 Young Brown (Willow AC) WP

1936
Mar   Jimmie Smith (Cleveland) - WKO
Part of an Inter-City Tournament in Cleveland
Apr   Stanley Murszyk (Chicago) - W
For Red Cross Flood Relief Fund-Raiser
Apr   Mario Duchini (Sacramento) - WP *
Apr   George G Morrow (Philadelphia) - WP *
Apr   Vincent Solders (Detroit) - WTKO3 *
Apr   Leo Sweeney (Pittsburgh Boys Club) - LP *
* *All the above indicated bouts were during the National AAU Tournament in Cleveland*
May   Al Anderson (Curry Rox Club) - WP**
May   Lou Gendle (Miami AC) - WTKO1**
May   Leo Sweeney (Pittsburgh Boys Club) - LP**
* *All the above indicated bouts were during the Allegheny Mountain Golden Gloves in Pittsburgh*
May   Eddie Wirko - WP

Professional Record

DATE (WEIGHT) OPPONENT (WEIGHT) LOCATION   RESULT(SCHEDULE)

1936
Sept-29	$(150^{3/4})$	George Liggins (145) Moose Temple, Pittsburgh, PA.	KO4 (4)
Oct-22	(147)	Ralph Gizzy $(146^{1/2})$ Duquesne Garden, Pittsburgh, PA.	W6
Nov-09	(150)	Eddie Wirko $(143^{1/2})$ Moose Temple, Pittsburgh, PA.	TKO5 (6)

1937
Jan-22	(148)	Ralph Gizzy (148) Knight of Columbus Aud, Oil City, PA.	KO2 (8)
Feb-08	$(147^{1/2})$	Ray Collins (148) Knights of Columbus Aud, Oil City,	TKO5 (8)
Apr-15	(149)	Johnny Folio (152) Palisades Rink, McKeesport, PA.	TKO5 (8)
Apr-19	$(148^{1/4})$	Ray Gray (151) Motor Square Garden, Pittsburgh, PA.	W6
May-03	(147)	Sammy Grippe (151) Duquesne Gardens, Pittsburgh, PA.	W6
May-27	$(148^{1/2})$	Keith Goodballet (152) Duquesne Gardens, Pittsburgh, PA.	TKO2 (8)
Jun-24	(146)	Mickey O'Brien $(146^{1/2})$ Hickey Park, Millvale, PA.	W10
Aug-09	(148)	Remo Fernandez (147) Hickey Park, Millvale, PA.	TKO 7(8)
Aug-16	$(145^{3/4})$	Sammy Grippe $(149^{1/2})$ Hickey Park, Millvale, PA.	TKO6 (8)
Sep-09	(148)	Eddie Dolan (139) Hickey Park, Millvale, PA.	L8

1938
Jan-27	(148)	Tiger Jackson (u/k) Duquesne Gardens, Pittsburgh, PA.	KO2 (4)
Feb-03	$(148^{1/2})$	Johnny Folio $(156^{1/2})$ Duquesne Gardens, Pittsburgh, PA.	W4
Feb-10	$(147^{1/2})$	Carl Turner (153) Duquesne Gardens, Pittsburgh, PA,.	W4
Mar-03	$(149^{1/2})$	Art Tate $(148^{1/2})$ Duquesne Gardens, Pittsburgh, PA.	KO2 (6)
Mar-21	$(147^{3/4})$	Fritzie Zivic $(146^{1/4})$ Motor Square Garden, Pittsburgh	L10
Jun-01	$(147^{3/4})$	Mike Barto $(142^{1/4})$ Hickey Park, Millvale, PA.	TKO4 (10)
Jun-13	(149)	Fritzie Zivic (148) Hickey Park, Millvale, PA.	W10
Aug-02	$(148^{1/2})$	Leon Zorrita $(145^{3/4})$ Hickey Park, Millvale, PA.	TKO6 (10)
Aug-22	$(145^{1/4})$	Cocoa Kid (144) Hickey Park, Millvale, PA.	W15

Billed for the 'Colored' Welterweight Championship of the World, Cocoa Kid defendng.

Nov-03	(151)	Werther Arcelli (147) Duquesne Gardens, Pittsburgh, PA.	KO1 (10)
Nov-21	$(152^{1/2})$	Billy Soose $(156^{1/4})$ Motor Square Garden, Pittsburgh, PA.	W10

1939
Jan-10	$(148^{1/2})$	Sonny Jones $(145^{3/4})$ Motor Square Garden, Pittsburgh,	TKO7 (12)
Jun-20	$(147^{1/4})$	Jimmy Leto $(146^{1/4})$ Hickey Park, Millvale, PA.	L10
Jul-17	$(149^{1/4})$	Fritzie Zivic (145) Forbes Field, Pittsburgh, PA.	W10
Aug-28	(146)	Jimmy Leto (146) Forbes Field, Pittsburgh, PA.	W10
Oct-23	$(149^{1/2})$	Mickey Makar (149) Moose Temple, Pittsburgh, PA.	KO1 (10)

Nov-01 (155) Holman Williams (148) Coliseum Arena, New Orleans. L15

1940
Feb-12 (155) Nate Bolden (156) Duquesne Gardens, Pittsburgh, PA. W10
Billed for colored middleweight championship
Apr-12 (149^{34}) Baby Kid Chocolate (149) Coliseum Arena, New Orleans. KO5 (15)
Apr-26 (151) Sammy Edwards (164) Coliseum Arena, New Orleans. KO2 (15)
Jun-17 (147$^{1/2}$) Carl Dell (145) Valley Arena, Holyoke, MA. W10
Jul-29 (156) Georgie Abrams (161) Hickey Park, Millvale, PA. D10
Aug-19 (149) Kenny LaSalle (149) Hickey Park, Millvale, PA. W10
Sep-03 (153) Jimmy Bivins (160^{34}) Hickey Park, Millvale, PA. L10
Oct-17 (150) Eddie Pierce (157) Butler Street Sports Arena, Pittsburgh. W10
Nov-11 (151) Vince Pimpinella (158) Turner's Arena, Washington, DC. W10

1941
Mar-31 (149$^{1/2}$) Babe Synnott (148) Duquesne Gardens, Pittsburgh, PA. TKO5 (8)
Apr-18 (149) Eddie Ellis (147^{34}) Boston Garden, Boston, MA. TKO5 (8)
Jun-02 (150) Ossie Harris (156) Hickey Park, Millvale, PA. TKO9 (10)
Jul-14 (152) Young Gene Buffalo (153) Gardens, Philadelphia, PA. KO5 (10)
Aug-25 (153) Otto Blackwell (145) Hickey Park, Millvale, PA, W8
Sep-25 (149) Antonio Fernandez (150$^{1/4}$) Convention Hall, Philadelphia.W10
Dec-12 (153$^{1/2}$) Ted Morrison (168) Armory, Minneapolis, MN. KO2 (8)
Dec-23 (155) Jerry Hayes (160) Eau Claire, WI. KO4 (10)

1942
Jan-09 (155) Shorty Hogue (163$^{1/4}$) Armory, Minneapolis, MN. TKO10 (10)
Jan-23 (150) Jackie Burke (151^{34}) Armory, Minneapolis, MN. TKO5 (10)
Feb-06 (u/k) Milo Theodorescu (u/k) Coliseum, San Diego, CA. TKO4 (10)
Feb-13 (151) Big Boy Hogue (159) Coliseum, San Diego, CA. TKO7 (10)
Feb-26 (148^{34}) Holman Williams (148$^{1/2}$) Armory, Minneapolis, MN. W10
Mar-13 (151) Jay D Turner (219$^{1/2}$) Armory, Minneapolis, MN. TKO7 (10)
Apr-10 (150) Cleo McNeal (146) Armory, Minneapolis, MN. KO5 (10)
Apr-20 (154) Phil McQuillan (147) St. Nicholas Arena, New York. KO1(8)
Apr-24 (152) Joe Sutka (162$^{1/2}$) Coliseum, Chicago, IL. KO4 (10)
Apr-30 (153) Sonny Wilson (160$^{1/4}$) Armory, Minneapolis, MN. KO2(8)
May-25 (155) Ezzard Charles (161$^{1/2}$) Forbes Field, Pittsburgh, PA. L10
Jun-23 (157$^{1/4}$) Holman Williams (157$^{1/4}$) Crosley Field, Cincinatti, OH. W10
Jun-29 (151) Ezzard Charles (160) Hickey Park, Millvale, PA. L10
Aug-14 (160) Holman Williams (156^{34}) Victory Arena, New Orleans. TKO9 (15)
Billed for colored middleweight title

Oct-16 (157^{34}) Holman Williams (157) Municipal Auditorium, New Orleans. L15
Billed for colored middleweight championship

Nov-13   (156)   Cecilio Lozada (153) Coliseum, San Diego, CA.   TKO2 (10)

Dec-11   (152¹⁄²)   Lloyd Marshall (158¹⁄²) Legion Stadium, Hollywood, CA. L10

1943

Feb-03   (158)   Harvey Massey (159) Auditorium, Oakland, CA.   TKO9 (10)

Feb-19   (152)   Jack Chase (155) Legion Stadium, Hollywood, CA.   W10

Mar-03   (153¹⁄²)   Aaron Tiger Wade (157¹⁄²) Auditorium, Oakland, CA.   W10

Apr-19   (152¹⁄²)   Cocoa Kid (152) Pelican Stadium, New Orleans, LA.   D10

May-14   (154¹⁄²)   Holman Williams (153) Legion Stadium, Hollywood.   NC10 (10)

Jun-26   (158)   Bobby Birch (156) Lane Field, San Diego, CA.   W10

1944

Mar-03   (151)   Bobby Berger (154) Coliseum, San Diego, CA.   KO5 (10)

Mar-24   (153¹⁄²)   Aaron Tiger Wade (158¹⁄²) Coliseum, San Diego, CA.   W10

Apr-06   (153¹⁄²)   Jack Chase (160) Legion Stadium, Hollywood, CA.   KO9 (15)

California State Middleweight Title Chase defending

Apr-21   (155)   Archie Moore (161) Legion Stadium, Hollywood, CA.   W10

May-12   (158)   Al Gilbert (170) Coliseum, San Diego, CA.   TKO4 (10)

Jun-23   (160¹⁄²)   Frankie Nelson (159) Legion Stadium, Hollywood, CA,   TKO7 (10)

Aug-28   (158¹⁄²)   Young Gene Buffalo (152) Civic Auditorium, San Fran.   TKO5 (10)

Sep-11   (157¹⁄²)   Jack Chase (159) Civic Auditorium, San Francisco, CA.   TKO12 (15)

California State Middleweight Title Burley defending

1945

Mar-13   (156¹⁄²)   Joe Carter (157) Civic Auditorium, San Francisco, CA.   W10

Jul-11   (161¹⁄²)   Holman Williams (159¹⁄²) Civic Stadium, Buffalo, NY.   L12

Jul-26   (156)   Oscar Boyd (160) Forbes Field, Pittsburgh, PA.   KO2 (8)

Aug-20   (158)   Aaron Tiger Wade (161) Forbes Field, Pittsburgh, PA.   W10

Sep-04   (160)   Dave Clark (158¹⁄²) Music Hall Arena, Cincinnati, OH.   KO1 (10)

Sep-28   (156¹⁄²)   Speedy Duval (159¹⁄⁴) Coliseum Arena, New Orleans, LA. KO4 (10)

Oct-08   (160)   Oakland Billy Smith (166) Civic Auditorium, San Fran.   W10

1946

Mar-14   (157)   Charley Dodson (157) Aragon Gardens, Pittsburgh, PA.   TKO3 (10)

Apr-08   (158)   Paulie Peters (161¹⁄²) Civic Auditorium, San Francisco.   TKO2 (10)

Sometimes listed as being for the California State Middleweight Title (and for 15 rounds).

Apr-24   (160)   Oakland Billy Smith (172) Auditorium, Oakland, CA.   W10

Jul-16   (158)   Charley Banks (165) Zivic Arena, Millvale, PA.   W10

Aug-05   (157)   Bert Lytell (153) Zivic Arena, Millvale, PA.   W10

1947
Feb-17   ($160^{1/2}$)   Bert Lytell (159) Coliseum, Baltimore, Maryland   L10
Aug-08   (158)   Larry Cartwright (160) Huntington, West Virginia.   TKO8 (10)

1948
Mar-24   (165)   Battling Blackjack (176) Phoenix, AZ,   KO3 (6)

1949
Apr-03   ($160^{1/2}$)   Charley (Doc) Williams (166) Coliseum Arena, New Orleans. L10
Jul-25   (160)   Willie Wright (162) Zivic Arena, Millvale, PA,   W8

Oct-18   (158)   Jack Burns (198) Council Bluffs, IOWA.   KO4 (4)
This bout was part of a barnstorming trip arranged by boxing Promoter Ralph Hayes

Oct-21   (u/k)   Jack Brennan (u/k) Council Bluffs, IOWA.   KO3 (4)
This bout was part of a barnstorming trip arranged by boxing Promoter Ralph Hayes

Oct-21   (u/k)   George Hayes (u/k) Council Bluffs, IOWA.   KO1
This bout was the result of a challenge issued to anyone who felt they could last a round with Burley.

1950
Feb-02   (162)   Chuck Higgins (166) Aragon Gardens, Pittsburgh, PA.   KO1
Mar-02   (159)   Buddy Hodnett (165) Aragon Gardens, Pittsburgh, PA.   KO6 (8)
Jul-22   (u/k)   Pilar Bastidas (u/k) Plaza de Toros de Acho, Lima, Peru.   W10

(u/k) = weight unknown

References and Bibliography

Newspapers:

Many newspapers were utilised during my research. Many of the reports and results of fights came from the press clippings that Charley Burley had collected over his career and these did not always identify the source; the same can be said of the press clippings collected by Eddie Booker. Those identified are listed along with the newspapers, and their outstanding writers, that were uncovered during micro-film and internet archive searches.

Pittsburgh Courier (Wendell Smith); Pittsburgh Post Gazette (Al Abrams, Harvey Boyle, Roy McHugh, Bert P. Taggart, Regis M. Walsh); Pittsburgh Sun-Telegraph (Jimmy Miller, Harry Keck);
Minneapolis Daily Star (Joe Hendrickson); Minneapolis Daily Times (Dick Cullum); Minneapolis Tribune-Sun (George A. Barton); (Will Connolly, Harry B. Smith); L.A. Times (Jim Murray, Al Wolf); L.A. Examiner (Morton Moss); The Philadelphia Daily News (Lansing McCurley); The Philadelphia Bulletin (Matt Ring); Springfeild Massachusetts Union (Vic Wall); San Jose Evening News ('Buddy' Leitch); San Francisco Examiner (Eddie Muller); The Oakland Tribune (Alan Ward); The Nevada State Journal (Lisle Shoemaker). World Telegraph (Lester Bromburg).
New York Times; Oil City Blizzard; Oil City Derrick; Cincinnati Enquirer; Francisco Chronicle; Hollywood Citizen News; The Times Picayune; The (Baltimore) Sun; Arizona Republic; The Washington Post; The Washington Evening Star; The Philadelphia Enquirer; The Holyoke Daily Transcript & Telegram; El Comercio (Peru).

Every effort has been made to identify and acknowledge the original source. Any omissions and/or inaccuracies are purely my own. My apologies for those that are not duly cited. Please forward all amendments/corrections to the author.

Periodicals:

Ring Magazine (Ray M. Todd, Harry Winkler, Prof. Wilfred Stephenson, Angelo Prospero)
Boxing Illustrated, Boxing News.
The Knockout (Billy Van junior, Ray Fouts, Lester Bromburg). Referee and Redhead (Joe Williams, Hymie Levy, Sam Barber, Barney Kafka, Al Barbour, Speed Riley, Hap Navarro).

The Journal of the International Boxing Research Organisation (its members and contributors). Jerry Fitch (and his excellent features on Cleveland's great fighters); Robert Cassidy.

Books:

Anderson, Dave., (1991) Ringmaster. Robson Books.

Carroll, Peter N. (1994). The Odyssey of the Abraham Lincoln Brigade: Americans in the Spanish Civil War. Stanford University Press,

Bodner, Alan., (1997). When Boxing Was a Jewish Sport. Praeger.

Grimault, Dominique & Mahe, Patrick (1984). Piaf and Cerdan. Comet.

Fried, Ronald K., (1991). Cornermen. Four Walls Eight Windows.

Graziano, Rocky & Barber, Rowland., (1954). Somebody Up There Likes Me.

Heinz, W. C. & Ward, Nathan., (1999). The Book of Boxing. Total Sports Publishing.

Heller, Peter., (1975). In This Corner. Robson

Moore, Archie., (1960). The Archie Moore Story. The Sportsman's Book Club.

Moore, Archie and Peal, Leonard, (1971). Any Boy Can. Prentice-Hall.

Nagler, Barney (1964). James Norris and the Decline of Boxing. Bobbs-Merill

Robinson, Sugar Ray and Anderson, Dave (1970). Sugar Ray. Viking Press.

Roberts, Randy (2000). Pittsburgh Sports. University of Pittsburgh Press.

Rosenfeld, Allen S. (2007). Charley Burley: The Life & Hard Times of an Uncrowned Champion. Authorhouse.

Ruck, Rob., (1993). Sandlot Seasons: Sport in Black Pittsburgh. University of Illinois Press.

Sammons, Jeffrey T., (1990). Beyond the Ring. University of Illinois Press.

Schoor, Gene., (1951). Sugar Ray Robinson. Greenberg.

Skehan, Everett M., (1977). Rocky Marciano. Robson Books.

Sugar, Bert Randolph., (1988). 100 Greatest Boxers of All Time. Crescent Books.

Sugden, John., (1996). Boxing and Society. Manchester University Press.

Record Books:

Ring Record Book (1945, 1946, 1948, 1950, 1951, 1981, 1986-87); Everlast

Boxing Record (1927, 1929, 1937); Post Boxing Records (1935, 1936, 1937, International Boxing Register (1999).

Television:
International Boxing Hall of Fame interviews (by Norm Meekison) - Ike Williams, Eddie Futch, Hank Kaplan, The South-Bank Show: August Wilson. London Weekend Television (1991).

Interviews and Conversations (with the author):
Charley Burley (1990, 1991, 1992); Julia Burley (1992, 1995, 1997, 1998, 1999, 2000, 2001, 2002, 2003, 2004, 2005, 2006); Angie Burley (1995, 1997, 1998, 2000); Bobby Lippi (1997, 1999) ; Jack Godfrey (1997); A.J. 'Blackie' Nelson (1997, 1998, 1999, 2005); Irving Jenkins (1998); Edward Edwards (1998, 1999, 2000); Hank Kaplan (2001, 2002, 2006); David Jordan (2001).

Websites:
Cyber Boxing Zone; Ibroresearch.com; Boxrec.com; Ancestry.com; Newspaperarchive.com; Antiquities of the Prize Ring.

Miscellaneous:
Subcommittee on Antitrust and Monopoly, Hearings on Professional Boxing. (1960).
Photographs: (other than author's collection)

Julia Burley (pages 11, 259, 276); Jerry Fitch and Tony Liccione Snr. (page 276); Lou Weiss (page 44); Harry Shaffer - Antiquities of the Prize Ring (Page 151).

Acknowledgements

Many thanks are due to many people and, although it is a huge cliche, it is true to say that this book would not have been possible without them. I would like to especially thank - in no particular order - Charley Burley, Julia Burley and Angie Burley for the opportunity to be a very small part of their lives and for always making me feel welcome. I can't thank you enough and I hope this small effort does the man some justice.

The late Bobby Lippi, Leona Burley and Jack Godfrey. Also A. J. 'Blackie' Nelson, David Jordan and Irving Jenkins for sharing their memories of Charley and some of their own life experiences.

The family of Eddie Booker; Edward Edwards, Loretta Bailey and Hilton E. Booker Jnr. for the time, the effort the scrapbook and the letters. Lou Weiss (the grandson of Phil Goldstein), who was a massive help with regard to 'Chappy's boxing and political career. Thank you all.

The late Hank Kaplan and Jimmy and Betty Faux. Also Henry Hascup, Chuck Hasson, Howard Branson and Mike Fitzgerald. The Guys at the Cyber Boxing Zone - themselves boxing historians of the highest calibre: Mike DeLisa, Steve Gordon, Kevin Smith and everyone else that shared a press report or story.

Thanks also to author and historian Peter Carroll for his assistance on the Barcelona Olympics and directing me to the Bernie Danchik collection. Do read Peter's book on what is essentially a forgotten slice of American history (reference in the appropriate section of this book).

Thanks to Gary Edwards of Oil City, Pa. (Venango Genealogical Society), Charles Cutter and Victor Birch at Brandeis University, George Rugg at Notre Dame University, Nick Jarzinski of Eu Claire for his radio piece on the Burley-Hayes fund-raiser. Thanks also to Juan Carlos Ortecho for the reports on Charley's time in Peru, Deepak Nahar for the 'Tale of the Tape' and Bob Dye and his daughter Lori Grove for the information on his cousins Willis and Willard Hogue. Deborah Alward and Liz Grey at the Pittsburgh Post Gazette. All of the staff in the microfilm department at Carnegie Library, Pittsburgh for being so helpful. The same thanks are extended to the staff at Philadelphia, New York and Manchester libraries. Thanks to Ella and Michael for giving me a place to rest my head when in New York and for being true friends. A big thank you to Allan Cooper for the proof reading, to Sandra for the typing of the records, Lea Eldridge for the advice, encouragement and support and John Exshaw for the fine-tuning. Thanks also to the late Sean Odega for his fantastic series of paintings of Pittsburgh and of Charley Burley and the Black Murderers' Row. Last, but not least, thank you to the late Norm Meekison - coach, historian and friend.

Apologies to anyone I missed. It was not my intention to do so.

Lightning Source UK Ltd.
Milton Keynes UK
UKOW03f2206070414

229569UK00001B/88/P